Imad El-Anis is Lecturer in International Relations at Nottingham Trent University, and received his PhD from Nottingham Trent University.

LIBRARY OF INTERNATIONAL RELATIONS

Series ISBN: 978 1 84885 240 2

See www.ibtauris.com/LIR for a full list of titles

JORDAN AND THE UNITED STATES

The Political Economy of Trade and Economic Reform in the Middle East

IMAD H. EL-ANIS

TAURIS ACADEMIC STUDIES
an imprint of

I.B.Tauris Publishers
LONDON ● NEW YORK

Published in 2011 by Tauris Academic Studies
An imprint of I.B.Tauris & Co Ltd
6 Salem Road, London W2 4BU
175 Fifth Avenue, New York NY 10010
www.ibtauris.com

Distributed in the United States and Canada
Exclusively by Palgrave Macmillan
175 Fifth Avenue, New York NY 10010

Library of International Relations 50

ISBN 978 1 84885 471 0

A full CIP record for this book is available from the British Library
A full CIP record for this book is available from the Library of Congress

Library of Congress catalog card: available

Printed and bound in Great Britain by
CPI Antony Rowe, Chippenham, Wiltshire

Camera-ready copy edited and supplied by the author

FSC
www.fsc.org
MIX
Paper from
responsible sources
FSC® C013604

For My Parents

CONTENTS

LIST OF TABLES

LIST OF ABBREVIATIONS

ABJ	Association of Banks in Jordan
ACM	Arab Common Market
AFL-CIO	The American Federation of Labour and Congress of Industrial Organisations
ALICO	American Life Insurance Corporation
AMU	Arab Maghreb Union
APC	Arab Potash Corporation
APM	Arab Pharmaceutical Manufacturing Co Ltd
CAFTA	Central American Free Trade Area
CBJ	Central Bank of Jordan
CIA	Central Intelligence Agency (US)
CUIO	Compulsory Unified Insurance Office (Jordan)
DAD	Dar Al Dawa (Jordan)
DEF	Development and Employment Fund (Jordan)
EPC	Executive Privatisation Commission (Jordan)
EPU	Executive Privatisation Unit (Jordan)
EU	European Union
FDA	Food and Drug Agency (US)
FDI	Foreign Direct Investment
FTA	Free Trade Agreement

GAFTA	Greater Arab Free Trade Area
GATS	General Agreement on Trade in Services
GATT	General Agreement on Tariffs and Trade
GCC	Gulf Cooperation Council
GDP	gross domestic product
GID	General Intelligence Department (Jordan)
GNP	gross national product
HCP	Higher Committee for Privatisation (Jordan)
IC	Insurance Commission (Jordan)
ICBMs	inter-continental ballistic missiles
ICG	International Crisis Group
IGOs	inter-governmental organisations
IMF	International Monetary Fund
IO	international organisations
IPE	International Political Economy
IPRs	intellectual property rights
IR	International Relations
JAPM	Jordanian Association of Manufacturers of Pharmaceuticals and Medical Appliances
JCF	Jordan Cement Factories
JD	Jordanian dinar
JEDCO	Jordan Enterprise Development Corporation
JEUAA	Jordan–EU Association Agreement
JIB	Jordan Investment Board
JIC	Jordan Investment Corporation
JIEC	Jordan Industrial Estates Corporation
JIF	Jordan Insurance Federation
JPMC	Jordan Phosphate Mines Corporation
JUSFTA	Jordan–US Free Trade Agreement
MENA	Middle East and North Africa
MFA	Multi-Fibre Agreement
MFN	most favoured nation
MHRA	Medical and Healthcare Products Regulatory Agency (EU)
MNCs	multi-national corporations

MRBMs	medium-range ballistic missiles
NAFTA	North American Free Trade Area
NAIC	National Association of Insurance Commissioners (US)
NGOs	non-governmental organisations
NIPE	New International Political Economy
NPS	National Privatisation Strategy (Jordan)
NTA	National Textile Association (US)
OECD	Organisation for Economic Cooperation and Development
OPEC	Organisation of Petroleum Exporting Countries
PA	Palestinian Authority
PC	Privatisation Council (Jordan)
PLO	Palestinian Liberation Organisation
PPF	Privatisation Proceeds Fund (Jordan)
PSC	Privatisation Steering Committees (Jordan)
PTC	Public Transport Corporation (Jordan)
QIZs	Qualifying Industrial Zones
R&D	Research and Development
RIPE	Review of International Political Economy
SALT II	Strategic Arms Limitation Treaty 2
T&C	textiles and clothing
TPA	Trade Promotion Act
TRIPs	trade-related aspects of intellectual property rights
UN	United Nations
UNGA	United Nations General Assembly
UNSC	United Nations Security Council
USAID	United States Agency for International Development
WB	World Bank
WIPO	World Intellectual Property Organisation
WTO	World Trade Organisation

ACKNOWLEDGEMENTS

This study is the product of a demanding four years of research and writing which, while difficult in many ways, has also been enlightening and fulfilling. For all the challenges and rewards these past four years have presented there has always been someone there to share them. A great many people have in one way or another been involved in this research project. To all I would like to express my sincerest appreciation. Paramount among all who I would like to acknowledge here are my colleagues at Nottingham Trent University's Department of International Studies, Dr Chris Farrands and Dr Roy Smith, whose intellectual support, collegiality, patience and friendship has been irreplaceable. To both I give my sincerest thanks.

The immeasurable importance of my family must also be acknowledged at length. This book is dedicated to my parents, whose support in so many ways allowed me to embark on this project and who helped to keep me determined throughout with their encouragement. To my friend and colleague Mohammed Al-Khraisha I would like to express my gratitude for his intellectual insights into Jordan–US relations, for reading through much of this study and offering his thoughts without hesitation and for his friendship. The support and encouragement of my good friend Dr Payam Mehrshahi also was invaluable over the past four years and deserves mention.

Nottingham Trent University has been a second home to me for many years and there are many people who deserve my appreciation.

I would like to thank Professor Lloyd Pettiford, Dr Cerwyn Moore and Dr Sagarika Dutt for their academic support and collegiality; and Janet Elkington who is in many ways indispensable. Members of other institutions have also helped me in one form or another and so my appreciation also goes to Professor Adam Morton, Professor Gerd Nonneman, Dr Katerina Dalacoura and Dr Aslaug Asgeirsdottir.

This research project would not have been possible without the help and time of many individuals whom I encountered on research trips in the UK, Jordan, the United States and Switzerland. In no order of merit I would like to thank the following: Khowla Al-Badri, the Managing Director of the Jordan Enterprise Development Corporation; Yousef Al-Shamali, the Deputy Director of the Foreign Trade Policy Department of the Ministry of Industry and Trade; Maha Ali, Director of the Foreign Trade Policy Department of the Ministry of Industry and Trade; Halim Abu-Rahmeh, Chief Executive Officer of the Jordan Exporters Association; Sabri Al-Khassib, Head of Research and International Agreements at the Amman Chamber of Commerce; Elias Farraj, Advisor to the Chief Executive Officer of the Jordan Investment Board; Fakhry Hazimeh, Lead Counsellor of the Jordanian Delegation at the World Trade Organisation; Ali Zeud, Head of Public Relations at the Jordanian House of Senate; Taroob Al-Zu'bi, Communication Officer for the Jordanian Executive Privatisation Commission; Samuel Munyaneza, Head of Trade Analysis and Information at the United Nations Conference on Trade and Development; Maire Ni Mhaidin

Kiiamov, Information Assistant at the Information and Media Relations Division of the World Trade Organisation; Carl Kress, Regional Director for the Middle East and North Africa at the United States Trade and Development Agency; Jeffrey Schott, Senior Fellow at the Peterson Institute for International Economics; Mohammad Abu-Atmeh, Chief Executive Officer of the Jordan Industrial Estates Corporation; Donna Thiessen, Communications and Policy Advisor at the United States Trade and Development Agency; Jorge Castro, Counsellor at the Legal Affairs Division of the World Trade Organisation; Halim Ghani, Librarian at the Jordanian Association of Banks; Said El-Hachimi, Counsellor at the External Relations Division of the World Trade Organisation; Taraneh Bastani, Evaluations Consultant at the United States Trade and Development Agency; Peg O'Laughlin, Public Affairs Officer at the United States International Trade Commission; Margaret Hilton, Librarian at the London City Business Library. A final mention of thanks should be offered to my editors at I.B.Tauris, Joanna Godfrey and Maria Marsh who both offered me a great deal of support and to Allison McKechnie who did a fabulous job of copyediting this manuscript.

There are undoubtedly many others who deserve acknowledgement here that through error have not been mentioned above. My sincerest thanks go to all.

PREFACE

This study considers the political economy of trade between Jordan and the United States. In so doing it asks a number of questions regarding the national interests which have led to the facilitation of bilateral trade, the nature of contemporary trade and market integration and the impacts of these on inter-state cooperation. Throughout this study the role of Jordanian and US engagement in international institutions is considered and conclusions formed regarding the utility of this engagement in trade relations and inter-state cooperation.

It is found that the Jordanian government's key interests over the past decade or so have been the pursuit of economic growth and stability. It is also found that these interests have been pursued through economic reform at the domestic level and trade liberalisation through international institutions at the international level. It is also concluded that the United States is pursuing a number of key policy goals in the Middle East and North Africa – it is important to note that this book assumes that states from Morocco to Egypt can be classed as being in the Middle East, as is common in much literature, but can also be defined as being within North Africa, which is geographically-speaking a more suitable term – (MENA).

These are: securing sustainable access to the region's resources, gaining greater access to the region's markets and achieving inter-state cooperation with MENA states.

It is demonstrated that the United States is pursuing these goals by encouraging states in the region to engage in international institutions and liberalise trade with one another and with the United States to increase economic integration and inter-state cooperation. The convergence of the two states' policy directions has led to inter-state cooperation in the facilitation of trade between Jordan and the United States.

In order to assess the nature of contemporary trade between Jordan and the United States and what the impacts of inter-state cooperation have been, trade in three economic sectors has been studied. It is demonstrated that trade in textiles and clothing, a low value-added manufacturing sector, has increased significantly since the process of trade liberalisation began in 1997. However, this form of trade consists almost exclusively of exports from Jordan to the United States. Trade in pharmaceutical products is also studied. It is found here that, while bilateral trade in these goods does exist, this form of economic activity is quite limited and has not greatly increased in the post-liberalisation era. Thus, economic integration has been limited in these high value-added goods. The study is taken further when trade in financial services is considered. The conclusion here is that this form of trade is extremely limited and has not been impacted upon in any significant way by inter-state cooperation and engageement with international institutions.

The overall conclusions are that Jordan and the United States as state actors have engaged with international institutions and liberalised bilateral trade in the hope of pursuing national policy goals. However, the impact of international institutions and trade liberalisation on economic growth, economic integration, interdependence and inter-state cooperation has been limited. Some significant growth in trade has occurred, but only in certain sectors, and some economic growth has been witnessed in Jordan as a result. However, wide ranging integration between the two markets has not occurred because non-state actors are largely not engaging in trade and economic activity between the markets. Furthermore, inter-state cooperation has been restricted to specific economic issue-areas. It is found that the utility of international institutions and trade liberalisation in this case is restricted by the agency of non-state actors and their roles in trade and market integration.

The originality of this study lies in both what is studied and how it is studied. In short, this study attempts to address a gap in the literature on Jordan and US–Jordan trade relations. Furthermore, this study acknowledges the Trans Atlantic divide in the study of International Political Economy and the related contemporary debates but refrains from advocating one or the other camp. Instead, a reflective approach is adopted in the use of a critical form of liberal institutionalist theory which remains free from these constraints and develops a non-Western-centric approach.

INTRODUCTION

This study is a broad assessment and analysis of a number of contemporary processes and related actors in the relationship between Jordan and the United States. What follows is an assessment and analysis of the political economy of trade relations between these two states within the disciplinary framework of International Political Economy (IPE). The purpose of this study is to understand and offer explanations of contemporary change in the relationship between the United States and Jordan. This is done by examining the United States and Jordan as state actors and as markets comprising non-state actors. Furthermore, this is done by studying state relations and the subsequent impact upon the framework within which the two markets interact, as well as studying the actual interaction of the markets through the activity of non-state actors. This study also addresses the significance of these elements of change and develops a set of predictions and prescriptions for both state and non-state actors pertaining to the future of US–Jordan trade and wider political and economic relations.

The main premise tested in this book is grounded in liberal political and economic thought and holds that trade liberalisation between Jordan and the United States has led to, and will continue to lead to, greater levels of bilateral trade, economic growth, economic integration and subsequently an increase in inter-state cooperation. In this endeavour four core research questions are addressed.

The first question considers whether or not trade liberalisation through the engagement with international institutions in the forms of international organisations (IOs) and trade regimes has led to greater levels of trade between Jordan and the United States. The second core question considers whether greater levels of trade have led to greater levels of bilateral market integration. The third question is whether increased trade and market integration have resulted in greater state-level cooperation between Jordan and the United States. The final research question considered in this study asks what the interests of the two state actors have been with regard to their bilateral relations, and if these are being met as a result of contemporary trade between them.

This book is presented in three main sections, the first of which is Chapter 1, which establishes the disciplinary framework within which the analysis takes place, and the theoretical approach used. The second section then uses the approaches outlined in Chapter 1 to examine relations at the state level, assessing relations and policies determining how the United States and Jordan (as state actors) have shaped the framework within which trade takes place. This section thus contains two chapters, one studying Jordanian domestic, foreign and trade policy and one studying US foreign and trade policy (the inclusion of domestic policy in the former chapter is explained below).

The third section of this book uses the theoretical approach established in Chapter 1 to study the actual trade relations between the US and Jordanian markets. This is done by studying non-state actors as well as state actors and their roles in three economic sectors and the interaction of

INTRODUCTION 3

these sectors in the two markets. This section consists of three chapters each addressing one economic sector (outlined below). It must be noted here that the three chapters in this section each draw upon various components of the conception of critical liberal institutionalism. However, the analyses in these chapters in some ways constitute individual elements of the overall theoretical analysis. As such they do not necessarily draw upon all of the elements of the theory used here. The conclusions to each of these chapters will, however, draw the analyses together into an overall theoretical analysis. The second and third sections of this book are based, to a certain extent, on primary data collected on field research trips to Jordan, the United States and Switzerland. A conclusion follows this third main section of this book.

Chapter 1, 'Twenty-First Century International Political Economy: Towards a New Understanding of US–Jordan Relations', critically assesses the disciplinary framework within which the remainder of this study takes place. The aim of this chapter is to introduce and engage with the debate within IPE regarding the nature of the discipline in the early twenty-first century[1] and how relations between the United States and the MENA region (including US–Jordan relations) have been included,[2] and to review relevant literature. It traces the emergence of the debate between the two main schools within IPE (discussed below) from the 1990s and highlights the shortcomings of a discipline which has to some extent failed to keep pace with a changing international political economy and changing US–Jordan and US–MENA relations. The argument in this chapter is that IPE has been dominated by an orthodox or hegemonic *version* of the discipline which is mostly, although not exclusively, rooted in the US academy.[3]

There have been significant efforts to develop a more heterodox discipline and this book aims to contribute to what has been termed a 'new' IPE.[4] However, this is not done by defending one of the two main IPE camps and contributing to it. The nature of IPE is introduced in order to give an overview of the discipline as a whole, but this study intentionally remains outside of the Trans-Atlantic debate. This is done in order to remain free from the constraints of this debate and to focus on the topic of study. Furthermore, Chapter 1 argues that the study of the MENA region and US–MENA relations have been relatively limited in IPE and are often state- and conflict-centric. The discussion in this chapter then indicates how the elements of IPE which are problematic are addressed in this book. The chapter also discusses the development of liberal institutionalism in IPE, demonstrating how the approach addresses the weaknesses of traditional IPE and studies of US–MENA relations. The development of a critical version of liberal institutionalism is also presented, outlining the specific theory and key concepts used in this study.

Chapter 2 examines Jordanian domestic, foreign and trade policy since the 1990s. The core focus of this chapter is a discussion of how changes in the domestic and international economic and political spheres have encouraged dual processes of reform.[5] This chapter therefore studies how processes of political and economic reform have interacted, resulting in the primacy of the latter over the former leading to contemporary Jordanian foreign economic policy aimed at facilitating trade through engaging with international institutions. The change in Jordanian foreign economic policy and economic reform at home, it is argued here, is a result of changes in demands and constraints – largely economic in nature – on national interests.

Chapter 3 presents a discussion of change in US foreign and trade policy since the early 1990s and how this is related to political and strategic policies and interests. This chapter argues that US foreign and economic policies are in fact largely one and the same.[6] Furthermore, the United States has, throughout its history, used economic and political policies in conjunction with each other in order to pursue various interests in the MENA region. Since the 1990s there has been a change in foreign and economic policy towards the region, exemplified by the drive towards bilateral economic integration through trade liberalisation.[7] An analysis of the state facilitation of trade between the US and Jordanian markets is then presented, outlining how this relates to broader US trade facilitation.

It must be emphasised at this point that this study, while seeking to discuss the political economy of trade between the United States and Jordan by looking at a range of state and non-state actors, explores these types of actors in differing levels of detail. As is discussed further in Chapter 1, a plurality of actors is assumed in the theoretical framework which is used in this study. Furthermore, the assumption is made that no single form of actor has universal primacy over all others. Thus, within this project it is claimed that in order to understand the complex relationship between Jordan and the United States as both state actors and markets of non-state actors we must discuss and analyse a range of actor types. These non-state actors will include corporations, trade associations and inter-governmental organisations (IGOs). However, the roles of the various state and non-state actors in trade between Jordan and the United States differ in character and often in significance.

As this study progresses state actors are seen to have an important role in defining the framework in which bilateral trade takes place. Non-state actors as a whole are discussed in detail. However, no individual non-state actor receives as much attention as the individual state actors discussed. The difference in the level of detail in the discussion of state and non-state actors should not be seen as either an assumption of the primacy of the state as actor or a conclusion of state actor primacy. This point is taken further in the conclusions.

The final section of the study begins with Chapter 4,

'Bilateral Trade in Textiles and Clothing'. The trade relations studied in this chapter are situated in a low value-added, labour-intensive manufacturing sector which is dominated by non-state actors (corporations and multinational corporations (MNCs)) operating in the Jordanian market and exporting their goods to the US market, so that the classification of the exports is 'Jordanian'. This chapter aims to study how US–Jordan textiles and clothing trade relations have changed as a result of state facilitation of trade, discuss which actors are involved in this trade and explain the impact of international institutions. The chapter demonstrates that the change in state policy has had a significant impact on change in non-state actor activity between the two markets in this sector.

Continuing the analysis of trade relations and market integration, Chapter 5 examines both the nature and level of trade in pharmaceutical goods between the US and Jordanian markets. The discussion develops the examination of how the change in regulatory framework within which trade takes place has begun to reshape the interaction between the two sectors in the two markets. In doing so, the assessment of the political economy of trade relations between the United States and Jordan is developed by analysing what can be classed as a second form of trade activity. This form of trade takes place in a high value-added, capital-intensive and high-technology manufacturing sector. This chapter demonstrates that this form of trade is characterised by low but more even levels of trade in value terms but dominance by the United States in determining the framework within which the bilateral trade takes place. Furthermore, this chapter examines how the World Trade Organisation (WTO)-negotiated agreement on trade-related aspects of intellectual property rights (TRIPs) has shaped both bilateral trade in pharmaceutical products as well as the nature of the Jordanian pharmaceutical sector. This analysis is developed by examining the significant differences between TRIPs regulation of the pharmaceutical sectors and the Jordan–United States Free Trade Agreement (JUS-FTA) which embodies so-called TRIPs-Plus provisions (which are far more stringent than TRIPs provisions as agreed upon at the WTO).

Chapter 6 completes the analysis of market interaction and the nature of contemporary trade between the United States and Jordan by assessing bilateral trade in financial services in the form of banking and insurance services. This chapter considers another high value-added and capital inten-sive sector and demonstrates the limits to the trade liberalisation which has been facilitated by the Jordanian and US governments. As is the case in chapters 4 and 5, this chap-ter is based largely on primary data collected during field research and considers the activity of non-state actors and examines the institutional framework within which they oper-ate. The general observations and argument of this chapter are that despite the increasing interaction and rising trade levels between the two economies, the low levels of trade in financial services prevalent before 2000 period persist today. The significance of this lack of trade activity lies not in con-temporary economic opportunities being missed but in the overall potential for US–Jordan trade and the limits to the impacts of international institutions.

The Conclusions draw together the analyses of the previous four chapters within the framework established in Chapter 1 and present a discussion answering the core re-search questions. A discussion of the hypothesis tested in the study is also presented and a number of significant conclu-sions are made with relevance to the political economy of trade between the United States and Jordan and what this demonstrates for the future of US–Jordan relations and the role of trade liberalisation and economic integration in these relations.

Context of this study

The relationship between Jordan and the United States is often ignored (perhaps for reasons such as the perceived small size of Jordan in terms of population, economy, military power and so on) and attention paid to the relationship between the United States and larger MENA actors such as Egypt, Iraq or Saudi Arabia.[8] However, the Jordan–US relationship is extremely important and should not be underestimated. In the post-9/11 era the United States has pursued a number of more revisionist policies in the MENA region, the 2003 invasion and occupation of Iraq being the most obvious example.[9] If the aim of a research project is to analyse the impacts of forced regime change in a Middle Eastern state it would be useful to examine the US–Iraq conflict and relationship. In the same manner it is useful, and perhaps essential, to study the political economy of trade between Jordan and the United States if the aim is to understand the changing nature of US–MENA trade relations and how this impacts upon broader relations through processes of interaction and integration. This is because the state level framework established by the JUSFTA for trade and economic interaction and integration between Jordan and the United States was the first of its kind between the latter and an Arab MENA state. The JUSFTA has acted as a model for further regulation of trade and thus market interaction between the United States and other MENA states and represents the first step on the path to a desired US–MENA FTA.

Understanding the state-level facilitation of trade between Jordan and the United States by examining government policy goals and decisions as well as the nature of market interaction and integration is essential in understanding the directions in which relations between the two are going. An understanding of this relationship and the directions it may take will also be useful in understanding changes in US–MENA as well as Jordan–MENA relations.

While this book is relatively broad and encompasses a large number of actors, issues and processes in the contemporary relationship between Jordan and the United States, there is much scope for further study. Firstly, this study has focused on three different market sectors in order to examine the nature of trade between Jordan and the United States. Within these sectors (low value-added manufacturing, high value-added manufacturing and high value-added services) there is room for the study of other goods and services. This could further enhance the understanding of the nature of trade between the two states and reinforce (or perhaps even undermine) the conclusions presented in this study. Secondly, this study has examined US–Jordan relations over a relatively short period of time – mostly since 1999. Thus, the conclusions formed cover a relatively short period in the years immediately after a number of key changes in state-level cooperation and interaction between the two states. Further studies of the political economy of trade between Jordan and the United States would therefore be useful in the future as the bilateral relationship develops.

As discussed above, studying the political economy of trade between Jordan and the United States offers useful insights into both contemporary US–MENA and Jordan–MENA relations. It would be interesting and useful to study and perhaps compare the political economy of trade between Jordan or the United States and other MENA states. Furthermore, there are implications of Jordan–US trade relations on the endeavour to create a US–MENA FTA. Future studies could analyse why and how this broad-ranging alteration in the framework of trade between the MENA region and the United States could emerge and what its impacts could be, based on the analysis in this book.

1

TWENTY-FIRST CENTURY IPE:
Towards a New Understanding of
US–Jordan Relations

This chapter considers the development and contemporary nature of the discipline of IPE and how the discipline includes the study of contemporary relations between the United States and the MENA region, and Jordan in particular. In the case of the former, the purpose of the discussion is to highlight the shortcomings of a discipline which has struggled, analytically, to keep pace with a changing international political economy. Furthermore, following the discussion of the problems with IPE, suggestions are made as to how the elements of the discipline which are problematic can be managed with respect to this study. This forms the basis of how this study will be carried out. In the case of the discussion on US–MENA relations, the aim once again is to highlight the shortcomings of a number of disciplines, including MENA Studies, Foreign Policy Studies and International Relations as well as IPE, in their study of contemporary relations. This discussion also offers suggestions as to how problematic issues can be addressed.

In order to complete these tasks, this chapter is divided into a number of sections. The first section introduces the argument that IPE as a discipline is incomplete. The core issues addressed in the following sections on IPE are high-lighted and a blueprint is offered on how to critique IPE. The second section then presents an introductory examination of what is here termed 'orthodox' IPE. As is the case throughout this chapter, the work of a range of scholars, contributors to both IPE and other disciplines, is considered. The following section examines the methodology used by orthodox IPE, highlighting the problems of common approaches. The fourth section develops the critique of IPE further by ques-tioning the scope of issues which are considered to be part of the agenda of IPE studies. A critique of the primary posi-tion of trade as an issue of study is developed, along with a defence of the inclusion of trade as an issue of study in this work. The final section to deal exclusively with IPE assesses attempts that have been made to develop a heterodox or 'new' IPE since the mid- to late 1990s. This is done because this study draws on liberal institutionalism as a whole but also draws upon, and in some cases resists, some of the more recent criticisms of it.

The following sections address the issue of contem-porary studies of US–MENA relations. The insular and often state- and conflict-centric nature of studies of these relations is critiqued in section six. Included here is a discussion of how, while the range of issues studied in IPE is limited, the agenda of studies involving the MENA region is even more narrow, and how this region is largely ignored by IPE. The penultimate section offers an analysis of how US foreign and trade policy strategies may be re-conceptualised within a 'new' IPE. It is worth noting that these latter two sections of the chapter are designed to be brief critical overviews of these two areas of study as opposed to comprehensive reviews.

They are thus observably shorter in length than the review of IPE which precedes them. This chapter then concludes by presenting a summary of the main points and arguments as well as outlining how this study can offer new insights to the study of US–Jordan relations.

The problem with International Political Economy

There is no single accepted definition of IPE. It is, however, the position of this author, following in the footsteps of such great and varied scholars as Adam Smith, Norman Angell, Edward Said, Noam Chomsky, Susan Strange, Jagdish Baghwati, Robert Cox and Karl Polanyi that, broadly speaking, the purpose of social science is to understand and explain the human condition – how we got to where we are and the ways in which human activity is shaped and organised – as well as to contribute to the improvement of this condi-tion. The author here would like to acknowledge the disciplinary and theoretical divergences between the abovementioned scholars as well as to state that these dif-ferences are inconsequential in the debate about the purpose of social science and its contribution to the human condition. This is a debate far too great to be engaged with in this study, although one which should indeed receive far more attention in scholarly work. In short though, it is the belief of this au-thor that scholarly work limited to the development of understanding and explaining, which makes no attempt to develop predictive and prescriptive ability, is the true enemy of progressive social science. Many scholars have engaged with 'understanding' and 'explaining' in IPE through the use and development of theoretical approaches.[1] However, fur-ther development of the analysis undertaken to include prediction and/or prescription is not a given. A source of this failure is lack of consensus over what actually constitutes the field of IPE in terms of *what* issues are studied and *how* they are studied.[2]

It is largely acknowledged that there are two broadly defined schools within IPE. One is centred on scholarly institutions in the United States and associated with the American journal *International Organization* (IO), and the other on British academic institutions (although many members of this school are actually American or Canadian) which can be labelled the 'critical' school (and whose main outlets are journals *Review of International Political Economy* (RIPE) and *New International Political Economy* (NIPE)).[3] Amanda Dickens efficiently characterises the former school as based on positivist methodological approaches and dominated by the hegemony of rationalist knowledge production.[4] On the other hand, as Mark Blyth and Hendrik Spruyt have so effectively outlined, the latter has developed more as a critique to the hegemonic position of the 'American' school in IPE.[5] A more critical statement regarding the British School, which will be developed below, and has been suggested by Robert Keohane, is that it can be characterised by problem-highlighting as much as if not more than problem-solving.[6] However, despite their differences and seemingly polarised agendas, a deeper analysis of IPE as a discipline and the 'schools' within it highlights a number of common problems.

Roger Tooze identifies IPE as 'denoting an area of investigation, a particular range of questions, and a series of assumptions about the nature of the international "system" and how we understand this "system"'.[7] This characterisation of IPE is accepted by many IPE scholars, although debate exists about what should be included in the set of defining questions. Susan Strange, for example, entitled her seminal introductory text to international political economy *States and Markets*. In this text she highlights the argument that the questions of IPE concern the relationship between the state (as actor) and the market (as system) as two ways of organising human activity.[8] It must be noted, however, that for Strange the core characteristic of this relationship is concerned with the socio-political and economic arrangements that affect the global system of production and distribution – she is in fact criticising the states and markets approach.[9] Others such as Robert Gilpin, while also arguing for the focus to be placed on the relationship between the state and the market, are concerned with a different set of broad research questions. Gilpin is more concerned with the political and economic causes and effects of the market system and the significance of these at the domestic level.[10]

Underlying the problem of what to study is the problem of how to study it. Historically concerned with understanding and explaining the post-Second World War world and the international liberal economic order established in that period with the aim of strengthening this order, IPE scholars have often failed to achieve their goals.[11] However, as Roger Tooze asserts, the causes for this failure have rarely been the subject of scrutiny as most IPE scholars have been content with strengthening IPE as a discipline without examining the foundations on which it is based.[12] Importantly, there has been a lack of evaluation of the hierarchy of issues that IPE studies and a tendency to continuously attempt to produce 'more accurate' conclusions about a number of 'old' or over-studied issues. These tendencies have led to what Craig Murphy and Roger Tooze term the orthodoxy of IPE.[13] They argue that this orthodoxy consists of a restricted view of what the important issues that need to be studied are and what questions need to be asked regarding these issues.

Tooze and Murphy were among the first IPE scholars to call for a revision of IPE as a response to the embedded nature of orthodoxy in the discipline, in their edited book *The New International Political Economy* in 1991. Richard Stubbs and Geoffrey Underhill have also called for a revision of IPE, although their argument differs slightly from that presented by Murphy and Tooze. Stubbs and Underhill describe IPE in their book *Political Economy and the Changing Global Order* as a discipline which is often in a state of analytical and explanatory paralysis due to the internal debates of how to study the international political economy.[14] They argue that the majority of IPE texts tend to adopt one of the three main paradigms (neo-realism, neo-liberalism or historical structuralism/Marxism) or some form of synergy and then embark on defending their choice.[15] This focus on competing paradigms severs the connection between material interests of actors and the resulting relationships they have with the international system and other actors and thus reduces analytical power.

The key to understanding the growth of orthodox IPE is understanding how the growth of the discipline through the 1970s until the mid-1990s largely reflected an IR agenda and was not shaped by a political economy or economics agenda. As a result of this the debates which shaped IR from the late 1970s, through the 1980s and early 1990s also had an impact on IPE. Despite differences in the discrete aims of critical or 'revisionist' scholars, such as Karl Polanyi, Peter J. Katzenstein, Stephen Gill, E. Helleiner and P.G. Cerny, a core aim is constant: to attend to the problem of orthodox IPE. While most revisionist scholars do not argue that they have the answer to what a new IPE should look like, they do provide valuable directions that can be taken in order to further develop the discipline. Tooze and Murphy, for example, outline four key areas one should critique. Firstly, one must examine the conceptual foundations of IPE, bringing them into question. Second, one must use this to construct the argument that having a diverse range of approaches to IPE should be welcomed and not rejected. This is because, as Stephen Krasner has highlighted, arguing for a single new approach to IPE would simply be replacing one form of orthodoxy with another.[16] Third, one should evaluate the philosophical and conceptual framework of IPE in order to increase understanding of the complex global order. Finally, it is claimed that it is evident that a high level of understanding of international political economy is only achievable by including competing analyses within IPE and analyses of other subjects from the social sciences.[17]

While these four key themes for the revision of IPE are promising this is not necessarily the only 'broad map' for such a critique. However, Robert Denemark and Richard O'Brien warn that any critique of IPE must be done tentatively, for two reasons. In the first instance any attempt to challenge orthodoxy and current thinking *will* be met with a level of hostility and criticism.[18] Second, an essential feature of attempting to 'open-up' IPE concerns the issues being studied and the questions being addressed. One of the core criticisms of orthodox IPE, made by Ian Taylor in his work on 'globalising' IPE,[19] is that it has a narrow and replicated issue agenda that continues to ask the same questions.[20] It is possible to bring this feature into question simply by examining alternative issues and asking different questions. It is essential to note that simply stating that IPE has a narrow issue agenda that should be expanded to include other issues in contemporary international political economy does not necessitate the expulsion of issues which have already been studied. Colin Hay and David Marsh have argued that 'old' issues that have received much attention from IPE scholars such as bilateral and multilateral trade may have been studied at the expense of other issues, but are nonetheless still important.[21] Any research that primarily aims to study issues such as trade but at the same time attempts to move away from orthodox IPE will therefore run the risk of being contradictory if existing critiques such as that of Murphy and Tooze are followed precisely. Rather, it is necessary to build on existing critiques to develop new ones.

Nevertheless, there are a number of tasks that must be completed in order to critique orthodox IPE and develop heterodox and more effective approaches – although the ways in which these tasks can be carried out may vary. Any attempt at moving away from orthodox IPE must begin with an evaluation of what orthodox IPE actually is. This entails an assessment of its ontological and epistemological foundations in order to establish patterns of knowledge and knowledge production. Following must be an assessment of the methodological dimensions which define the range over which the methodology of orthodoxy varies. Thirdly, an assessment and critique of the orthodox issue agenda needs to be carried out. A successful critique of these areas of orthodox IPE will not necessarily yield precise answers as to how the limitations of the orthodox approach can be overcome. However, it will provide some insight as to how to develop more complete approaches to understanding and analysing various contemporary issues.

An introductory examination of orthodox IPE

The primary aim of theoretical discussion in IPE is to evaluate 'the appropriateness of the instrumental categories and theories used to "make sense" of the changing "reality" of a Global Political Economy'.[22] Many scholars and students of IPE have successfully engaged with this discussion, but many others have failed.[23] But it is relatively easy to test the competing narratives of IPE and their varying analyses against a 'reality' that is understood through common sense.[24] It is here that any critique of social understanding and explanation must start, for, according to Robert Cox, 'reality' as understood by common sense *exists* even before theoretical analysis is undertaken.[25] For this reason a degree of scepticism is needed about how knowledge that is taken as 'common sense' in IPE is attained. Antonio Gramsci went as far as to state that such a critique of common sense should be the starting point of all progressive social change.[26] Gramsci suggested that we should examine common sense in order to highlight the ways in which 'theory' often determines what are taken as facts, as well as outline the inconsistencies that exist in accepted pre-conceptions. Furthermore, the aim should be to reveal the historic and practical reasons behind the development of common sense ideas, and answer the question of who is and who is not served by ideas that are believed to be common sense.[27]

The discipline of IPE itself can initially be seen as one that is deeply contested because of the existence of a clear profusion of approaches and research programmes, and one that therefore has no universally accepted 'common sense' knowledge. Groom and Light, writing explicitly on IR and implicitly on IPE, argue that the broad range of contradictory approaches and the variations of these approaches project the image that IPE research can produce varying results and competing analyses.[28] This therefore allows for differing common sense arguments to advocate the most convincing explanation.

The view of a dynamic discipline is misleading. Robert Cox argues that there is a global political economy of the production of IPE knowledge.[29] This has over the last two decades evolved into an orthodoxy defined by a clear set of values, theories and a 'particular mode of production of IPE knowledge that specifies a particular relationship between the objective and subjective and uses appropriate epistemological and ontological categories to support this relationship'.[30] According to Cox a theory that is divorced from a particular standpoint in time and space simply cannot exist. Rather, he argues that 'theory is always for someone and for some pur-pose'.[31] Using this argument as a core principle, Richard Higgott suggests that an investigation of who benefits from knowledge production and re-production is beneficial in order to ascertain how best to avoid claims about the truth-fulness of certain types of knowledge.[32]

The core issue here is that the vast majority of IPE research is done within a framework of 'paradigm production' that is formed by a number of intellectual assumptions and practices. The implication of this is that the divergent paradigms that exist within IPE and that contradict each other on one level are in fact all created in a single, larger framework of 'knowledge production'. This argument, made by scholars including Cox, Strange, Tooze and Murphy,[33] has been met with the pro-orthodox response by scholars such as Ernest Haas,[34] pointing out that the competing paradigms within IPE are contradictory and hence must be divergent in their origins and their application to studying IPE. This is true to some extent in that the competing paradigms do contain differing views on how to understand and explain certain features of international political economy and can produce contradictory explanations. However, according to Ash Amin and Ronen Palan, the epistemological and ontological foundations of orthodox IPE allow for the synthesis of these paradigms (most commonly realist-liberal) to allow for the resolution of such incompatibilities.[35] In order to understand this framework of knowledge production we must first examine the process of 'intellectual production' by assessing the material and theoretical bases of knowledge in orthodox IPE.[36]

It can be argued that identifying a particular range of theories and empirical referents does not immediately lead to an identification of what actually constitutes orthodox IPE. In order to accomplish this, as Bob Jessop and Ngai-Ling Sum[37] indicated in their discussion of IPE, the distinct set of ontologies and epistemologies on which orthodox knowledge is produced and interpreted must be highlighted. This is because when combined with the existing range of theories in IPE, these produce the *culture* of orthodox IPE. This culture has its material bases and theoretical foundations for knowledge production and perception.[38] Unfortunately, simply being aware that there is a culture of knowledge production and interpretation within orthodox IPE that pre-assigns the researcher to participate in the processes of orthodox IPE's reproduction is not enough to prevent this from happening. All research that is undertaken will contribute in one form or another to orthodox IPE.[39] This is because orthodox IPE often encourages different positions and views in an attempt to be a contested discipline, only to either ignore such alternatives or to incorporate them into the orthodox mainstream.[40] It is certainly not the purpose of this research project to break entirely from orthodox IPE. The aim here is merely to offer critique the foundations of IPE research and produce a study which takes some steps towards heterodox research which incorporates a level of reflexivity in the analysis.

It is difficult to explain what the ontological and epistemological bases of orthodox IPE knowledge production are without briefly considering an example of how they materialise in research. Robert Gilpin in his text *The Political Economy of International Relations*[41] (which is considered by many to be one of the seminal IPE texts) offers an explanation of the nature of IPE, what its dynamics are and what constitutes the research agenda. Gilpin's opening remarks provide an insight into what he suggests IPE is concerned with:

> A significant transformation of the post-war international economic order has occurred. The Bretton Woods system of trade liberalisation, stable currencies, and expanding global economic interdependence no longer exists, and the liberal conception of international economic relations has been undermined since the mid-1970s. The spread of protectionism, upheavals in monetary and financial markets, and the evolution of divergent national economic policies among the dominant economies have eroded the foundations of the international system ... What has happened to the system? What are the implications of the failure of the system for the future?[42]

This introduction to IPE portrays the discipline as having a specific and narrow issue agenda. Here it is suggested that *trade liberalisation, stable currencies and economic interdependence* are the key issues that the discipline attempts to study and explain. Furthermore, this introductory paragraph exemplifies how IPE has often been concerned with understanding and explaining the US-dominated liberal economic order with a view to strengthening this order – something which Joan Spero highlights in her book *The Politics of International Economic Relations*.[43] While each of the seven editions of this book change the focus of IPE slightly, Spero is always liberal in her work and she provides little indication that IPE can be concerned with processes and events that do not immediately relate to the abovementioned issues.

Gilpin goes on to attend to the theoretical level of his text. He states that 'this work is part of an expanding body of scholarship on the political economy of international relations: it assumes that an understanding of the issues of trade, monetary affairs and economic development requires the integration of the theoretical insights of the disciplines of economics and political science'.[44] While Gilpin's work *does* incorporate economics and politics, the problem remains that the issues he regards as being relevant in terms of the 'common sense' of IPE are still few in number and narrow in scope.

Finally, as the text progresses Gilpin turns his attention to the paradigms used in IPE. It is interesting to examine how he refers to, and describes the place of, ideology in IPE. The key criticism here is that he refers to 'the ideologies of liberalism, realism, and Marxism'[45] as being the totality of ideology within IPE. There is no mention of, or explanatory space left for, alternative paradigms such as feminism, green thought or post-modernism. Furthermore, Gilpin refers to the three key paradigms as being unitary and makes no mention of the divergences within them and the cross-fertilisation amongst them. He goes on to declare that he refers to paradigms as being 'systems of thought and belief which [individuals and groups use to] explain ... how their social system operates and what principles it exemplifies'.[46] This highlights one of the core problems of orthodox IPE research in relation to paradigms.

Orthodox methodology

From the above example of what orthodox IPE research can look like and the results it may produce it is possible to take the examination of orthodox IPE further by examining the methodological range employed. According to Louise Amoore, Randall Germaine, Richard Dodgson, Paul Langley, Iain Watson and Barry Gills there are three main methodological dimensions by which all orthodox research is influenced.[47] The first stems from the orthodox perception of all IPE research being positivist and scientific. This 'positivist epistemology'[48] creates what has been termed the most restrictive methodological approach used by orthodox IPE. This is because this type of methodology is based on the assumption that subject and object can be separated, thus creating objective knowledge that can be tested using hypotheses against an objective and pre-existing 'reality'.

Russell Keat, John Urry,[49] Peter Halfpenny[50] and Chris Lloyd[51] claim that this process produces scientific understanding and explanation that is, in essence, 'truth'. However, this kind of approach can easily be brought into question. In the first instance, as mentioned above, there is the underlying question of how 'reality' is (pre-)determined. There is also the problem of tautological claims that stem from the question of *what* constitutes the 'real' world. Quine argues that the knowledge that is produced from positivist research is founded on assumptions about the presumed real world that are not necessarily as solid as they are believed to be.[52] The danger of accepting the notion that truth and what is 'real' can be determined unquestionably is, as E.P. Thompson explains, that there is not necessarily a distinction between what is 'out there' and what is 'inside here': 'Thought and being inhabit a single space, which is ourselves.'[53]

The advocates of positivist research, such as A.J. Ayer, have claimed that positivist knowledge (truth) is generated through infallible scientific research.[54] However, scholars such as Thomas Kuhn[55] and Paul Feyerabend[56] argue that research of this kind does not allow for the issue of inter-subjectivity to be addressed. In this sense inter-subjectivity relates to the non-material features of the international system such as values, ideals and beliefs. Positivist approaches disregard the possibility that non-material features can themselves be a part of and interact with the international political economy.

Alan Deardorff and Robert Stern, while defending the WTO, have in fact taken account of such factors in their work on anti-globalisation and anti-WTO currents.[57] In fact non-material features can be as important as material structures and agents such as international organisations. For example, the WTO is an agent that affects change within the international political economy in a profound way. However, both the actions of the WTO and those agents that respond to its actions are often determined by values or goals. John Dobson presents a good analysis of how anti-globalisation, anti-capitalist or simply anti-WTO organisations and movements can have a profound impact on international affairs.[58] According to Marjorie Mayo this can take the form of direct action such as protests or through the spreading of knowledge and awareness regarding issues relating to the WTO.[59] These movements are rarely inspired by any rational self-interest but by certain beliefs and opinions about various issues that they deem as being important. A positivist research approach, such as the three-volume, 3,000-page analysis of the WTO conducted by Patrick Macrory, Arthur Appleton and Michael Plummer,[60] is unable to account sufficiently for this type of phenomenon due to its exclusion of the study of non-material features. Murphy and Tooze also argue that positivist IPE produces inadequate explanations because it excludes phenomena which are not captured by its ontological foundations.[61] Regardless of what the explanatory framework is and what issue is being studied, if there are phenomena included in the study that are not found in the ontological foundation of the positivist IPE approach the explanations produced will be incomplete.

The second main methodological dimension of orthodox IPE is a clear and unwavering commitment to explaining events and issues as the results of the rational actions of unitary individual actors.[62] This commitment is not necessarily overtly advocated but is in fact often unstated. The dedication to this form of methodological individualism can lead to misunderstandings of IPE research that attempts to break away from mainstream approaches. As a result such research is often discredited by orthodox scholars. Therefore there is a need to address the shortcomings of using a methodology that advocates the analysis of the (supposed) rational actions of (supposed) unitary actors. As stated elsewhere, and as emphasised by Claire Sjolander and Wayne Cox, the problem is not rooted in orthodoxy's commitment to methodological individualism as opposed to the fact that there is a lack of openness to other types of explanation.[63]

Orthodox IPE tends to exemplify the argument that combining explanations of events and issues that are based on either the individual or on historical and contextual social structures is ineffective. Part of this is because of what is taken as common sense about explanation within orthodox IPE. For example, Stephen Krasner in his seminal essay on regimes[64] summarises a number of explanatory approaches that have been suggested by IPE scholars. In this essay Krasner suggests that regimes can be explained as a result of the interactions of rational individuals.[65] However, what

Krasner does not suggest is the possibility that individuals and their 'rational' actions may be explained as being constituted by broad historical and social institutions.[66] In contrast consider the work of other scholars such as Bernard Lewis.[67] In his work on the causes and patterns of the relative economic and social decline of the MENA region over the last three centuries, Lewis highlights the effectiveness of explanations that are based on the study of individual rational action. However, Lewis grounds his analysis within the framework of broader historical and contextual structures that determine what are considered to be rational actions and how the actions are constructed.

Alternatively, consider some of the later work of Karl Marx such as *Das Kapital*,[68] which can be taken as more obviously linked to the contemporary discipline of IPE as it deals with an analysis of capitalism and related economic theories. Here, Marx constructs conclusions about the social consequences of the combined actions of a number of rational individual actors, namely capitalists, within the context of historical social institutions. In short, his was a theory of action which linked issues of structure and agency (social causation and actions of the individual) into a single explanatory framework. Orthodox IPE lacks the ability to do this due to the explanatory boundaries created by its enduring reliance on and commitment to explanations which focus on rational individual actors.

Orthodox IPE scholars, such as Helen Milner, may argue that what are interpreted as rational actions and what constitutes an individual actor are not affected by historical social institutions to any great extent.[69] Such arguments do have their merits. However, if this were the case and common sense dictates what the rational actions that can be taken in any given situation are, and individual actors are unitary due to their very existence, there are still reasons to combine the study of rational individuals and over-riding structures. Chris

Farrands and Owen Worth claim that questions must be asked about the impacts that broad systemic structures may have on the options rational individual actors may take.[70] In this sense actors may have a set of rational choices but the number and scope of these choices may be bounded by broader structures.[71]

The final methodological dimension of orthodox IPE regards the three dominant paradigms of liberalism, realism and Marxism. According to Geoffrey Underhill, at the heart of orthodox IPE explanation and theoretical analysis is the contest between these paradigms, each of which offers a particular view of the world and contemporary political and economic life.[72] The place of paradigms within orthodox IPE research and the impact they have on the explanations produced needs to be examined. The incorporation of ideology into IPE study is equivalent to the evolutions seen in the social sciences as a result of the exposure to the 'problems of enquiry and explanation'.[73] However, as Y. Lapid noted as early as 1989, unlike other social sciences, orthodox IPE has not allowed the incorporation of ideology to undermine the positivist epistemology and methodology that orthodox research is based upon.[74]

During the 1970s the social sciences underwent a period of change in the way social forms were understood. Increasing scepticism about the possibility and utility of purely scientific research emerged during this period within both IPE and IR. Scholars (largely Western), such as Frances Cairncross[75] and Tadeusz Rybczynski,[76] began to adapt their approaches to accommodate ideologies and values into studies of social phenomena. An example of this is the attempt to understand the seemingly irrational support given by the vast majority of developing states to the Organisation of Petroleum Exporting Countries (OPEC) in its policies of raising oil prices and periodically reducing supply – which proved difficult. In this case non-material features such as values had to be taken into account in order to explain the situation. Simply relying on a positivist epistemology and a methodology that studies the rational actions of unitary agents did not produce sufficient answers.

The incorporation of ideologies into orthodox IPE was therefore necessary but often unwelcome. They were embraced as a part of international political economy as explanatory tools. However, the extent of and ways in which factoring in ideology as a reality of international political economy in theoretical understanding and explanation has been used has varied and is often contradictory. Firstly, ideologies are not used to explain fundamental actions. They have generally only been used to explain the differences between the communities that examine real events and issues.[77] Therefore, ideology is only assigned a limited role in orthodox IPE: the role of interpretation. But it is not seen as a material reality and orthodox scholars do not use ideology in an attempt to explain existing material reality.[78]

While the contradictory use of ideology in orthodox IPE's explanatory framework is the most important aspect of the use (or lack of use) of ideology, it is not the only point of contestation. As mentioned above the position of liberalism, realism and Marxism in analytical discussion means that the content of these paradigms is privileged. There are, however, a range of paradigms beyond these three that have much to offer the field of IPE, especially when expanding the issue agenda. Sandra Whitworth argues that it is often the case that if other paradigms are considered in IPE research they are viewed from the standpoint of one of the three core paradigms and are discredited or at best incorporated into the traditional approach being used.[79] Furthermore, the consideration of paradigms generally necessitates the inclusion of the debate over which one is most appropriate. The distraction of focusing on the competing paradigms immediately reduces the analytical power of any investigation.[80]

The orthodox IPE issue agenda

Having highlighted to some extent the ways in which ortho-dox IPE studies and offers explanations of events and issues it is worth addressing the problem of *what* to study. For scholars calling for a revision of IPE there is a distinct prob-lem with orthodox IPE relating to how the discipline is constructed and how this reflects the issues that it deals with. Ben Rosamund claims that the way in which the framework of knowledge production within IPE is organised results not only in the restrictive patterns of how to study international political economy but also in certain issues being privileged.[81] This prevents the inclusion of 'new' or different issues on the IPE agenda. As Hay and Watson assert orthodox IPE 'renders specific views of the world "correct" by reducing them to the status of common sense'.[82] The problem of a relatively narrow and exclusive issue agenda has its roots also in the social realm in which IPE was established. Matthew Watson argues that the social sciences in general, including IPE, have developed largely as a reflection of the policy con-cerns of the main powers (traditionally state powers) within the Western world and in particular the United States.[83] These policy concerns include US supremacy, the spread of democ-racy, capitalism, economic growth and international trade. In addition to the dominance of Western interests and concerns, IPE has tended not to give credence to potential changes in the interests and concerns of peripheral states and regions. Ian Taylor has argued that 'the global division of wealth and power is taken, if not as natural, then certainly as something seemingly normal and not to be interrogated too deeply'.[84]

This is the case in practically all research undertaken with regard to the economic and political relationships between Jordanian and US state and non-state actors. For example, William Lovett, Alfred Eckes Jr. and Richard Brinkman use the 2001 FTA between the two states as a case study in US foreign trade policy.[85] Robert Lawrence also studies the FTA as an element in US foreign trade policy: surprisingly little is mentioned of Jordan in his study.[86] Equally selective is Howard Rosen, who suggests by way of ignoring Jordanian involvement in the process leading to the FTA that the JUS-FTA was only signed by the US and forced upon Jordan.[87]

When the FTA is considered as an issue in Jordanian foreign trade policy it is done in a manner which prioritises Western or US interests. Bashar Malkawi, a leading Jordanian academic studying trade law and policy in Jordan, for example, largely concentrates on what is better for the global economic system − bilateral FTAs or the pursuit of multi-lateral agreements. Malkawi makes limited reference to why the Jordanian government pursued the FTA and how Jordanian state and non-state actors have been impacted by it from a Jordanian perspective.[88] This is a question which is at the core of the purpose of this study.

The issues, values and methods of interpretation that IPE is founded on exist within a broader framework of post-1945 industrial society. For Deborah Johnston this translates into (largely) American values and issues of interest being presented in a privileged and materialistic manner as well as determining what constitutes the questions of IPE.[89] The core problem with this form of agenda creation is that, as Peter Vale has stated, the system of states and the majority of issues seen as important by the core of this system is often of little relevance to large parts of the world's population.[90] For example, the issue of development has been seen as important and currently appears to be gaining increasing attention. The fact that development has been determined as an issue that IPE should address is welcomed by both orthodox and heterodox IPE scholars. However, as stated by Bjorne Hettne, Development Studies has evolved into a discipline of relatively low academic standing.[91] The core problem with development studies in IPE is the underlying question of *what* it is that we should be studying when we say 'development'. The answers to this question may vary greatly. Of most importance is that the key prescriptions as to what to do in order to 'develop' alter significantly depending on the basic assumptions about what development is. According to B. Dasgupta, in practice, it has been Western conceptions of development and prescriptions which have been focused on and generated with little real understanding of the processes and concerns of the very people under consideration.[92]

A further key assumption often made within orthodox IPE research that helps to determine the issue agenda, relates to the extent to which economics and politics are (still) held as separate. This distinction is based on the definition of *economics* as the scientific area of investigation that deals with the production and distribution of wealth, while *politics* is defined as the area of scientific research that investigates the organisation of (non-economic) human activity.[93] The study of politics and economics as related but separate spheres is an inherent trait of traditional IR. IPE exists as a separate discipline[94] from IR in part due to the lack of analytical and explanatory power that this separation produces. However, while IPE research does not always (at least overtly) express this separation of politics and economics, the interaction between the two is founded upon an ahistorical conception of the relationship between them. This conception derives from the political and ideological influences of early liberalism. The result is a 'value-based political economy utilizing a closed set of economic techniques and analytical schemes'.[95]

Orthodox IPE has largely inherited the agenda of traditional IR. For Gerard Strange, orthodox IPE *claims* to study the politics of international economic relations but often it does little more than simply study the issues of international economics.[96] At the same time Alison Watson agues that the adoption of a largely economic issue agenda is inherently restrictive and produces a hierarchy of issues of importance, with some more privileged than others.[97] There are a number of ways in which this manifests itself. First, the issues which are privileged are assumed to be more important in both theory and policy terms than those issues that are not, which are subsequently marginalised. Stephan Haggard and Sylvia Maxfield's analysis of financial internationalisation in the developing world offers a good example of this type/form of hierarchy.[98] Second, the issues which are privileged are not only seen as being more important but also act as the basis of assessment and evaluation for all the marginalised issues. For example, an issue such as the importance of nepotism in low ranking regional government decision-making entities in the less prosperous states of the MENA region only becomes an important issue when evaluating its impacts on international trade.[99]

It is widely acknowledged that the most privileged issue within orthodox IPE is international trade (and perhaps finance). Barry Gills claims that the fact that international trade is so privileged is an example of the incorporation of the agenda of international economics into mainstream IPE, as well as the impact of liberal economic thought on the formation of the discipline.[100] At its fundamental level, liberal international economics is founded on the perception of the international political economy as an international economy of trading states where the totality of economic interaction is trade. Thus for liberal economists the international economy is the principal structure of human activity and therefore all other issues and forms of human interaction are understood as being determined by this structure. Orthodox IPE adopts this perception in large part. However, this limited view can be easily discredited by the study of the phenomenon of 'international production' and the global division of labour and their implications for the belief that the international economy is merely trade between states.[101]

In order to understand fully the pre-eminence of the

issue of international trade it is necessary to refer back to the claim that orthodox IPE largely reflects the issues and policy interests of the United States. Following the end of World War Two and the beginning of the era of US supremacy, international trade emerged as an area of significance in US domestic politics.[102] In the post-1945 international political economy the United States clearly dominated most global economic activity, producing a vast majority of goods and having the largest share of international trade. Thus the issue of trade became increasingly important to certain classes, sectors and firms within the United States.[103] The interest of these groups translated into political pressure on the way the US government acted with regard to the interaction between the international and US economies.[104] Also, the emergence of the United States as the most significant power in world affairs after 1945 meant that it was at the forefront of managing the restructuring of the world economy.[105] In part due to the status of the issue of international trade within US decision making circles, along with basic economic principles, the task of restructuring the world economy was undertaken with structures of trade as the focal point.

It must be conceded that in contemporary world affairs the issue of international trade remains highly significant both to the United States and the majority of other states and actors. This is for a number of reasons. In the first instance, in the decades since the rise of US supremacy there has been a reversal of the nature of the patterns of US trade. As the French historian and anthropologist Emmanuel Todd pointed out in his book *After the Empire: The Breakdown of the American Order*, the United States currently imports far more than it exports. Growing reliance on the world's true productive centres,[106] Japan, Western Europe and now arguably China, for goods and services has led to record trade deficits in recent years. Second, the ability of the United States to 'manage' the world economy and global trade has been under question since the late 1970s. For these reasons, among others, Daniel T. Griswold is quite accurate in his acknowledgement that trade is one of the more important features of the study of international political economy.[107] Even a critic of the orthodox IPE issue agenda must concede this point.

The hegemony of 'trade' in orthodox IPE began to be challenged in earnest in the early 1990s, not least of all by Susan Strange whose favourite and chosen area of study became money and international finance. Unfortunately the result has been a further polarisation within the discipline. There are orthodox scholars who remain intent on analysing trade on one side and so-called heterodox scholars who focus on money and finance on the other, and others still who focus largely on other issues such as development. Rather than leading to a diversified 'new' IPE, these processes have given rise to competing hegemonies within an increasingly indecisive discipline.

There exist other confrontations over the range of issues within IPE. Orthodox IPE seems to have largely ignored security as an area of study, for example. Susan Strange had gone some way in addressing this issue by developing ideas pertaining to the international political economy of security in her work on the 'security structure', and technology in her work on knowledge structures.[108] However, this work, along with similar research, has too often been excluded from orthodox IPE research. Other issues such as resource scarcity and depletion, by scholars such as Thomas Homer-Dixon;[109] technological developments, by scholars such as M. Talalay;[110] demographic change, and culture, also hold a subordinate status to the issue of international trade in orthodox IPE. However, within heterodox IPE the problem of hierarchy in the issue agenda has resurfaced. In short, the issues mentioned above as subordinate to international trade in orthodox IPE have, individually, become the primary focus in the 'new' IPE.

A realisation is needed that IPE can be, perhaps above all other social sciences, the most diverse discipline in terms of scope and methodological approaches and capacity for change. Adopting a hierarchical issue agenda which has as a core formative element the principle of selectivity is perhaps the most serious hindrance to the development and generation of IPE research. Barry Gills, for example, warns against the 'colonisation' of IPE by specific issues such as identity, stating that this will not prove 'fruitful' and will lead to unwanted conflict within the discipline.[111] As with theoretical and methodological approach, the issue agenda should be permanently opened to practically all possible issues of study. If it is not, the result will be the continued stagnation of IPE and the continued fracture of the invisible college of academics and scholars.

Beyond orthodox IPE

Following the above assessments of what constitutes orthodox IPE, what methodological range orthodoxy employs and the issue agenda to which attention is paid, it is now important to return to the question of how to transcend the limits of orthodox IPE. There are four important steps that should be taken in order to develop an IPE approach to the study of US–Jordan trade relations. The first step is required in order to overcome the restrictions on the range of issues that can be studied and the hierarchy of issues that are studied. It is necessary here to reject the existing orthodox hierarchy, thus refusing to place international trade as the primary issue of study. This does not necessitate the refusal of the study of international trade. Rather it simply means rejecting 'the means of constructing the universe of (orthodox) IPE'.[112] As Diana Tussie states, this means questioning the ahistorical distinction between politics and economics and recognising the impacts that Western, largely American, cultural values have had on orthodox IPE.[113] This constitutes the second step. It is often the case that this step will need to be taken simply because the issue that is being brought into question may not be located within the realm of US policy interests.

The third step, and something that Owen Worth and Carmen Kuhling have highlighted, is to be self-conscious of the research that is being undertaken.[114] While it is easy to criticise orthodox scholars for only studying issues that are of significance when viewed in the sense of US policy interests or Western values, the same criticism can be made of most IPE research. As stated above, this research project represents a set of specific interests which include the issue of US–Jordan relations from a dual perspective. It is also important to realise the connection between the research project and the interests and values of the author. Carrying out this research project thus may be construed as being contradictory, exchanging one set of values and interests in IPE research for another. However, the difference is that the connection between the researcher and the research here is explicitly made and reflected upon, therefore acknowledging the subjective relationship.

Incorporating such self-consciousness and reflexivity into the research process allows for the IPE researcher to take a further step towards producing a heterodox piece of work. This is the step of addressing the epistemological inadequacies of the methodology that orthodox IPE uses.[115] The three main methodological dimensions as explained above have specific problems which must be addressed and resolved in order to produce a more complete IPE study. Initially there is the problem of the reliance on positivism's awkward distinction between subject and object in an attempt to achieve objectivity. Orthodox scholars attempt to produce scientific understanding of the world and its events, processes and structures and present this understanding as 'truth' through truth-seeking research. Heterodox IPE scholars on the other hand tend to offer an alternative version of research and truth-seeking: the self-conscious identification with a certain set of values, interests and perhaps group(s) of people. As Murphy and Tooze state, 'The scholar ... *needs* to understand the world in order to change it'.[116] By taking this fourth step it is possible to present a solution to the problem of objectivity by reflecting multiple *sources* of objectivity or even multiple sources of subjectivity.

The second problematic methodological dimension of orthodox IPE is the commitment to explaining events and issues in terms of the rational actions of individual actors. Attempts to study and explain the actions of individual actors should be included in IPE research in most instances, depending on the area of study. However, in order to fully understand these actions it is important to also study the historical construction of these actors and the broader structures that they operate within.[117] This does not necessarily mean agreeing on specific explanations of historical and contextual structures and events. For example, there are varying explanations on the historical evolution of the post-Second World War international economy as well as varying interpretations on the impacts that the different processes of globalisation may have on the economies of the MENA region.

One final criticism of the epistemological difficulties of orthodox IPE relates to the use of theory. Acknowledging the diverse range of theories that exist and not simply *labelling* or approaching research using one of the three main paradigms (realism, liberalism or Marxism) has two main results. First, this allows the researcher to understand the arguments, theories, explanations and interpretations offered by other social scientists. Second, the problem of communication between different research programmes[118] can be resolved, which in turn can lead to the understanding that heterodox scholars do not necessarily claim their research agendas should be everyone else's[119] – as orthodox scholars do.

State-centric and conflict-centric MENA studies

According to F. Gregory Gause, the majority of research and scholarly work focusing on the MENA region has traditionally been carried out by Western academics or Western educated academics.[120] For Fred Halliday this has led to the majority of work on the international relations or international political economy of the MENA region being dominated by a narrow range of approaches and a limited range of issues being considered.[121] In short, the study of the MENA region in IPE, IR, Foreign Policy Analysis and MENA Studies, among other disciplines, has been dominated by Western conceptions of the region and Western interests. Thus there is a distinct problem of when and how IPE takes into consideration the actors, issues and processes of the MENA region. In the case of the actors of the region, the vast majority of scholarly work concentrates on a system of states. L. Carl Brown's *International Politics and the Middle East* is a prime example of the state-centric approach.[122] With regard to the issues and processes of relevance, Edward Said has argued that mainstream approaches focus on inter- and intra-state conflict and natural resources.[123] The result is that a range of issues of importance, such as the integration of legal frameworks governing various international economic activities, are not studied.

With regards to the dominant state-centric approach there are two main critiques. The first, according to Tariq Ali, is that the MENA region has not historically been constituted by states.[124] The modern state in the MENA region is a relatively new type of actor. The second critique is, as Peter Mansfield argues, that human forms of social organisation in the region have historically taken the form of a number of hierarchical entities very much unlike the modern state.[125] At the top of this hierarchy of actors is the *Dar al-Islam*, or House of Islam, the singular yet not unitary empire of Islamic peoples.[126]

Progressing down the hierarchical structure, Fernand Braudel claims that sub-regional entities with some of the characteristics of modern states can be found, although these entities were organised along geographical, ethnic and tribal lines.[127] The most discrete form of organisation in the region has been and still is the tribe – which this author likens to contemporary non-governmental organisations (NGOs) in other regions.

An old and resurgent form of actor also exists parallel to the tribe. This is the corporation or multinational corporation (MNC). Thus in the first instance simply analysing the state as the dominant form of actor in the region risks producing inaccurate conclusions due to the historically 'foreign' nature of and relatively recent arrival of the state as a type of actor in the region. In the second instance, as Kenichi Ohmae has highlighted,[128] failing to incorporate other forms of actors such as the MNC in any study of international political economy produces incomplete analyses. This is because the agency and impact of a large number of actors is not understood or considered, thus producing false or incomplete conclusions.

In relation to the range of dominant issues which are studied, Andrea Teti and Claire Heristchi claim that conflict has more often than not been the focus.[129] Tariq Ismael meanwhile argues that the study of the region's natural resources and their importance to extra-regional actors and systems comes second on the hierarchical issue agenda.[130] Studies of the international political economy of the MENA region have focused on other issues such as trade, poverty alleviation, education, environmental protection and so on; however, these issues and the research done on them are consistently excluded from the 'core intellectual discourse' on MENA studies. For Larbi Sadiki this is a disciplinary weakness which must be rectified by 'bringing in' to mainstream discourse previously excluded and under-studied issues and research topics.[131] It is the belief of this author that while the study of the politics, economics, international relations and international political economy of the MENA region in the social sciences in general has been limited, the most extreme case of exclusion and selectivity is within IPE. This is for the reasons highlighted above regarding what is studied and also for how these issues are studied.

The unfortunate truth is that the majority of issues pertaining to the international political economy of the MENA region that are studied are examined from a non-MENA perspective. Edward Said's work on Orientalism has led to the emergence of a new paradigmatic approach to studying the MENA region which does not reduce the actors – and most importantly the people – of the region to mere subjects of study by 'others'.[132] Despite this, however, as mentioned above, scholars such as Rashid Khalidi and Bashar Malkawi, who originate from the MENA region, have often produced studies which use a Western approach in the sense that the study does not take sufficient account of MENA actors and interests. Worthy of mention here is a recently established academic journal entitled *Arab Insight* published by the World Security Institute, whose remit is to provide a platform for research on international relations done by MENA-based academics with a non-Western approach. It is the aim of this study to break with the mainstream tradition and use a more holistic approach to the study of US–Jordan trade relations. Thus, this study will not focus solely on any one *type* of actor such as the state; nor will it focus on conflict as a central theme. Furthermore, the actors, interests and processes of the Jordanian element of this study will not be ignored. This does not, however, equate to this study being Jordanian or non-Western focused – this would simply be replacing one incomplete approach with another.

Re-interpreting US strategies and interests

Of the three areas of academic enquiry which are reviewed in this chapter, the study of US foreign and trade policy is perhaps the most complete. However, there are still issues and processes which have not been fully considered or analysed. As Eugene Wittkopf, Charles Kegley and James Scott claim, attention has generally tended to be directed towards *either* the United States' strategic interests and the use of foreign and trade policy as a mechanism to achieve these interests *or* on the economic impacts of such policies.[133] In short, there has too often been a divide between research focusing on the political aspects of US foreign and trade policy on the one hand and economic aspects on the other. John Rothgeb Jr. argues that consideration of the *political economy* of US interests and policies has not tended to be the traditional route of analysis.[134] This has historically been the case with regard to US–MENA relations.

Concerning US–MENA relations, there are a number of key political, economic and social issues within the MENA region which have been seen as the root causes of the major problems the region has faced. As Peter Hahn[135] has highlighted, the attention to what is essentially the domestic structure of a foreign region stems from the vested political and economic interests that the United Sates has in this region.[136] Douglas Little argues that for the United States, the threat of instability and conflict in the MENA region is the primary challenge to these key strategic interests.[137] For exxample, the threat of military action in the region can easily disrupt the flow of oil to the world market. The second major concern for the United States since the end of the Cold War has been international terrorism.[138] Prior to 11 September 2001, terrorism emanating from the MENA region was seen mostly as a threat faced by the ruling elites of the region and US interests abroad. However, the phenomenon has since become a direct threat to the territory of the United States. Furthermore, slow economic growth, impassable barriers to trade and relatively isolated economies in the MENA region have become key obstacles not only to regional stability but also to US access to the region's markets.

According to Michael Oren any study of US governmental and non-state actor policy towards the MENA region, whether foreign or trade policy, must take these broad interests into account.[139] However, as Richard Feinberg has argued,[140] this must be done in a manner which allows for the synthesis of political and economic interests and policies to enable a study of the political economy of such policies. For Tom Hanahoe this entails moving away from focusing solely on one key interest at a time and critically assessing how US governmental interests interact with the interests of US non-state actors such as MNCs.[141] In the post-9/11 era, it has too often been assumed that the US government desires above all else a re-structuring of the state system of the MENA region through forced regime change in order to secure its main interests in the region. Thus, attention has been drawn mostly towards security issues and military conflict. Geoff Simons' book *Future Iraq: US Policy in Reshaping the Middle East* is a prime example of this type of approach.[142]

This study aims to demonstrate how it is possible to develop more comprehensive and eclectic analyses of US foreign and trade policy towards the MENA region. However, the approach taken in order to accomplish this does not necessitate ignoring the traditional key interests of the US government and non-state actors. Instead, what is necessary is a re-interpretation of these interests and what the political economy of US governmental and non-state actor policy is and how it remains oriented towards securing these interests.

This chapter has critically assessed the nature of contemporary IPE and the shortcomings of orthodox research. Within the discipline there are prevalent characteristics which limit the effectiveness of research carried out. In the first instance there are limitations to the range of methodological tools employed, which often result in research which has more in common with the natural sciences than the social sciences. These are the commitment to positivism, rationalism and only three main paradigms. Second, the issue agenda included in IPE has been constructed and perpetuated in a manner which excludes certain types of issues as well as alternative interests and competing analyses. Within these limitations, the areas of MENA studies and US foreign and trade policy studies present even greater problems. Studies of the international political economy of the MENA region have been dominated by the hegemony of state- and conflict centricism. In the case of US foreign and economic policy, studies have focused on state actor interests and conflictual relationships as the means of pursuing these interests. Furthermore, politics and economics have either been separated or studied in a dominant–less dominant manner, favouring the former.

It has been argued that the first step in undertaking a heterodox IPE research project is to establish the framework within which the issue(s) to be studied can be assessed and analysed. Initially this means determining *how* the issue(s) will be studied. There are a number of problems that must be resolved in relation to the paradigmatic choices the project makes and the methodology employed. As explained above, a major shortfall of much IPE research is the unnecessary amount of attention paid to the debate surrounding the three main paradigms of IPE. This debate will not be engaged with in greater detail in this book. It is important, however, to outline the paradigmatic approach that will be used.

This study utilises an approach which rejects the totalitarianism of positivism and the fallacy of objectivism. However, this is not an entirely post-positivist and subjective study. Rather, the possibility of objective and positivist research is acknowledged and the benefits of empirical observation and data collection are also utilised in chapters 2 to 6. Furthermore, an ontological position is acknowledged which allows for the analysis of varying types of actors, including non-state actors such as MNCs, as well as the varying forms these types of actors may take between different regions.

The second key feature of the research framework that must be decided upon and highlighted before a heterodox research project can be undertaken is to produce an outline of what the issue agenda of the project is going to be. As stated above, the traditional issue of most concern to orthodox IPE scholars has been international trade. The lack of ability of orthodox scholars to incorporate other issues into the issue agenda has been their most important failure. However, there exists an equally important problem with the commitment to preserving the issue of international trade as the primary issue on the agenda. When a 'secondary' issue is the focus of a research project the result has tended to be that the project is undertaken with the purpose of assessing the issue and analysing its impacts on primary issues such as trade. The reader could be forgiven here for assuming that this research project is therefore in contradiction with the aims of diversifying and developing IPE as this is a study about international trade. However, there is a key difference between this research project and other such studies that are orthodox in their approach and their findings.

While this project aims to assess the political economy of international trade between the United States and Jordan, there are a number of more subtle issues that are engaged with. As highlighted above, a common misunderstanding is that international trade is the primary issue and all other issues are always understood as part of its processes. While this is sometimes the case, this study does not aim to simply assess the impacts of international institutions on trade levels. Likewise this project does not aim to assess perceived 'secondary' issues of US–Jordan relations such as cultural animosity, forms of governance and so on, on current and future levels of bilateral trade. However, this study also does not ignore trade as an issue simply because it has received such a significant amount of attention in IPE. In fact the study of trade in IPE has often ignored the MENA region and Jordan in particular. Furthermore, US–Jordan relations and US–MENA relations in general have focused largely on issues of conflict and issues of resources.

The intention of this study is therefore to offer alternatives to both the orthodox approach of studying trade *and* the critical approach of ignoring trade. This study thus assesses the relationship between state and non-state actors in both the United States and Jordan in forming patterns of trade in order to evaluate current and future patterns of political and economic cooperation and integration between the two states. In this sense the primary issue of this study is international cooperation and interdependence while the secondary issue is international trade.

The value of institutionalism

There are a number of demands and constraints regarding the theoretical approach to be used in this study. The critique of the discipline of IPE and the pursuit of a more heterodox approach to studying international political economy accounts for much of these. Analysing the political economy of trade between the United States and Jordan at the domestic, state and international levels also places yet more demands and constraints on the theoretical tools to be used. A third set of demands and constraints are generated by the need for a theoretical approach which allows for the inclusion in this study of multiple types of actors.

It is *not* necessary, here, to outline and discuss other theoretical approaches in IPE. Rather it *is* necessary, for the purpose of this research project, to introduce and discuss liberal institutionalism, considering some of the main developments in the history of the approach, its ontological and epistemological foundations and how these relate to those of this study, in order to introduce the exact variant of the liberal institutionalist approach to be used here. In defence of this position it will also be necessary to briefly relate this approach to others. A final look at the use of liberal institutionalism in IPE will be followed by a summary of how exactly it will be employed in this project as a critical liberal institutionalist approach.

Within political science and the broader social sciences there exists a relatively broad school of theory which is labelled by many scholars of IPE and IR as 'liberal institutionalism'.[143] It must be noted, however, that there is no single institutional approach. Instead, there are a number of approaches, related but occasionally contradictory, which are classed as institutionalist.[144] It is this variety and the way this has come to be that constitutes one of the strengths of this approach and thus one of the reasons why it has been chosen for this research project. The variety of institutionalist approaches stems in part from the ever-changing nature of social science theory and the debates that continue, seemingly endlessly, about how best to do social science research.[145] Institutionalism has gained much from reacting to this debate after coming under criticism in the early post-war era. As Vivien Lowndes points out, '[u]ntil the 1950s the dominance of the institutional approach within political science was such that its assumptions and practices were rarely specified, let alone subject to sustained critique'.[146] This would soon change.

The study of the role of international institutions in international political economy has been central since the end of the Second World War and admittedly has been a focus of orthodox IPE research.[147] In the first decades following the war a highly practical organisational analysis emerged that focused on the issue of how well the newly formed international institutions addressed the problems for which they were created.[148] A central assumption in this debate was that post-war institutions would be shaped and limited by the international politics of the time. As a result few scholars held the view that such organisations would be able to have a significant impact on international relations and live up to the tasks they were assigned.[149] The United Nations (UN),[150] the International Monetary Fund (IMF)[151] and the General Agreement on Tariffs and Trade (GATT)[152] were the subject of a large number of studies – a large proportion of which were highly critical.

A number of these early studies assessed the impacts that international institutions could have on the policies of the major powers in Europe and North America, as well as the military relations between them. Howard C. Johnson and Gerhart Niemeyer, for example, investigated the impacts and roles that international norms and the organisations to implement them had on state behaviour.[153] They asked the important question of whether states would be willing and able to use force in order to preserve public law and order rather than for the sake of gaining relative advantages over other states.[154] Johnson and Niemeyer ultimately saw more value in the balance of power approach. Nevertheless, they called for a specific mechanism that could explain the effects of institutions on actor behaviour.[155]

Following this call for such a mechanism, a large number of studies throughout the 1950s focused on the question of institutional impact on state behaviour. Understandably, the majority of these studies focused on international institutions and the role of the United States in world affairs. The United States' role, for example, in decolonisation was seen as being influenced by a range of institutions that were believed to be raising US consciousness about pressing issues that affected American interests.[156] One of the results of this surge of research was the conclusion that the UN had in fact had an impact on some of the most important international issues of the time (although this impact was seen as being marginal).

Lisa Martin and Beth Simmons argue that 'though lacking the elaborate theoretical apparatus of current research, early studies of post-war organizations had many of the same insights that have informed "modern" institutionalism'.[157] However, it is worth noting that much of the research carried out in the 1950s on institutions would be abandoned for the following two decades and only re-emerge in the late 1970s. Of the most significant 're-discoveries' of early institutionalist research, and one that is instrumental to this research project, was the idea that international institutions can have a significant impact on state behaviour by acting through political channels at the domestic level. B.E. Matecki, writing in 1956, even went so far as to say that international institutions had the ability to encourage national forces that could directly influence the making of national policy.[158] Other key findings of the early institutionalist research included: that the nature of international political economy impacts upon the effectiveness of international institutions; that it is worth studying this effectiveness in order to understand and predict actor behaviour; and that elaborate organisational structures are not always the best way to ensure international cooperation.

More importantly, scholars writing on international institutions in the 1950s and 1960s were concerned not only with whether international institutions have an impact but also *how* they have an impact. However, the lack of a theoretical framework within which to understand and answer these questions meant that the insights developed were simply replaced by other methodological tools borrowed from the broader social sciences. Attention was subsequently paid to the internal politics of international institutions as opposed to their external characteristics and 'actions' in order to explain their impacts on international political economy. This was largely encouraged by issues such as the use of the veto in the UN Security Council (UNSC), which in many ways resulted in the paralysis of this organisation. The UN General Assembly

(UNGA) too was scrutinised as it increasingly became a workshop for East–West confrontation throughout the Cold War. Furthermore, following the influx of newly independent states in the 1960s, the UNGA developed also into an arena for North–South conflicts.[159]

Regardless of the advancements in institutionalist theory, its dominance in social science research would be challenged and discredited by the behavioural revolution of the 1960s. Behaviouralist scholars were insistent upon dismissing the formalisms of social science and political science in particular, such as institutions, organisational charts, legal assumptions and so on.[160] Over the next three decades theorists sought to find a more comprehensive way of doing social science research. Rational choice theorists such as Anthony Downs sought to explain international relations in terms of the independent individual unit's rational self-interests.[161] At the same time theorists of a neo-Marxist orientation attempted to understand and explain the human world via the roles of structures and systemic power.[162]

The influence of behaviouralism and the study of US domestic politics have been highly significant in developments in institutionalist research. This is not least of all because the many scholars in IPE have traditionally been Western (often American) in origin or in education. The majority of the emerging literature on the internal politics of the UNGA throughout the 1960s, for example, could be traced back to developments and literature in the study of US domestic politics. Hayward Alker and Bruce Russett's study *International Politics in the General Assembly*, for example, acknowledged 'that studies of the American political process by Robert Dahl, Duncan Macrae, and David Truman were theoretically and methodologically suggestive of ways in which roll-call data could be used to test for the existence of a pluralistic political process in a quasi-legislative international organization'.[163]

By the 1970s a new research path in understanding international institutions had been taken. Rather than focus on the formal character of international institutions, Robert Cox and Harold Jacobson's study of eight specialised UN agencies in an edited volume focused on the structure and processes of influence of these institutions and their outcomes.[164] Their underlying assumption was that IOs could be analysed as though they are unitary political systems which had evident patterns of influence. This research path subsequently led to an inter-governmental model of the influences of IOs. The core assumption of this model was that there exist intimate inter governmental and transnational relationships between different government bureaucracies as well as between domestic pressure groups.[165]

A final strand of institutionalist research during the 1970s emerged from Ernst Haas' neo-functional work. According to Haas, 'political integration is the process whereby actors shift their loyalties, expectations, and political activities toward a new centre, whose institutions possess or demand jurisdiction over pre-existing national states'.[166] Building on this assumption, the roles of interest groups and individuals in the processes of integration and institutionnalisation were emphasised. The involvement in the national policy-making process of individuals and groups was seen as being highly significant. Furthermore, these actors were hypothesised to perceive benefits in involvement in international institutions and thus present them in a favourable light.[167] In this study a range of actors are considered and it is the interaction of this plurality of actors which is examined rather than processes of integration brought about by consensus building. The developments within institutionalist research since the end of the Second World War were rapidly disrupted during the early 1970s. The two decades of predictable and relatively stable monetary relations under the Bretton Woods institutions were shattered by the unilateral US decision made in

1971 to abandon dollar-gold convertibility and later to float the dollar.[168] The sudden emergence of OPEC and its power with respect to oil pricing and supply further shook the foundations of the liberal economic order. The 1973 oil embargoes of the United States and Holland exemplified the newfound power and influence that OPEC had in international political economy.[169] As a result a multitude of responses to the series of events that undermined the international order during the 1970s were presented. The most advocated approach was to strengthen IOs in order to combat the problems of an increasingly interdependent world.[170] The majority of the responses suggested were often contradictory; however, one similarity was evident. The focus on formal structures and agreements based on multilateral treaties such as the UN was no longer sufficient in understanding and explaining international issues and events.[171]

Confronted by a world characterised by complex interdependence, scholars began to expand the study of international institutionalism by including international regimes – where an international regime is defined as a set of rules, norms, princeples and procedures, or in other words a set of non-tangible institutions.[172] By encompassing international regimes in institutionalist research it became possible to study how international rules and norms *as well as* IOs affect actor behaviour. This allowed for the substitution of an understanding of the workings of IOs for a more thorough understanding of international governance.[173] Through the late 1970s and early 1980s the study of international regimes developed in order to analyse in more detail the circumstances and ways in which states cooperate with each other. A key part of this is the inquiry into how international institutions affect the potential for cooperation.

The study of international regimes developed in three main directions. First, distributive consequences of actor behaviour were replaced by a greater consideration of how international regimes are created in the first place and how they change over time, and what role norms and values have in this process.[174] Second, specific attention has been paid to the subjective meaning of the norms and values which influence the nature of international regimes.[175] Third, explanations began to emerge by the mid-1980s that overtly connected international regimes with broader international cooperation. Here the realist-based critique that states' relative power, national interests and relative gains[176] are key features of much international politics has been adopted and built upon. Robert Keohane, for example, developed research in the 1980s on how international institutions provide ways for states to overcome the problems of high transaction costs (an economist's term which means the cost of making and enforcing agreements), collective action, and information deficits or asymmetries.[177] It must be noted that Keohane's work, while developing the institutionalist approach in one direction, also reneged on some institutionalist work by viewing states as unitary rational actors and ignoring transnational coalitions. Furthermore, the strength of Keohane's work lies in the value of explaining how institutions are created and maintained as opposed to how they affect state behaviour.[178]

So, despite the tide of new approaches to social science there remained many scholars who saw the institutionalist approach as the most complete way of doing research. Scholars such as R.A.W. Rhodes[179] have argued that the institutional approach is still useful and claim that *adapting* the approach to meet the criticisms of others has been successful. The result is a range of *new* institutionalisms which specify and defend the assumptions and practices of traditional institutionalism. These approaches have six core characteristics which as a whole make *new* institutionalisms much more complete. First, there has been a shift from focusing on organisations and other tangible institutions to include non-tangible institutions such as rules, norms, values and procedures. The second characteristic is that institutions are no longer held to be exclusively formal, but include informal conceptions too. Third, the view of IOs has therefore become increasingly dynamic as opposed to fixed. Fourth, the values embedded in institutionalism which have come under scrutiny, have explicitly been defended and included in institutionalist research. Furthermore, the conception of institutions has become more disaggregated whereas traditionally it had been holistic. And finally there has been a major shift from the view of institutions as independent actors to one where they are embedded in particular contexts.[180]

James March and Johan Olsen, who coined the term 'new institutionalism',[181] have helped to redefine what the term 'institution' means for social science. Thus:

> The bureaucratic agency, the legislative committee, the appellate court are arenas for contending social forces, but they are also collections of standard operating procedures and structures that define and defend interests. They are political actors in their own right.[182]

This argument prompts a number of important questions for this study which must be answered. These include: what actually constitutes an institution; how do institutions operate; what is the capacity for individuals to influence the functions and nature of institutions; and in turn how do institutions shape and influence the functions and nature of individuals and other actors? There seems to be no single answer to any of these questions; instead, institutionalist theorists offer differing, but sometimes similar and overlapping answers.[183] The result of these differing answers is the range of institutional approaches, which Peters identifies as the following: normative institutionalism; rational choice institutionalism; historical institutionalism; empirical institutionalism; followed by sociological institutionalism; and network institutionalism.[184]

The differences in institutionalist approaches arise from the answers given to the questions mentioned above. These answers are based on slightly differing epistemological positions. All institutionalist approaches seek to understand and explain social phenomena and relationships and as such are largely foundationalist in ontology. However, they vary in the manner in which the world is understood and explained. On the one hand there are the normative institutionalist approaches (normative institutionalism; sociological institutionalism; and network institutionalism) and on the other, approaches which are rational choice variants (rational choice institutionalism; historical institutionalism; empirical institutionalism and international institutionalism).[185] The normative strand views institutions as organisations, sets of rules and values that determine appropriate behaviour.[186] In international political economy this could mean institutions such as international copyright laws which determine when, where and by whom certain goods and services are eligible for production and sale. A further example could be the Most Favoured Nation (MFN) principle of the WTO. The rational choice strand views institutions as organisations, rules, values, norms, and procedures as determinants of interactions between utility-maximising actors.[187]

Referring back to the epistemological foundations and the core aims of this study provides some clarity to the utility of the institutionalist approach in this case. The general theme of this research project is to study the nature and characteristics of trade relations between states on a bilateral and multilateral basis. The aim is to understand these relations in the context of the international institutions that have helped to determine them. This is in order to explain the nature and characteristics of these relations and provide some insight into the future prospects of cooperation and integration between these states and others. It is not, therefore, simply a normative project but one that is interested in the inherent interests of actors and how these are pursued in the context of international institutions. These themes and aims are best exemplified in the institutionalist approach which aims to assess how the behaviour of actors determines the nature of and is in turn steered by the formal and informal structural constraints of international political economy.[188]

However, this approach does not leave much room in terms of analytical power for the inclusion of the impacts of international institutions on actor behaviour in the normative sense. In short, an implicit assumption of this project is that international trade can in certain circumstances lead to increased cooperation between actors and thus increased stability at both the domestic and international levels. With this consideration, it seems most appropriate to conceptualise the theoretical approach to this project as one which allows for a synthesis of both rational choice and normative elements. This can best be accomplished by using the liberal institutionalist approach used largely, but not exclusively, in IPE and IR by theorists such as Robert Keohane, Joseph Nye, Daniel Griswold and Brink Lyndsey.

IPE theorists often point to the importance of certain types of actors and relationships for the management of international relations. The most often cited are international institutions and hegemony.[189] As mentioned above there have traditionally been two types of international institutions that are of significant interest to IPE scholars:[190] first IOs and second international regimes. International regimes often attempt to promote an international system of cooperation in the areas of monetary relations and international trade.[191] In more recent institutionalist work as outlined above there has been the expansion of what is classed as an institution to include abstract and non-tangible elements of the social world. These include: values, norms, beliefs, procedures, structures and processes. At the same time many IOs attempt to promote both economic and political cooperation in a system which is characterised by a high level of interdependence between actors.

Liberal institutionalism focuses on the use of international institutions and a liberal international economic order to promote peace and prosperity among states through greater interdependence.[192] Achieving cooperation[193] in a system of states and other actors is highly problematic as there is no centralised authority which can establish and enforce rules of behaviour. Nevertheless, liberal institutionalists contend that a strong set of IOs provides the framework upon which states can settle their disputes peacefully, without resorting to violent conflict.[194]

Liberal institutionalists further contend that a liberal international economic order created and maintained by regimes leads to greater economic interdependence between states.[195] This economic interdependence helps to prevent conflict by increasing the profits of peaceful coexistence while at the same time increasing the costs of conflict.[196] According to liberal institutionalism, power is primarily economic in nature, and therefore much competition between actors takes place in the economic sphere. Hence, by increasing economic interdependence and thus economic cooperation, competition between actors is reduced. Liberal institutionalists, furthermore, argue that two conditions are required in order to sustain a state of peace: interdependence and liberal democracies.[197]

One way in which interdependence is fostered is through inter-state cooperation and economic integration by greater international trade. In a globalising world system these trends are ever-increasing. However, greater levels of international trade between states do not only affect relations at the international level. Rather, there is also a significant impact at the domestic level.[198] Daniel T. Griswold has argued that increased trade can have significant socio-political and socio economic impacts within states. In the first instance trade can help to influence the political system of a state through increasing interaction between that state's citizens and those of other (perhaps freer) societies.[199] This interaction can take the form of face-to-face meetings as well as via electronic communications such as phone, fax or email. Furthermore, increased communication between groups of people who are involved with the processes of trade can bring a sharing of ideas along with exposure to alternative ways of thinking and organising civil society and business. The flow of books, magazines and other forms of media can often have a political and social context, helping to further spread different ways of thinking. By exploiting the opportunities for foreign travel and study that come with foreign investment and trade, citizens can experience the political and civil liberties of others, thus further influencing the direction of domestic political demands.[200]

For liberals a key constraint on individual political freedom is the extent of governmental power. Economic freedom and trade can provide a counterweight to this. This is because the free market diffuses economic decision-making from the control of a small number of governmental actors and into the hands of a broader range of actors. This reduces the power of the centralised actors, who often use the power gained by monopoly over decision-making to marginalise other actors. David Held claims that the subsequent dispersion of economic control creates space for non-governmental actors and private sector alternatives to central political control and authority, such as civil society.[201] The presence of private sector corporations creates an alternative source of wealth, influence and leadership. Furthermore, non-state institutions can be funded by the private economy. According to March and Olsen these institutions can provide new ideas as well as influence and leadership outside the control of the government.[202]

Anthony Downs claims that increased international trade is often accompanied by faster growth and greater levels of wealth.[203] These in turn promote democratic practices by creeating an economically independent and politically aware middle class. A larger middle class means a larger number of people who can afford to be educated and take an interest in political affairs. Authoritarian systems of governance can be prone to acute shifts in economic policy. As citizens gain more assets and establish businesses and careers in the private sector they will be more likely to desire continuity.[204] At the same time that increased international trade and integration at the international level can lead to impacts at the domestic level, actors, institutions, and processes at the domestic level can impact upon the emergence, nature and success of international integration.[205]

Liberal institutionalism, like other theoretical approaches, as mentioned above, is very broad and complex, and encompasses a large number of key principles. Furthermore, how these key principles relate to each other often deviates from one version of the theory to another. It is, however, possible to identify and present the key principles used in any particular approach and how these relate to each other. The exact nature of these principles and their relationship to each other determine the unique nature of any theoretical analysis. In this study a critical version of liberal institutionalism is used which shares much in common with the institutionalisms used by scholars such as Robert Keohane, Joseph Nye, Ernest Haas and Robert Axelrod as highlighted above. Some amendments and re-interpretations are made, however, which while limited in scope are significant in terms of impact on what is studied here and how.

With regard to the similar key principles and assumptions adopted in the theoretical approach, this project shares a number of common elements with broader institutionalist approaches. In the first instance is the assumption of a global system which is characterised by limited global governance and regulation of state and non-state behaviour. Here, while some elements of global governance can be seen with regard to some issues and processes in particular regions, the belief in the existence of a global system which is closer to the conception of anarchy is adopted. Furthermore international institutions are aimed at addressing the anarchic system and allow for greater interaction, which helps reduce anarchy. Secondly, institutions are seen here as being IOs and regimes. Thirdly, a plurality of actors is assumed. No single type of actor, whether a state or MNC and so on, can ultimately be defined as universally dominant over time and space. Rather, all types of actors can be relevant and can have differing levels of importance with regards to different issues, processes, relationships in different places and at different times.

A fourth key principle which forms the version of liberal institutionalism used in this study is the belief that all actors have aims and objectives which they pursue – whether through cooperation or conflict. However, a rationalist approach is not fully adopted here. Instead while actors have interests which they pursue these interests and the actions taken to achieve them may not come as a result of wholly rational calculation under circumstances of perfect information. The belief here is that often interests and subsequent policies are based upon imperfect information and imperfect calculation. In short we can only go so far as to claim that actors have interests which they pursue but we cannot assume rationality. We must therefore include a deeper discussion of the formation of actor interests and policies.

Issue linkage or issue interdependence is also a key principle discussed in this project. This point is linked directly to a sixth principle, which is that international relations are a plus sum game (this point is discussed below). The assumption of issue linkage and interdependence is pivotal to this study as it allows for a complex analysis of the political economy of trade between Jordan and the United States in a heterodox manner. The issue of bilateral trade facilitation at the state level, for example, is directly linked with other issues such as state-level cooperation on foreign policy matters, non-state actor activity in domestic markets as well as societal interaction, and so on. Furthermore, international relations and domestic relations are intricately linked and often inseparable. Thus the Jordanian government's decision to facilitate trade with the United States should be discussed not only by examining Jordanian foreign policy but domestic policy and interests as well. Also, repercussions of processes and relationships at one level of analysis can be extremely important in leading to repercussions at another level – such as the arguments put forward by Brink Lyndsey and Daniel Griswold regarding the link between trade and democratic processes at the domestic level.

While the developments in institutionalist study over the past several decades have been significant in relation to the broader fields of study encompassed in IPE and IR, they have often been ignored by mainstream research. However, in relation to assessing and evaluating the political economy of trade relations between the United States and Jordan a critical liberal institutionalist approach will prove highly effective. This is for a number of reasons: first, current trends in these trade relations suggest a greater move towards political and economic reform. Second, there is an emerging broad-ranging adoption of liberal trade policies by Jordan and other states in the MENA region, coupled with a strengthening impetus within the United States to encourage this adoption. The move to liberal policies could precede a move to greater integration with the global economic system and to greater integration with the United States in particular.

At a more basic level, employing a critical liberal institutionalist approach allows for the reconciliation of a number of basic components essential to this study. In the first instance this approach allows for the study of a range of different actors without giving primacy to any single one. In this study this is important as states, MNCs, IGOs, NGOs and individuals as actors are all studied. At the core of the approach used here is the assumption that all of these actors may have agency; however, no single one may have ultimate primacy. Furthermore, while some of these actors are studied as tangible institutions in the form of IOs, this study also examines non-tangible institutions such as trade liberalisation agreements and regimes. Finally, this theoretical approach allows for the fusion of an anti-foundationalist and realist scientific approach with an interpretativist approach to a certain extent, and does not require exclusively positivist research to be carried out.

2

STATE FACILITATION OF TRADE:
Jordanian Interests and Policy

In the endeavour to study the political economy of trade between Jordan and the United States it is necessary to address a number of questions regarding how state actors have created and engaged with international institutions. This chapter thus begins the assessment of state-level facilitation of trade by discussing Jordanian state interests at the domestic and international levels and the links between them through issue interdependence. This is done in order to determine what the state's main interests are, what policies taken to pursue these interests and how both these issues are decided. By analysing the demands and constraints on government decision-making within the context of an anarchic international system with limited international governance, the main state interests can be identified. It is then possible to offer a description and an explanation of how Jordan has engaged with international institutions in the form of both IOs and regimes pertaining to trade in order to achieve its main aims through more cooperative relations. The main premise is that dual processes of reform in both the political and economic spheres at the domestic level have been encouraged by changes in the domestic and international environments. Furthermore, these processes of reform have interacted, resulting in a reinforcement of change in the domestic and international interests of the Jordanian government.

Under the rule of King Hussein, Jordanian interests had largely been determined by external actors and processes, much the same as today.[1] However, the international relations of the Middle East and the broader international system, coupled with the level of socio-economic development within Jordan, historically resulted in a security-oriented set of government interests.[2] While socio-economic interests were evident, they were constantly subservient to the greater interests of national security, regime survival and regional stability.[3] In the twenty-first century the accelerating processes of globalisation, economic and strategic regional transformation and the changing socio-economic characteristics of Jordanian society have produced a far different environment. In short, there has been a shift from the focus on security interests and a set of security-oriented domestic and foreign policies to a focus on socio-economic interests and a political economy-oriented set of domestic and foreign policies. This new policy focus has led to state-level facilitation of international trade through engagement with international institutions.

In the endeavour to explore the current set of national interests it will be necessary to first briefly explore the transformation of Jordanian domestic and foreign policies over the past two decades. The first section briefly explores changes in government decision-making in the 1990s and the early King Abdullah II era. Changes through the 1990s provided the basis from which government interests were been redefined after 1999. Gil Feiler argues that, in part a result of the reorientation of national interests and in part a cause of it a vast range of interdependent issues are now having a significant impact upon the decision-making process.[4] Subsequent sections of this chapter address these issues. Two broad categories of interests can be identified at both the domestic and international levels: socio-economic and security. As will be shown through this chapter, the majority of contemporary interests fall within the former category. At the same time some interests and policy responses fall in the last category and continue to impact decision-making. For the purposes of this chapter and in order to allow for a cohesive argument to be made, socio-economic interests will be explored in detail.

Philip Dew and Anthony Shoult claim that policy making under King Abdullah II can best be described as reformist.[5] Political and economic liberal reform has been the calling card of the various governments and main institutions since 1999. The second section of this chapter outlines efforts towards political liberalisation and the processes of democratisation supported by the government since 2000. Economic liberalisation is dealt with in the following sections. There are three elements to economic reform pursued by the Jordanian government over the past two decades. The first element is macro-economic structural adjustment. Section three addresses the relevant adjustment policies taken by the government through the 1990s and early twenty-first century. The next section examines the second element of the government's economic reform: privatisation. The fifth section develops the previous discussions by assessing the government's move towards facilitating external trade through FTAs. In all of the areas of economic reform, the Jordanian government has engaged with liberal economic international institutions.

A conclusion will re-emphasise the main points of the evolution of governmental domestic and foreign policy in the twenty-first century. A summary is also provided of the framework within which current political economy-orientated policy is made.

Political and economic reform: 1989–99

In 1989 the Jordanian government announced the temporary suspension of external debt repayments. A financial crisis had befallen the kingdom that evolved into the worst economic crisis in the short history of the country. One of King Hussein's responses was to implement an adjustment and austerity agreement which had been made with the IMF in return for assistance.[6] It must be noted, however, that this agreement (and indeed economic reform in general) was disrupted in 1990 and did not re-start until 1992. The agreement's main recommendation was the cutback of government subsidies on food and other basic goods.[7] The result was a gradual easing of budgetary demands on the government and resumption of debt servicing. Such moves were not welcomed at home, however, as a large part of the population was heavily reliant on government subsidies and in particular the subsidy for bread. Riots broke out across Jordan from Amman to Ma'an, Karak and Salt. In response to calls for greater governmental accountability and transparency the government announced that parliamentary elections would be held in November 1989. A national charter to guide the democratisation process was adopted in June 1991. The following year martial law was lifted, political parties were legalised and restrictions on freedom of expression were relaxed.[8]

The pace of change drastically slowed following the 2 August 1991 Iraqi invasion of Kuwait. Once again security concerns seemed to negate all other interests and the Jordanian government reverted back to advocating a strict security state with a slow and tightly controlled programme of political reform.[9] With the economic situation still in crisis and the likely prospect of the Iraq–Kuwait conflict evolving into a broader international conflict involving regional and extra-regional states, the prospect for domestic political change seemed extinguished. King Hussein, weary of domestic sentiment which strongly favoured Saddam Hussein, officially adopted a neutral stance in the Gulf Crisis and subsequent war.[10] This neutrality was seen as being pro-Iraq both at home and abroad.

With regard to the international relations of the region and broader international system, this stance proved to be extremely costly. Members of the Gulf Cooperation Council (GCC) feared an Iraqi invasion further south down the Persian Gulf as well as domestic rebellions by 'foreigners' from neighbouring Arab states who resided within their borders.[11] Their response was to side with the US-led coalition against Iraq, to expel large numbers of expatriate workers (most of whom were of Palestinian, Jordanian, Egyptian and Sudanese origin) and to reduce or cease aid to those states seen to be siding with Saddam Hussein's regime.[12] The cost to the Jordanian economy verged on catastrophic. Approximately 300,000 expatriate workers 'returned' to the kingdom, adding to the demand for housing, services, jobs and government subsidies.[13] The halt in discounted oil coupled with the drop in financial aid from the GCC states and the West (most notably the United States) had a further negative impact on the economy.[14]

At home the result of the government's position was far different. According to Ranjit Singh, King Hussein's popularity in 1991 was as high as it had ever been and popular sentiment towards the government was extremely accommodating.[15] This wave of popular support and satisfaction further slowed the pace of change at home. Parliament was postponed in the fall of 1991 (seen by most as an attempt to prevent a no-confidence vote on the government of then Prime Minister Tahir Masri). Changes to the electoral law were made in November 1993, which subsequently enhanced the electoral chances of pro-regime candidates.[16] The government then seized on the opportunity to conclude the 1994 peace treaty with Israel, which was assured to be unpopular at home among both the approximately 60 per cent population of Palestinian descent and the remaining 'East Bankers'.

The following five years saw a decline in support for the government and a rise in the expression of anti-government sentiments through independent media, political associations and popular movements.[17] The government's response was to re-introduce restrictions on the media. The final reversal of the hard-won political liberalisation which had taken place through the late 1980s and early 1990s came when in 1997 'the opposition parties, professional associations and prominent independent figures boycotted the elections'.[18] With only pro-regime candidates, parliament was solidified as an adjunct to the regime.

By February 1999 and the passing of King Hussein, the democratic gains made in the 1989–93 period had been reversed and the kingdom had once again become a state where the security apparatus was omnipresent, and security interests and concerns defined government policy. However, the seeds had been sown and for the first time in its history the Jordanian government had seriously considered reform over a significant period of time. The preponderance of high politics in the making of policy had for a time been interrupted by issues of low politics. With the death of King Hussein and the ascension to power of a young, inexperienced and relatively unknown head of state the opportunity for change once again presented itself.

Political liberalisation and democratisation

While 1999 brought potential for change with a new head of state with arguably a more 'contemporary' outlook, the ascension of King Abdullah II did not translate into immediate political change. It was hoped, although not expected, that Abdullah would instantly initiate a broad ranging programme of political liberalisation that would result in an opening up of the political system in Jordan and usher in more democratic practices. As the initial months of his reign passed it became clear that the analysts who had suggested the transition from one ruler to another would mean tighter controls were in fact correct. The actual succession had in the first instance been 'rocky' as the ailing King Hussein removed the designation of Crown Prince and heir to the throne from his brother Hassan Bin Talal in favour of his eldest son, Abdullah. Hassan had been Crown Prince for almost the whole of King Hussein's rule and was widely expected to take power once his elder brother had passed away.[19] It came as a relative shock therefore that this would not be the case and that Abdullah, a figure of unknown political capabilities, would lead the kingdom into the twenty-first century. With a plethora of destabilising forces (economic, political and regional) against him King Abdullah II cautiously retained the role of the security services. Security issues became ever more important and the *Mukhabarat* (the Jordanian secret police) increased in importance.[20] Over the first year and a half of King Abdullah II's reign press freedoms receded further, there was a general crackdown on protests and academics, journalists and others were dismissed for perceived political offences.[21]

As has become a hallmark of Abdullah's leadership, he managed to escape the subsequent negative response from the masses. Instead it was the Director of the General Intelligence Department (GID), Samih Batikhi that was the target of blame for the worsening political environment.[22] Critics scorned Batikhi for his dual role as Director of the GID and Royal Advisor and laid the blame for the tightening of the political system on him. In November 2000 Batikhi was replaced by Major General Saad Kheir, who remained out of the public eye and as such also escaped blame, although the prospects for political liberalisation still remained small.[23] The following November King Abdullah II postponed parliamentary elections, saying that more time was needed to implement procedures that had been mandated by a newly drafted electoral law. This postponement evolved into an indefinite suspension of parliament, signalling that there were still no intentions of loosening the government's grip over the political sphere.[24]

Regardless of who became the target of condemnation, further government controls on the political system continued through the following years. In 2001 an amended Article of the Penal Code, article 150, was passed by royal decree establishing severe penalties for those who published news that could damage national unity, incite crimes and hatred or jeopardise stability. The amendment to article 150 further built upon the 1999 Press and Publications Law – a law which in itself was seen as harsh. A range of other laws were passed that same year, including the Public Gatherings Law,[25] the State Security Court Law[26] and the Municipalities Law.[27] It must be noted, however, that while the introduction of these new or amended laws was unwelcome, the suspension of parliament was seen by some as a blessing in disguise. One opinion was that parliamentarians, who were conservative and deprived of any real power, were corrupt and inefficient. Others (generally within the government) viewed parliament as a liability which would offer only criticism of the government's foreign policy and would act as a hindrance to economic reform. Former Finance Minister Michel Marto claimed that 'the absence of parliament was essential for the introduction of legislative reform, because in the past gaining parliamentary approval proved very difficult'.[28]

Throughout this period of consolidation of control the government was split into two camps. On the one hand were those who advocated strict controls and further roll-back of the processes of political reform begun in 1989. According to Bouillon, the rationale for such a position was two-fold: first that security in the kingdom was under increasing threat as a result of the destabilising impact of the transition in rule and the more worrying march to war by the international community against Iraq.[29] Second was the recognition that the vast majority of the population were more interested in economic issues such as increased employyment and income as opposed to democratic freedoms.[30] On the other side were those who called for greater liberalisation and reform such as entrepreneur and former Prime Minister Ali Abul Ragheb. However, within this camp there was a general consensus that economic liberalisation and reform was of greater immediate importance. Furthermore, it was believed that this would be more readily accomplished under a more closed political system.[31] The then Minister of the Royal Court, Faisal Al-Fayez, argued that once economic reform was well underway then democratic forces could emerge.[32] Despite their numerous different objectives, both camps shared the belief that political liberalisation should be slow and managed.

It was the advocates of the latter camp that eventually gained more influence within government by 2002 and in October of that year the 'Jordan First' campaign was launched.[33] The launch of this reformist campaign was not solely a result of the disposition of those in the government. External factors coupled with economic processes within Jordan also contributed. Jordan has the misfortune of being located in what has been termed the 'rough neighbourhood' of the Middle East, sandwiched between two conflict zones. On the east lies embattled Iraq, which by October 2002 was on the verge of being invaded for the second time in just over a decade. To the west lies Palestine and Israel, between whom the Second Intifada was raging at that time. With economic woes remaining largely unchanged since the late 1980s and early 1990s and with large parts of the population living below the poverty line (see later discussion), pressure on the government was mounting. As Faisal Al-Fayez had argued, ordinary Jordanians were more interested in their own economic well-being than in political freedoms. However, by 2002 neither economic nor political expectations were being met, thus putting more pressure on the government to act in some manner.

Throughout the build-up to the third Gulf War King Abdullah II had managed successful brinkmanship by satisfying popular pressures at home and international (largely US) pressure abroad.[34] At home the vast majority of the Jordanian population was overwhelmingly against any further confrontation between Iraq and the international community. Abroad, Washington was applying immense pressure to its regional allies in the attempt to drum up political and military support. For Jordan this meant use of Jordanian territory in the eastern desert region bordering Iraq for use by Special Forces – deployed by the United States and United Kingdom in an effort to seek out and destroy Iraqi Scud missile units.[35] With these dual pressures increasing, the government was aware that the general public needed some way to express their feelings. Coming away from a meeting with President Bush at the White House in the summer of 2002, King Abdullah II knew that the United States would invade Iraq in the coming winter or spring. According to Alan George he also knew he would have to offer some support to this endeavour.[36]

In order to win support from his Western allies and at the same time keep the Jordanian street quiet, Abdullah embarked on an active period of diplomacy. Following his meeting at the White House in 2002 he shuttled across the globe in an effort to drum up support for a peaceful solution to the crisis. This was done carefully to show his people at home that every effort was being made to avert war and help the Iraqi brethren (not necessarily the regime) while not annoying Washington. He also ensured that his government denied that there were US and UK troops stationed in his country beyond the acknowledged several hundred troops there for the defence of the kingdom – manning Patriot anti-ballistic missile units and so on. Other measures included assuring the public that oil would continue to be subsidised in the event of a loss of Iraqi supply (which was guaranteed when war started); issuing stern warnings that while the public were allowed to express displeasure with events they were not allowed to disrupt the stability of the kingdom; and to continue to issue condemnations of the conflict once it had gotten underway.[37]

As was expected, the initial military-engagement period of the conflict was over in a relatively short time. Coming as a great relief to many regimes in the region and especially to the Jordanian government, this meant that the storm had so far been weathered successfully. However, public opinion was outraged and condemnation over the king's international decisions was common.[38] Furthermore, the economy had suffered in the months leading up to the invasion with continuing problems in the early 'post-war' period. Most badly hit were sectors which affected the people more directly than others. Tourism, for example, had seen a serious plunge in revenues earned, leading to lower incomes and loss of jobs. The result was the decision made by the government, led by those who supported political reform first followed by economic reform, to once again attempt to open up the political system.[39] In order to defuse public pressure, parliamentary elections were announced for 17 June 2003 (less than two weeks after the official end of combat operations in Iraq). This was followed by the repeal of the temporary amendments to Article 150 of the Penal Code that had been implemented in 2001.[40]

By late summer 2003 it appeared that calls were being made for further democratisation and political liberalisation in the future. The then Foreign Minister, Marwan Muasher, in an interview conducted by the Brussels-based think tank International Crisis Group (ICG) claimed that the way to greater security and stability was through political liberalisation.[41] One reason given was that Jordan needed to pre-empt calls for democratisation from Washington which, he claimed, were counter-productive. The vast majority of the Jordanian population mistrust the Washington administration and viewed President Bush's insistence on democratisation, in the same way as other US prescriptions, as part of an imperialist plot.[42] According to Muasher those Arab regimes which heed such calls are therefore seen as stooges of the United States. Furthermore, Muasher argued that those who advocate true reform have subsequently been marginalised by this interpretation. He went on to describe Jordan's strength as lying 'in the fact that we are more open – politically and economically – than the rest of the region. This is how we managed to capture the attention of the West in the first place.'[43] It was the belief of many in the government that in order to maintain Jordan's position as a reliable and competitive partner and to continue to receive economic support, the government must pursue greater political liberalisation.

Others have agreed with Muasher's call for greater liberalisation but for differing reasons. The common fear seems to be that as a result of economic stagnation and in the absence of legitimate political means of expression Jordanians will pursue undemocratic means to express their frustration.[44] With conflicts on two of its borders and with a population which is highly sensitive to these conflicts, the risk of extremism taking root in the kingdom is very real. Some realise this, including Ahmad Obeidat who has acted as Prime Minister, Head of the GID and director of the National Centre for Human Rights. Obeidat has argued that total democracy as well as absolute political closure would harm national security. Rather he argues that:

> The government needs to balance between risks and needs between security, human rights and democracy. It is all a matter of wise state management, you need a vision, a strategy, a system and regulations. Jordan is not a new state, it has been in existence

for more than seventy years. It should not be that worried about opening up politically. Regional problems are bound to be felt here but this should not mean that the government must place a limit on political openness.[45]

Since 2003 the call by those in government such as Muasher and Obeidat has been heeded and greater political freedoms have been implemented. With economic reform well under way prior to 2003 and continuing liberalisation in this sphere taking place, further reform seems likely in the short to medium term.

Economic reform: Structural adjustment

Following the 1989 financial crisis and economic slowdown in Jordan, epitomised by the 1989 default on debt repayments by the government, poverty and unemployment rose dramatically to unofficial figures as high as 70 per cent of the total population[46] and 40 per cent of the active labour force.[47] Macro economic restructuring throughout the 1990s was difficult and detrimental to large parts of Jordanian society but was largely accomplished by the time King Abdullah II took the throne.[48] The process of economic reform in Jordan dates back to the 1989 financial crisis. Through the 1980s the drop in oil prices on the international market led to a general slowing down of the region's economy as a whole. The effect on Jordan was relatively severe, with lower remittances coming from expatriate workers living and working in GCC states and lower demand for export goods and services.[49] The government responded by increasing public spending, which was financed by external borrowing, in order to stimulate the economy. This did not have the desired effect, however, as external debt quickly expanded but the economy remained weak with high inflation and an increasing budget deficit.[50]

Following the economic difficulties that the kingdom

faced in 1989 came a series of tough economic reform measures aimed at stabilising the government's budget in order to reinstate the servicing of external debt. Initially these reforms were prescribed by external actors such as the IMF, World Bank (WB) and various donor states such as the United States. As such they were not domestically constructed plans implemented with the sovereign intent of improving the economic standing of the nation's citizens.[51]

The reforms centred on restoring growth and reducing economic imbalances. In mid-1989 the WB and IMF both supported the process: the former with a $150 million Industrial and Trade Policy Adjustment Loan (approved in December 1989 and closed in 1992),[52] and the latter through a macro-economic stabilisation programme in the form of a Standby Arrangement. A WB report on the reform process initiated in 1989 states that the Jordanian government's response to the crisis included three elements:

1)   Macroeconomic policy adjustment to reduce internal and external imbalances, mainly by reducing the fiscal deficit and maintaining a flexible and competitive exchange rate.

2)   Trade liberalization and industrial policy reforms to induce a strong supply response.

3)   Protection of the poor through restructuring of public expenditures and provision of targeted safety nets. The policy changes were to be accompanied by reforms of the legal and regulatory regimes to stimulate investment.[53]

Reforms were directed towards four main areas of the economy. These were: obtaining macro-economic balance by fiscal adjustment, reducing inflation through tightening the monetary policy, liberalisation of the trade regime and protecting the poor (according to Carlos Silva-Jauregui, a task manager in the WB's Social and Economic Development Sector MENA Region department, this latter aim was more popular within the Jordanian government than with external actors such as the IMF and WB).[54] The main problem faced by the government in 1989 was the fiscal deficit, which had grown to record levels. The IMF supported a programme to reform the tax system while the WB supported programmes to cut public expenditures, including food subsidies. In 1988 the government's total expenditures had topped 49 per cent of GDP.[55] This figure was reduced to 39 per cent by 1992 after the government implemented the IMF- and WB-backed programmes.[56] Efforts included cutting military spending, implementing a targeting mechanism for the poorest segments of society to replace food subsidies and, in 1992, increasing oil prices, practically eliminating oil subsidies. Higher tax revenues due to increased trade levels and a conversion from quantitative restrictions into tariffs (doubling revenue from trade between 1990 and 1992), along with reduced budget expenditures, led to a decline in the deficit. Between 1989 and 1993 the deficit had dropped from 18 per cent of GDP to 6 per cent.[57]

With the account deficit declining, inflation rates within Jordan also declined. In 1989 inflation had stood at approximately 26 per cent.[58] By 1993, following the implementation of broad economic reforms, this figure had dropped to the relatively low figure of just over 4 per cent. At the same time the government adopted a policy of tightening monetary policy, which included liberalising the financial sector. By decontrolling deposit and lending rates the government was able to avoid higher inflation and encourage short-term capital inflows due to domestic interest rates climbing. This process was briefly interrupted by the Gulf Crisis and War in late 1990 and early 1991.[59] However, while the crisis had negative effects on the Jordanian economy including the return of 300,000 expatriate workers, the return of these citizens also meant the repatriation of savings. Coupled with the increase in capital inflows this resulted in foreign reserves within Jordan increasing ten-fold between 1989 and 1993.[60]

This was significant, not least because the Jordanian economy was burdened with a large external debt. By the middle of 1990 total external debt accounted for 180 per cent of the kingdom's GDP. The government managed to reduce this figure to 132 per cent of GDP by the end of 1993.[61] This was initially achieved mostly by pursuing policies of debt restructuring, which leads only to the short-term relief of some of the pressure caused by debt servicing. However, following success in reducing the budgetary expenditures and increasing capital inflows and currency reserves, the government was able to pursue more aggressive debt reduction policies by 1992. Supplementing the policy of debt restructuring the government pursued market-based operations such as debt buybacks and debt swaps. While these policies led to a greater reduction of external debt they were nevertheless still limited, as was realised towards the late 1990s.[62] What was needed was an increase in the ability to service external debt and to repay it.

Due to the perceived limitations on the structural adjustments discussed above, the Jordanian government was encouraged by the IMF and WB to embark on a process of trade liberalisation in the mid-1990s in the hope of further stabilising the economy and increasing revenues through exports. In order to do this a broad-ranging liberalisation programme was initiated. This programme had a number of elements, both demanded by external actors and devised by domestic policy planners. Before the WB would release its $150 million loan it requested that the majority of quantitative restrictions and import bans be removed and replaced with import tariffs.[63] As a response to this condition of the loan the Jordanian government was instructed to rationalise the tariff structure in order to conform to the WB's standards but at the same time not to undermine the increase in revenues sought after. In 1990 the vast majority of domestic price controls were lifted, including thos on food, although essential commodities such as bread remained under a tight monetary policy to ensure that they remained available to the entire population. Like many other countries, Jordan at the start of the 1990s had a fixed exchange rate which prevented depreciation of the Jordanian dinar (JD). However, this policy acted as a brake on international trade levels and so was adjusted and a policy of a 'managed' floating of the JD was adopted – the result was an almost immediate depreciation of the JD by 50 per cent. This policy remained until 23 October 1995 when the JD was pegged to the US dollar.

To complement these international trade reforms domestic adjustments were made. In 1991 the investment law was revised to allow for the licensing of domestic investment to become more efficient and less discretionary. According to Sabri Al-Khassib, the Head of the Research and International Agreements Unit at the Amman Chamber of Commerce, this streamlining of the process led to a two-fold increase in the number of privately owned enterprises operating in the kingdom between 1989 and 1992.[64] In the same year Jordan's primary mechanism for financing exports, the Export Discount Facility (EDF), was reformed to become more accessible to exporters. However, this policy had little effect on increasing exports. Commercial banks were not attracted to the EDF's low interest margins and rigid administrative procedures. Again, further steps had to be taken to improve domestic conditions for export-oriented economic activities and increase overall international trade.

It is worth noting that while the macro-economic structural adjustments were being implemented in the first half of the 1990s extensive measures were taken to protect the most vulnerable segments of the kingdom's population from any detrimental effects. During the period of adjustment the government employed two main policies to acheive this. The first policy was aimed at restructuring public spending so that the reduced amount of resources directed to the public sphere was targeted at those who needed it the most. For example, while military spending and fiscal spending for general price subsidies were reduced, spending on key sectors such as health and education were not.[65] General food subsidies and price controls were removed and replaced with a rationing system that targeted those house holds with the lowest income to receive subsidies and other financial support.[66]

The second policy aimed at protecting the poor from the economic shocks of the adjustment process was to improve the efficiency of the kingdom's networks for supporting the poor. The main component of this policy was the establishment in 1990 of the Development and Employment Fund (DEF), which coordinated the activities of the government and NGOs involved in poverty alleviation.[67] However, while the policy of targeted support was relatively successful, the DEF was not. Initially the creation of the fund helped to win support for the adjustment process and was relatively active. Over time the role of the fund evolved and the DEF became involved more in direct lending as opposed to coordinating poverty alleviation activities.

In short the kingdom's first major encounter with economic reform had been significant. Some successes had been seen, such as the decline in the fiscal budget and subsequent decline in the budgetary deficit, decreasing levels of debt and the resumption of debt servicing. However, overall macro economic adjustment in the 1990s did not translate into high levels of economic growth or a general strengthening of the economy. Rather, the process of structural adjustment allowed the Jordanian economy to recover from the immediate effects of the 1989 financial crisis and resume servicing of its external financial obligations.[68] Efforts to strengthen the economy and press forward into the twenty-first century with strong economic growth were in large part unsuccessful. This was partly due to the fact that policies that would have led to greater economic growth were not pursued until the royal succession of 1999.

Economic reform: privatisation

Although macro-economic restructuring and subsequent economic policy allowed the Jordanian government to resume relatively healthy external debt servicing, overall debt remains at approximately 30 per cent of GDP and stood at almost 50 per cent at the end of 2007.[69] One medium-term goal professed by the Jordanian government is to reduce this figure. In this endeavour further economic restructuring is likely. According to the Jordan Investment Trust Corporation, in the government's pursuit to achieve the abovementioned socio-economic goals, as well as the pursuit of overall economic growth, attracting foreign direct investment (FDI) is of prime importance.[70]

The structural adjustment programme and macro-economic reforms employed through the first half of the 1990s as mentioned above were aimed at economic recovery and stabilisation and not growth. In order to pursue sustained economic growth the Jordanian government embarked upon a process of wide-ranging policy reforms in late 1996.[71] A linchpin of this drive for economic development was the privatisation of government-owned enterprises and service industries. Implementation of this programme had been slow through the 1990s[72] but began in earnest in 1998 with the general aim of rebalancing the role and scale of the public sector in the economy by reducing the government's stake in industrial sectors dominated by state-owned enterprises.[73] According to the Executive Privatisation Commission (EPC), which was established in 1996 and was initially called the

Executive Privatisation Unit (EPU), to spearhead the privatisation process – the goals of the programme are:

> To increase the efficiency and hence production
> levels of privatised firms, creating a competitive
> market where demand and supply can freely inter-
> play, attracting FDI, allowing the private sector to
> participate in infrastructure investments, deepening
> and developing the Jordanian financial market, and
> most importantly, limiting the government's role to
> that of the regulator rather than that of the ineffi-
> cient producer of goods and services.[74]

Prior to 1996 the government had founded and managed
most of the kingdom's infrastructure, including power generation, telecommunications services, transport services and
water supply. The government also had a major role in other
industries such as mining and manufacturing, for example,
majority shares in Jordan Phosphate Mines Corporation
(JPMC), Arab Potash Corporation (APC) and Jordan Cement
Factories (JCFC). The possibility of embarking on a privatisation programme had been discussed as early as 1989,
however, the ongoing structural adjustment programmes
along with worker resistance, bureaucratic red tape and an
overall lack of government support prevented any serious
attempt at privatisation.[75] With the structural adjustment programmes implemented and largely accomplished by the mid
1990s, the Jordanian government was able to address the
issue of reducing the level of public sector involvement in the
economy.

According to Taroob Al-Zu'bi, the Chief Communications Officer of the EPC, there have been five main
methods of privatisation. The first and most common
method has been the sale of government shares in public
share holding companies, or *Capital Privatisation*.[76] This has

been relatively effective and the government has to date sold the majority of its stakeholdings. A second approach has been to sign *Management Contracts* with private sector actors.[77] These contracts usually have a relatively short initial timeframe allowing for assessment of the management and possible extension of the contract, as happened with the water and sewage systems management in the Greater Amman area. The third main method employed so far has been to sign *Concession Agreements*, or *Exclusivity Agreements*, where the private sector is given the responsibility to build a particular enterprise, exploit and operate it pursuant to the concession, as in the case of the Public Transportation Corporation (PTC) which was privatised in 1998.[78] This latter example signifies the initial completion of the privatisation of a major company.

Another method employed has been to sign *Lease Agreements* where the operation of a facility is leased out to a private sector actor but where the government remains the sole owner.[79] The private sector actor will operate the enterprise and reap the profits in exchange for a fee paid to the government. *Private Infrastructure Development and Operation* contracts constitute the final approach. Of these there are four types, it is worth quoting the EPC directly here:

1) Build-Operate-Transfer: The private sector designs, finances, builds, and operates the facility over the life of the contract at the end of which, ownership reverts to the government.

2) Build-Transfer-Operate: The private sector designs, finances and builds the facility then transfers it to the government while retaining the right to operate it for a specific period of time.

3) Build-Own-Operate: The private sector designs, finances and builds the facility, retains ownership and

operates it.

4)   Build-Operate-Own-Transfer: The private sector builds
      the project, owns it for a specific period, operates it and
      then relinquishes it to the public sector.[80]

In order to successfully carry out the privatisation of inefficient and uncompetitive government-owned enterprises, and
to open up public sector-dominated industries but at the same
time to utilise the revenues from such a programme, the
Jordanian government has created a legal and institutional
framework. This framework was not drafted until 1999 after
King Abdullah II took power and consists of three elements.
An organisational structure was needed in order to oversee
the privatisation programme and so the Higher Committee
for Privatisation (HCP), the EPC and the Privatisation Steer-
ing Committees (PSC) were created. According to the WB
'this form of institutional structure provided the right balance
of effectiveness and transparency'.[81]

A National Privatisation Strategy (NPS) was also created
and ratified by parliament in 1999. This document acts as a
general guide for the government on privatisation and also
addresses the use of the proceeds from such a programme.
The NPS specifies three general uses for the proceeds:
'resolving the employees' issues of the privatised enterprises;
paying back foreign debts; and financing infrastructure projects'.[82] The following year the Privatisation Law (No. 25) was
passed. It provides the procedural, legislative and institutional
basis for the programme and allows the government to decide
on the main issues of privatisation including the allocation of
proceeds.

As of the end of 2009 over 70 transactions had been
completed, including the sale of the government's shares in
54 companies under the Jordan Investment Corporation (JIC)

portfolio. The total proceeds of the privatisation programme equal approximately $2.6 billion,[83] while total investment (both domestic and FDI) has surpassed $850 million – mostly in the water, telecommunications, transport and power sectors.[84] The issue of how to use these proceeds has perhaps been the area of most concern, and the legal and institutional framework briefly detailed above is focused on resolving this matter. The NPS stipulated that the proceeds should not be allocated to cover the contemporary expenditures of the Treasury.[85] Article 13 of the Privatisation Law sets out the allocation of proceeds from the privatisation programme. The initial step was the creation of a Privatisation Proceeds Fund (PPF) where all the revenues are deposited. This fund is supervised by the Privatisation Council (PC) and regulated and administered by the EPC. Once the proceeds have been deposited in the PPF they are allocated for seven different purposes, once again it is worth referring to the EPC directly:

1) Settlement of government debts accumulated by the institutions or enterprises undergoing a restructuring or privatisation process and covering the expenses resulting from such a process.

2) Purchase of government debts to benefit from deductions on these debts or to settle such debts through debt-swap deals or by any other method approved by the Council and consented to by the Council of Ministers.

3) Investments in financial assets.

4) Financing economic activities and new investments in infrastructure sectors with feasible economic and social returns which will assist in achieving sustainable development, provided that such financing is included in the government's budget.

5) Re-qualifying and training employees working at institutions and organisations undergoing a restructuring or privatisation process and settlement of their ensuing financial rights.

6) Retrospective subscription with the Social Security Corporation on behalf of employees of privatised institutions who will become subjected to the Social Security Law.

7) Proceeds of investments of the Privatisation Proceeds Fund shall be considered revenues for the Treasury.[86]

At the time of writing the Jordanian government has largely followed these guidelines and used proceeds in six main areas. The area of most importance appears to have been external debt settlement, with proceeds used to the sum of $111.827 million.[87] Approximately 66 per cent of the proceeds generated by the JICP, totalling $91.1 million, have been spent on recurrent expenditures of the general budget.[88] This constitutes the second-largest area of expenditure from the PPF. The government has also spent $64.134 million on the settlement of domestic banking loans including $21.449 million to the Housing Bank for Trade and Finance and $18.721 million to the Savings Fund and Social Security Corporation.[89] Development projects have also been a key area of concern for the government and have been the focus in later rounds of economic reform. Using PPF revenues, $63.973 million has been spent on projects such as the construction and maintenance of rural and agricultural roads ($11.63 million), the Lejoun and Corridor Water Projects ($21.6 million) and sewerage projects ($2 million).[90]

In terms of the rate of the privatisation of government-owned or affiliated corporations and the relative number of such entities being privatised, the programme as a whole has been quite successful, to the point where the WB has stated that it ranks as 'one of, if not the most, successful in the Middle East region'.[91] It is worth briefly highlighting some of the projects undertaken as part of this programme in order to identify how the government's policy has been implemented. On 23 January 2000 40 per cent of the government's shares in the Jordan Telecommunications Company (JTC) were sold for $508 million to an international consortium which included France Telecom and the Arab Bank.[92] The transaction was a fee-based management contract. A further 1 per cent of shares were allocated to the JTC employees' Provident Fund that same month. The following month a further 8 per cent of the government's shares were sold to the Jordan-based Social Security Corporation for $102 million. The remaining 51 per cent of total shares still owned by the government were endorsed for sale through Initial Public Offering in 2002 with JP Morgan and the Jordan Investment Bank as the lead managers for the transaction. The 'IPO was completed on 29 October 2000 with the sale of 10.5 per cent of JTC total shares whereby 3.5 per cent were acquired by retail investors and 7 per cent by local and non-Jordanian financial institutions; total proceeds amounted to around $86.2 million'.[93] Throughout the privatisation of JTC US-based Merrill Lynch acted as the consultant and financial advisor for the project while legal firm Macarthy, of Canada, was the legal consultant. As a result of the privatisation of JTC, over 7,000 jobs have been created and over $500 million invested in the telecommunications sector in Jordan. Since 2000 and the initial steps towards privatisation of the sector, two more telecommunications operators have established themselves: Mobilecom (2000) and Fastlink (2002). Total revenues from the project stood at $691 million.[94]

There are a number of other major projects that have been completed in a number of fields, as outlined above. It would be useful in other studies to outline these projects and provide some form of assessment of their success and implications. However, for the purpose of this study the above discussion is sufficient to develop the analysis of contemporary Jordanian economic policy. The next logical step in the analysis is to examine Jordanian efforts towards trade liberalisation. This is the most relevant issue area in this chapter in terms of this study. However, it has been the intention to create a picture of contemporary Jordanian interests and so the previous sections should be viewed in this light.

Trade liberalisation

As part of the government's efforts to maximise the benefits of the structural adjustments of the late 1980s and mid-1990s, as well as to further the process of economic reform in order to boost economic growth, a broad-ranging policy of external trade liberalisation through domestic legislation and international institutions was established in the late 1990s.[95] Efforts towards greater intra-Arab trade have been underway for many years, dating back as far as 1953 and the establishment of a treaty between the member-states of the League of Arab States aimed at facilitating transit of trade (one element of what is termed the first wave of Arab regionalism).[96] Further attempts at greater Arab integration were pursued throughout the following decades, including the 1964 creation of the Arab Common Market (ACM) which envisaged the elimination of all tariffs between Arab states.

In 1981 the Agreement for Facilitation and Promotion of intra-Arab Trade was signed by all Arab states.[97] This was followed by another declaration for the elimination of all tariffs and non-tariff barriers to trade in manufactured and semi-manufactured goods. However, the impact of these and other agreements on intra-Arab trade has, until recently, been minimal, leading to what appears to be a new wave of regionalism.[98] The latest round of integration goes much further than previous attempts and it could be argued that this wave of regionalism has more in common with the broader processes of globalisation than with regionalism and is powered by the increasing importance of international institutions.

For the Jordanian government, this wave of integration has not been ignored. Unlike some regional governments, such as those of the GCC states, the Jordanian government has been active in promoting policies aimed at greater economic integration with the Arab world as a whole and, perhaps more importantly, with the global economy.[99] There are six main elements to the government's process of trade liberalisation and economic integration. These elements are as follows: accession to the WTO, the Jordan–EU Association Agreement (JEUAA), the Greater Arab Free Trade Area (GAFTA), the Mediterranean Arab Free Trade Area (MAFTA), the European Free Trade Association (EFTA), and bilateral FTAs such as the JUSFTA.

Within the government's decision-making bodies there exists a debate that dates back to the establishment of the latest round of trade reform in 1996. The trade policy issue in debate is whether the process should focus on *regional* or *global* integration.[100] Referring back to the discussion in Chapter 1, there is much evidence that suggests that trade liberalisation and economic growth, are directly and positively related.[101] There is even more evidence that suggests that non-discriminatory trade liberalisation leads to higher economic growth than preferential liberalisation.[102] Preferential trade liberalisation is likely to cause a diversion in trade. This can include diversion away from sources of efficient production and lower costs to sources of less efficient production and higher costs. Furthermore, trade diversion could mean that access to larger or more lucrative markets is prevented.[103] For the Jordanian government these implications have been considered and a non-discriminatory and broad-ranging process of multilateral trade liberalisation has been pursued.

Accession to the WTO is a clear indication of the government's chosen route to trade liberalisation.

The Hashemite Kingdom of Jordan became the 136th member of the WTO on 11 April 2000 following initial negotiations that began in late 1994.[104] The accession negotiations were largely focused on the major economic and legislative reforms discussed above, whose implementation was required before admission to the organisation was possible. According to the Jordanian Ministry of Industry and Trade the government had to make 'amendments to the [kingdom's] Trademarks and Copyrights laws' and new laws had to be created 'on Patents, Models and Industrial Design, Integrated Circuits, Trade Secrets and Unfair Competition, Geographical Indications, and Plant Variety Protection'.[105] Furthermore, existing laws on 'Standards and Metrology, the Customs Law, General Sales Tax Law, and the Law on Unifying Fees and Taxes' had to be revised in order to conform with WTO standards and regulations.[106]

The JEUAA is just one of a number of Association Agreements signed between the EU and MENA states and is just one element of the broader Barcelona Process between the two regions.[107] The agreement also replaces the 1977 Co-operation Agreement signed by the EU and Jordan. The JEUAA itself was signed on 24 November 1997 but was not ratified by the Jordanian parliament until September 1999. The implementation of the agreement was delayed still further until 15 May 2002 as it had not been ratified by all of the then 15 EU member states until that time. As an element of the process of regional integration between the EU and MENA, the JEUAA incorporates three issue areas which are of importance to greater bilateral and multilateral integration: these areas are in the political, economic and financial, and socio-cultural spheres.[108]

Article three of the JEUAA states that a regular political dialogue shall be established between the two parties, and in particular between the EU parliament and the Jordanian parliament.[109] The aim of the political aspect of the agreement is to develop mutual understanding and cooperation between the parties with emphasis placed on the achievement of peace, security and human rights. To quote the text directly, the political dialogue aims in particular to do the following:

> develop better mutual understanding and an increasing convergence of positions on international issues, and in particular on those issues likely to have substantial effects on one or the other Party; enable each Party to consider the position and interests of the other; enhance regional security and stability; and promote common initiatives.[110]

The economic component of the JEUAA aims to establish in progressive steps an FTA between the EU and Jordan by 2010. The agreement covers the following sectors: industrial and agricultural products, services, right of establishment, payments and movements of capital, competition, intellectual property rights (IPRs), standards and measurements, financial cooperation, economic cooperation in the field of industry, agriculture and investment, transportation, telecommunications, science and technology, environment and tourism as well as energy.[111] This element is based upon the provisions existing in the General Agreement on Tariffs and Trade (GATT) and in the General Agreement on Trade in Services (GATS). Also important to the development of links between the EU and MENA are socio-cultural issues. In this respect the JEUAA also has provisions established in order to increase the interaction between civil society actors.[112] Emphasis is placed upon education, training, the role of women in society, migrant population groups, health and cooperation in justice and home affairs and in particular action to combat international crime such as drug trafficking and terrorism.[113]

Significantly the JEUAA has had limited impact in both the total value and total quantity of trade between the Jordanian and the EU markets. Furthermore, the sectors within which this trade takes place have remained constant. This is important for two reasons. First, there is a stark contrast between the results of the JEUAA and the JUSFTA in the value and quantity of trade in goods and services as well as the sectors within which trade takes place. Note that the JEUAA is some three years older than the JUSFTA. The second way in which this is important is in the implications for the positive returns on FTAs for the Jordanian economy. The later discussion on non-state actors (chapters 4, 5 and 6) engages with this anomaly and offers an explanation. Significantly, trade between the EU and Jordan has remained quite constant since 2001 with Jordanian exports totalling approximately $350 million in 2001 and $445 million in 2008. Imports from the EU are much higher and have witnessed some growth, with 2001 imports totalling around $2.7 billion and the 2008 figure over $3 billion.

A number of MENA economies are liberalising their trade regimes. However, there has been a distinct lack of political will and commitment to integrating fully with both the regional economy and the global economy. There has also been a serious lack of cohesion and agreement on the ways in which to pursue an overarching MENA free trading-economy.[114] This is shown by the number of regional economic integration projects ongoing as of late 2009. These are as follows: GAFTA, GCC, the Arab-Maghreb Union (AMU), and MAFTA. All of these preferential trade agreements have the same aim of reducing tariff and non-tariff barriers to intra-Arab trade and promoting greater economic integration. However, they often overlap and contradict one another and often lose internal cohesion.[115]

The largest and most comprehensive agreement, in terms of the scope of states involved and the range of issues dealt with is GAFTA, signed at the League of Arab States General Meeting in Amman on 19 February 1997.[116] Jamel Zarrouk argues that to some extent GAFTA was created as a result of the fear that the EU–MENA Association Agreements would divert intra-Arab trade away from the MENA regional economy to Europe.[117] It can also be argued that GAFTA came as a response to the Uruguay Round of trade negotiations which it was believed would hinder Arab access to the European economy. At the same time as the Barcelona Process was born so too was an Executive Programme, established under the auspices of the League of Arab States. The aim of the Executive Programme was to revive the 1981 Agreement for Facilitation and Promotion of Trade, which had largely been abandoned. It was realised that the main flaw of the 1981 agreement was that it was merely a statement of intent and did not include any concrete steps or targets for implementation. GAFTA was established to reduce traditional barriers to intra-Arab trade at the rate of 10 per cent per year with the end target being 0 per cent tariff on all intra-Arab trade by 2010.[118]

However, progress in implementing the negotiated steps towards tariff reduction in GAFTA since 1998 has been sporadic and uneven.[119] Nevertheless, on 1 January 2005 the full removal of customs duties on all merchandise traded between the member states came into effect. Bernard Hoekman and Jamel Zarrouk claim that the Jordanian government, and the Ministry of Industry and Trade in particular, was instrumental in the early stages of negotiating and implementing GAFTA. The result of Jordan's involvement has been a three-fold increase in trade exchange between the Jordanian market and those of the other member states of GAFTA.[120]

As a result of what Hassan Al-Atrash and Tarek Yousef call the uneven development of GAFTA[121] a number of other regional trade agreements have been signed by various members of the original 17 Arab states that created GAFTA, as well as other states. The Jordanian government signed the MAFTA agreement (also known as the Aghadir Process) on 25 February 2005. The agreement involves Egypt, Morocco, Tunisia and Jordan and was initially agreed at a meeting between the foreign ministers of the abovementioned states in Aghadir, Morocco on 8 May 2001.[122]

Table 2.1: Jordanian trade levels with GAFTA members in US$ million[123]

Year	Imports	Exports	Total	Balance
2000	1092.9	608.6	1701.5	-484.3
2001	1162.1	961.6	2123.7	-200.5
2002	1282.7	1046.3	2329	-236.4
2003	1584.3	977.1	2561.4	-607.2
2004	2506.4	1335.8	3842.2	-1170.6
2005	3552.7	1547.6	5100.3	-2005.1
2006	4137.2	1763.6	5900.8	-2373.6
2007	4532.6	1967	6499.6	-2565.6
2008	5639.7	2567.1	8206.8	-3072.6

The Aghadir Declaration has three key objectives, which are as follows:

1)   To enhance mutual Arab cooperation and to further develop the Pan-Arab Free Trade Agreement and the efforts exerted to establish an Arab Common Market.

2)   To establish a strong economic alliance responsive to challenges of sustainable economic development and global economic developments.

3)   To arrive at a proper mechanism for trade liberalisation between the Mediterranean-Arab countries and the EU,

and which will be compatible with contemporary economic trends in both the regional and international arenas.[124]

Initially it seems unclear why a secondary regional economic integration initiative should be taken three years after the GAFTA agreement was signed and came into effect. A closer analysis of the MAFTA agreement, though, shows that this initiative – while having the same aim of reducing trade barriers within the MENA region – has two main differences from GAFTA. Firstly, MAFTA is relatively exclusive in the sense that it includes Arab states on the Southern Mediterranean (granted Jordan does not actually have a Mediterranean coastline).[125] Second, the medium- to long-term intention is to increase the prospects specifically for EU–Arab integration. In this respect, the initiative aims at developing a single block with which negotiations with the EU can commence.[126] It is worth noting that GAFTA also seeks to create a single block with which other regions could negotiate economic cooperation. The creation of MAFTA signifies a desire of the member states' governments to further encourage the process of greater integration with the global economy – a process which is rather slow in the context of GAFTA.[127]

Due to the relevance of the JUSFTA to this current piece of work a slightly more in-depth look is necessary here than has been granted to the other FTAs signed by Jordan and outlined above. However, as it is just one element of trade relations between the two states (as will be shown in the following chapters) only an introduction and brief evaluation is required here. Thus the following section discusses the origins of the JUSFTA, a breakdown of the main elements, a summary of its implementation up to the point of this work and the overall impacts seen thus far on US–Jordan trade levels in terms of total value and quantity.

One could argue that the JUSFTA is merely a reward to

Jordan by the United States for supporting US policy in the MENA region. During an interview held in Amman in December 2006, Yousef Al-Shamali, the Deputy Director of the Foreign Trade Policy Department of the Ministry of Industry and Trade, described this position as viewing the FTA as granting Jordan access to the world's largest market as a form of support for the Jordanian government's pro-Western stance.[128] This assumption would be based on the belief that the Jordanian economy will benefit by greater exports to the US market – a development that is seen as contributing to economic growth and employment in Jordan.[129] This may all be true: for certain the fact that Jordan was the first Arab state to sign an FTA with the United States and only the fourth globally did have something to do with the support the Jordanian government has given the United States over the past decade or so. This support has come in the forms of cooperation in military missions in the region and diplomatic and economic efforts to promote stability in the Palestinian territories. However, one must not accept this interpretation without delving deeper into the FTA's origins.

Accepting the argument above prevents the researcher from examining a number of other factors that may have been involved in the creation and ratification of the JUSFTA. For one, the position of the United States should not be seen simply as a reward for an ally. As mentioned above Jordan was only the fourth country globally to sign an FTA with the United States. This alone adds more importance to the FTA. To reward the Jordanian government's cooperation and political stance, the United States need only extend the numerous grants given Jordan under the United States Agency for International Development (USAID) project there.[130] Or simply provide the Jordanian military with new or upgraded equipment as happened in 1996 as a result of the signing of the Jordan–Israel peace treaty in 1994.[131] In fact, there are overarching factors which the Bush Administration took into account when ratifying the JUSFTA.

The JUSFTA was a first in many ways in US trade policy. It was the first with an Arab country and only the second in the MENA region – the first being with Israel. It was also the first time a bilateral FTA between any states included provisions for labour, the environment and IPRs.[132] As will be shown below and in later chapters, the impact of the JUSFTA on trade levels between the two states has been significant and has evolved into a model for FTAs between the United States and other MENA states. This latter point is perhaps the most compelling in light of the position of the US government towards the MENA region and its current political, military and economic activity there. In chapter three it is shown that the Bush Administration spearheaded a comprehensive change in US policy towards the region. The United States wishes to transform its relations with the MENA region.[133] In this way, the JUSFTA was not merely a reward but an initial step on the way to transforming economic relations with the MENA region. If this is true then the 'reward' is greater for the United States than for Jordan – this will be discussed in more depth in the following chapters.

What is also important and often overlooked in the discussion of the JUSFTA is the position and contribution of the Jordanian government in the formation of this agreement. It is often assumed that the Jordanian government was handed out charity and gratefully took it. However, this view only hinders a deeper analysis of the agreement and its implications. As has been shown above, and indeed has been the purpose of this chapter, the interests and foreign and trade policy of the Jordanian government have undergone a transformation in the last decade. Pursuit of membership in the WTO, the signing of multiple bilateral (such as the Jordan–Singapore FTA of 16 May 2004) and multilateral FTAs (GAFTA, MAFTA, JEUAA) have been a priority of the Jordanian government. The Ministry of Industry and Trade has transformed Jordanian foreign trade policy since 1997 and pushed for greater economic liberalisation and reform. As part of this process, negotiations for the JUSFTA were launched in 1998 under the Clinton Administration – the JUSFTA was in fact finalised while the Clinton Administration was still in office and the Bush Administration merely ratified it.[134] The desire for greater access to the US market went hand in hand with the overall diversification of Jordanian foreign trade. The results of the agreement with the United States have been very significant for the Jordanian economy, as will be shown below. However, the greater significance lies in the pursuit of trade liberalisation and the repositioning of the Jordanian economy in the global economy as a result of this process (to be discussed in the following chapters).

With regard to trade in goods, the FTA requires the removal of all tariffs by 2010. The transition to 0 per cent tariffs is scheduled in four main stages, as shown in Table 2.3 below. The exception is a list of 250 Jordanian products which were granted immediate 0 per cent tariff access to the US market.[135] Regarding trade in services, Jordan already had complete access to the US market at the time the FTA came into effect.[136] The United States, however, did not have reciprocal access to the Jordanian market. The FTA calls for the total liberalisation of this market in Jordan for access to US-based and US-affiliated corporations over a ten-year transitional period. The sectors to be liberalised include: energy distribution, convention services, printing and publicshing, courier services, audiovisual, education, environmental, financial, health services, tourism, recreation and transport services (an assessment of trade in financial services is the focus of Chapter 6 of this book).[137] The agreement also stipulates in annex 2.2 that 35 per cent of the value of any good that is traded between the two states must originate in the exporting country.

The JUSFTA came into effect on 17 December 2001 and has seen success in the implementation of the phased reduction in trade barriers. The target year of 2010 to have eliminated all barriers to trade between the two economies looks set to be met. To summarise, tariffs on all goods outlined in the agreement have been reduced according to schedule: unhindered access to the Jordanian services market has been granted to US-based corporations; studies have been completed according to the labour and environment provisions of the agreement and joint committees established; and the dispute mechanism (although not tested) has been confirmed.[138] The impacts have been significant and have transformed Jordan–US trade relations in terms of value, quantity and to a certain extent sectors involved. As can be seen from Table 2.3 the overall value and quantity of trade between the two markets has increased from $568.2 million in 2001 (the last year before the FTA came into effect) to a total of $2.1 billion in 2008 with an expected slight increase in 2009.[139] Furthermore, while traditionally the United States held a surplus trade balance with Jordan ($109.8 million in 2001), since the FTA came into effect the trade balance has been in Jordan's favour ($8 million in 2002 and $771.7 million in 2006, and down to $197.1 million in 2008).[140] While the pattern of trade seems to have altered in 2009 with a trade balance in favour of the United States, this fits with the pattern of bilateral trade relationships between the United States and others in that the recession beginning in 2007 reduced most US imports to a significant extent. At the same time US exports, to the MENA region in particular, have not declined in the same manner. Jordan's levels of trade have remained largely the same overall through the global recession.

An analysis of the sectors in which this trade has taken place and within which this growth in trade has been witnessed is important and revealing. It offers an insight into the nature of trade relations between the two economies and will provide the basis for the analysis of the impact of non-state actors in Jordan–US trade in the following chapters. The main Jordanian exports to the US market are in the following sectors: textiles and clothing, Dead Sea cosmetics, ortho-paedic appliances, olive oil, chemical fertilisers, paints and varnishes, luggage, antibiotics, household appliances and arti-cles of jewellery.[141] Other sectors which appear to be on the rise in total export value are phosphates, aluminium bars and insecticides.[142]

Table 2.2: Removal of tariffs between Jordan and the USA[143]

2000 Tariff level	Phase-out period
<5%	2 years
5%-10%	4 years
10%-20%	5 years
>20%	10 years

The aim of this chapter has been to discuss state-level facilitation of trade in Jordan. This has been done by tracing the changes in the main interests in contemporary Jordanian domestic, foreign and trade policy and the domestic and in-ternational environment within which these take place. Towards this endeavour a number of key interests and proc-esses have been identified. These signify a break from traditional interests, which have been largely focused on national security and regime survival. An overarching shift has been made in the key objectives of Jordanian decision-making. With an analysis of the major policy directions taken by the Jordanian government over the past decade it can be discerned that the main policy focus is now on issues of eco-nomic reform and international cooperation, which are aimed at achieving economic growth and sustained development. It must be noted, however, that issues and interests of an eco-nomic nature are directly linked in an interdependent relationship with political issues and interests. One element of the reform pursued has been to reform the regulatory framework within which trade takes place to facilitate greater levels of trade between Jordan and international markets in the anarchic international system. This has been done by engaging with international institutions in the form of IOs, such as membership of the WTO and regimes such as the GAFTA and JUSFTA.

This transformation from security to economic interests dates back to the mid-1990s. However, with the ascension to the throne of King Abdullah II came a re-configuration of how government interests in Jordan are formulated. This has led to subsequent reform-oriented governments which have pursued economic reform more aggressively in the form of structural adjustment, privatisation and the liberalisation of trade. The implications of this reorientation for the political economy of trade relations between the United States and Jordan have been significant and will remain so in the medium to long term.

As outlined in Chapter 1, this study is not state-centric and in fact aims to diversify the study of actors in trade relations. However, it is important to include the relevant state actors – or national governments – as part of the analysis. The Jordanian government is one of the central actors that impacts trade between the United States and Jordan. This impact comes in many ways but the most important here are in the forms of government control of state borders, administration and the creation and enforcement of international agreements. In this way the government of Jordan has adopted a policy direction which has overtly facilitated trade. By pursuing economic liberalisation and reform the government has attempted to develop an environment where economic activity can evolve, seeing this as being in the state's best interests. By creating a more transparent political environment states can attract economic activity. Coupled with privatisation this political reform has led to greater inward investment and economic activity. The government's efforts at structural adjustment and trade liberalisation have complemented this process and have spawned greater economic integration with the international economy, thus facilitating trade – a key goal in the pursuit of economic growth.

Table 2.3: Jordan trade levels with the United States 2000–09 in US$ million[144]

Year	Exports	Imports	Balance
2000	73.3	316.9	-243.6
2001	229.2	339	-109.8
2002	412.4	404.4	+8.0
2003	673.5	492.4	+181.0
2004	1,093.45	51.5	+541.9
2005	1266.8	644.2	+622.7
2006	1422.1	650.3	+771.7
2007	1328.9	856.2	+472.7
2008	1137.5	940.3	+197.1
2009 up to September	709.5	863.9	-154.5

As this and the following chapter show the governments of the United States and Jordan have pursued policies aimed at facilitating trade between the two states which have culminated in the JUSFTA. This agreement is an integral element in the regulatory regime governing bilateral trade. While both governments have pursued their respective national interests, these overlap and have resulted in a synthesisof interests in the overall facilitation of trade. In the case of Jordan links between and the interdependence of economic and political issues at the domestic and international levels have shaped a set of state interests. Full rationality is not assumed in state identification of interests and the decisions taken in order to pursue national goals. However, the analysis above presents the argument that the Jordanian government has identified various state interests and has generated policy decisions which it is believed will achieve these goals. Furthermore, these policies include as a main element the reform of political and economic forms of governance at the domestic level and the engagement with international institutions at the international level.

The Jordanian government has in the past decade and a half or so pursued a slow and uneven process of political liberalisation as well as macro-economic structural adjustment, privatisation and engagement with international institutions. While there are unique characteristics to all of these policy areas they have one broad common characteristic. They are all, in one form or another, aimed at achieving economic growth and stability. Facilitating trade is a key element in fostering economic growth in Jordan and the engagement with international institutions as a means of inter-state and inter-market cooperation is a pivotal component of this facilitation.

The assumption that international institutions encourage cooperation and stability, offering a level of governance of international relations in an international system which is characterised largely by anarchy, seems to be less important in Jordanian policy-making than the benefits to economic growth through international trade. This would suggest that liberal economic thought and the importance of international institutions in facilitating trade are more important in understanding the Jordanian government's involvement in IOs and trade regimes. A similar discussion of US interests, foreign and trade policies and involvement in international institutions follows in the next chapter. This analysis presents a clearer assessment of state actor belief in the utility of international institutions in fostering cooperation and stability in international relations. Broadly speaking the United States has different interests to Jordan and different policies are pursued in order to achieve these goals. However, the engagement with international institutions and with Jordan in these institutions is a key convergence of the two states' policies. The following chapter thus develops, in line with the discussion in this chapter, the argument that cooperation between Jordan and the United States through international institutions is overall a positive-sum game but with multiple levels of zero-sum and positive-sum games.

3

STATE FACILITATION OF TRADE:
US Interests and Trade Policy

This chapter completes the analysis of state actor facilitation of trade between Jordan and the United States. The focus here is on the continuities in US interests in the MENA region and Jordan, and changes in foreign and economic policies there. The main argument here is that US foreign and economic policies towards the region are in fact largely one and the same and have been used in conjunction with each other to pursue policy goals and interests. These goals and interests have remained largely constant but major foreign and economic policy directions have changed – as is exempl-ified by the move towards bilateral economic integration through international institutions and trade liberalisation. There are two broad categories which need to be discussed in order to understand US facilitation of trade with Jordan. These are firstly, US interests and second US foreign and economic policies. This chapter is therefore constructed in four main sections. The first section offers a brief discussion of the three main US policy goals with regard to the MENA region and Jordan. The second section then offers historical examples of US policy in pursuit of these interests from the onset of the Cold War to the present. This section demonstrates the differences between policies which rest upon military or hard power and those which rest upon soft power and international institutions.

Understanding broader trends in US trade policy is essential to the discussion of US–Jordan trade policy and so must be included at this stage of the study. Section three thus offers an analysis of US trade policy as a whole and not simply towards Jordan or the MENA region. The move from focusing on multilateral trade liberalisation to bilateral liberalisation since the mid-1990s is discussed here. The following section then develops an assessment of US trade policy to the MENA region as a whole and how US–Jordan trade policy fits into this, adding to the discussion of the JUSFTA included in the previous chapter.

A concluding section then summarises the main policy goals and interests of the United States with regard to the MENA region and Jordan, as well as contemporary US trade policy. A conclusion of how US–Jordan trade policy is shaped by these interests and policies is then offered. What this section does not do is offer an overall summary of US foreign economic policy or trade relations. This is an important issue area, but this chapter exists to serve a much more specific function within this this particular argument. So more general issues of US external economic policy are only touched upon to the extent that they make sense in terms of this discussion. To discuss them in greater detail would be a large, and unnecessary, diversion.

US interests in the MENA region

It is possible to identify three core interests that the United States has in the MENA region which act as demands and constraints on US policy there. It must be made clear that the

United States, as both state and market of non-state actors, has an incalculable range of interests with regards to the states and markets of the MENA region. However, for the purpose of discussing US foreign and economic policy in the region three core interests are primary and dominant. These interests have developed since the late nineteenth century and have grown in importance since the 1950s.[1]

The first core interest to develop was access to the region's markets for US exports of goods and capital, as well as markets to import from.[2] This interest emerged as the first major US policy interest in the region and has remained relatively constant. The second core interest has been the maintenance of secure access to the region's natural resources – mostly oil and gas.[3] Here it must be noted that access to these resources for the broader global economy has been as important to the United States as securing access for the US economy. This interest developed from the early twentieth century but was not overly significant until the 1930s. The final core interest emerged *after* the 1950s as the MENA states became independent from European patrons and the former imperial powers largely withdrew from the region. The subsequent power vacuum, growing importance of oil and gas in the global economy and instability in inter-state relations led to the US interest of creating stable and cooperative relationships with the states of the region.[4] This third core policy goal has developed in large part in order to achieve the first two policy interests (and during the Cold War reinforced broader US policy vis-à-vis the Soviet Union).

Throughout this period of core US interests and especially after the third core interest of achieving inter-state cooperation, Jordan has been less important than some states, such as Saudi Arabia. However, following a series of developments which resulted in a decrease in US-friendly regimes in the region (discussed below), Jordan became a more significant potential partner for the United States.[5] Since the 1990s

Jordan has developed into one of the more important states for US–MENA cooperation. This has mostly been due to worsening relations between the United States and other states in the region (such as Syria, Iraq and Yemen) since the 1990s, as well as instability in other states that norrmally maintain healthy relationships with the United States (such as Lebanon and Saudi Arabia).[6] Thus, while Jordan only represents a small market (and prior to 2001 trade with the United States was insignificant) and possesses no natural resources of significance, the importance of Jordan in inter-state cooperation and regional stability have made US policy to Jordan partly synonymous with broader US–MENA policy. The following discussion offers examples of how US policy in pursuit of its core interests has developed and how US–Jordan policy has been impacted.

The development of US–MENA policy

The United States, while arguably the most influential and important external actor in the MENA region, has not had core interests in the region for much more than 70 years. While some, such as Douglas Little,[7] would argue this is not the case and US interests and policy goals in the region date back to the mid- to late nineteenth century, one must examine the commitment of the United States to pursuing its interests in the region over time. Let us start in the late eighteenth century, when the newly independent United States was far from possessing the capabilities and resources of the great European powers of the time. One of the areas of greatest disparity was in naval power. The United States did not possess adequate naval capacity at that time and as a result could not protect its shipping. Britain had formerly guarded American shipping while it was a colony but that privilege had been revoked following the American Revolution in 1776.[8] By the turn of the nineteenth century US shipping in the Western Mediterranean and Eastern Atlantic had to be protected by relying on payments of goods and money to the Barbary States of the North African coast.[9] However, such agreements were constantly breaking down either because the United States did not pay on time or because the Barbary States raised their demands.[10]

An action of this kind by the Caramanli ruler of Tripoli in 1801 prompted a war between the United States and Tripoli that lasted until 1805, as well as a series of wars with the broader Barbary Coast that lasted until 1815. The most famous event of the war was the march from Alexandria to Tripoli by the US consul in Tripoli, William Eaton, and a small number of US Marines.[11] This expedition was ultimately a failure but it signified the first US military engagement in the region and a significant commitment to pursuing policy goals. General Eaton (as he was later entitled) was able to redeem his initial lack of success when in 1815 the newly formed US Navy was able to send a squadron to Algiers under Commodore Decatur and secure a favourable treaty from the Algerians, thus ending US reliance on 'protection' payments.[12]

In the following century there was little active US policy-making or engagement in the region.[13] Unlike the European powers which had ventured into the quagmire of the region in the previous decades and remained involved,[14] the United States remained largely detached from the region. This was largely because of broader isolationist tendencies within US government.[15] Wider US foreign policy during the nineteenth century reflected the tendency to remain disengaged from international affairs except for the promotion abroad of the principles on which the American nation was founded. Thus John Quincy Adams, who would become the sixth President of the United States in 1825, in an 1821 address warned against seeking 'Monsters to Destroy' and greater involvement in the broader world.[16] During the first half of the twentieth century US interests in the MENA region were significant. However, US policy toward the region remained less active than that of European powers and much less vigorous than US policy towards other regions such as South America or South East Asia.[17]

It is more appropriate to identify US interests in the MENA region and then discuss how vigorously these have been pursued through foreign and economic policy to determine how and when they became central in US foreign policy overall. Thus the following section highlights key periods of US policy to the region as a whole and demonstrates some of the policies taken in pursuit of the three core US interests. It is important to note that there is a distinct difference between the two main types of US policy towards the region. The first is characterised by hard power in the form of military power and coercion. The second form of policy is characterised by what Joseph Nye has termed soft power[18] in the form of liberal institutions and integration. Both forms, however, demonstrate the commitment of the United States to pursuing its interests in the MENA region.

By the onset of the 1948 Arab–Israeli war both the US government and academic scholars had acknowledged that the MENA region was increasingly important in world politics. In the inaugural issue of *The Middle East Journal*, the first American scholarly quarterly that was established to study the contemporary Middle East, it was declared that 'the region was now "very near" the United States, both in point of time-distance and with respect to the United States' new involvement there in questions of power politics'.[19] Yet, even with the realisation of the strategic, economic and political importance of the MENA region, US policy towards the region remained to a large extent non-committal until the 1950s.[20]

The importance of the MENA region to the United States increased further following the first Arab–Israeli war in 1948. However, this was not due to any normative response to the plight of the Jewish nation. Instead it had more to do with an assessment of the *utility* of securing access to the region's resources and markets, in no small part in the pursuit of US supremacy and the defeat of international Communism.[21] In the 1950s and 1960s the United States was increasingly concerned with surging Soviet influence in the MENA region and a perceived threat to US allies and interests there.[22] This concern was justified by two key assumptions. The first was that the Union of Soviet Socialist Republics (USSR) was an expansionist power whose motivations, while ideologically based, were nothing more than imperial designs and confrontational to the West.[23] The second was that the strategic interests of the Arab states would leave them susceptible to Soviet influence if the United States did not present itself and its support as a second option.[24]

Developments following the end of the Second World War and their interpretation by US scholars, analysts and politicians led to the embedded assumption that the USSR did pose a threat to US interests.[25] As a result of this interpretation of the international political environment the policy of *Containment* was conceived and implemented. George F. Kennan a former advisor, diplomat, political analyst, and historian, is regarded as the author of the Containment strategy.[26] By analysing Soviet foreign policy, traditions, ideology and Russian history Kennan argued that the USSR was an expansionist power.[27] Furthermore, regardless of its historical interests, Kennan argued that the USSR would pursue new avenues of expansion in any region of the world – including the MENA region.[28]

The United States was increasingly concerned with the rapid increase in Soviet influence in the MENA region throughout the 1950s and 1960s.[29] This concern was coupled with the realisation in the 1940s that the Arab world was strategically important to the West and the United States in particular for a number of reasons. First, in the geographical sense the Arabs sit astride the Suez Canal, beside the Straits of Gibraltar, and they control the northern approaches to the

Indian Ocean.[30] The second reason for the Arab world's importance is that a small percentage of the region's people control a vast amount of the world's oil and gas reserves.[31] Regardless of the growing US interest in maintaining the MENA region independent of the Communist sphere of influence – if not within the US sphere – Soviet advancements were made. In late 1955 it was revealed that Egypt under Colonel Gamal Abdul Nasser had negotiated a massive arms deal with Czechoslovakia – tantamount to a Soviet–Egyptian arms deal.[32] Egypt was able to purchase some 200 tanks and other advanced weapons systems. This arms deal signalled the gradual opening up of the Soviet arsenal first to Egypt and subsequently also to Syria and Iraq.[33] Along with severely altering the balance of power in the region, this arms deal allowed the Soviet Union to develop a foothold where it previously had to accept Western exclusivity.

As a result of the announcement of the Czechoslovakian arms deal the then Secretary of State John Foster Dulles offered the Egyptians US aid for the Aswan High Dam in return for a revocation of the arms deal and future Soviet assistance. By February 1956 Nasser was ready to sign an agreement; however, Dulles had trouble selling the project to the United States.[34] Pro-Israeli politicians denounced the dam, southern Congressmen wondered why the United States should build a dam that would allow the Egyptians to produce more cotton, thus threatening their industries, and the Cabinet feared supporting the project would unbalance the budget.[35] The matter was made worse when in April 1956 Nasser formed a military alliance with Saudi Arabia, Syria and Yemen and refused to cancel the Czechoslovakian arms deal.[36] For Secretary Dulles there was only one option – to withdraw the backing for the Aswan High Dam. He had believed at the time that the Russians would not be able to take the United States' place and back the dam project due to a lack of technical and financial capabilities.[37] However, the Russians had both capabilities and began work on the project at the invitation of Nasser in 1957.

With thousands of Russian technicians and engineers and their families as well as large amounts of Soviet money now in Egypt, a firm foothold in the region had been established. The US position in the MENA region was not strengthened by the pan-Arab sentiments emanating from Egypt. Nasser continued to spread propaganda for Arab unity and socialism while continuing to take increasing amounts of Soviet economic and military aid.[38] Secretary of State Dulles and President Eisenhower grew increasingly concerned that the Soviet Union would move into the region and fill the vacuum left by the withdrawal of the European powers and were convinced this must not be allowed to happen.[39]

In light of this expansion of Soviet influence in the region a new foreign policy doctrine was called for. In a message given to Congress on 5 January 1957 then President Dwight D. Eisenhower presented the *Eisenhower Doctrine*, which stated that the United States would use armed force upon request in response to imminent or actual aggression from Communist forces in the MENA.[40] Furthermore, countries that took stances opposed to Communism would be given aid in various forms.[41] The military provisions of the doctrine were applied in the Lebanon Crisis in the following year. The intervention in Lebanon perfectly illustrated Eisenhower's methods and the solidification of US strategic policy towards the MENA region. It was a unilateral action not approved by the UN that was undertaken in haste and with the aim of supporting an undemocratic government that had very little popular support amongst its own people.[42] The Lebanon intervention was indeed a far cry from the normative policies employed by the Wilson Administration. Nevertheless, the Eisenhower Doctrine and the intervention in Lebanon demonstrated the importance of US interests in the region and the significance of US policies aimed at securing these interests.

Premier Khrushchev had not wanted to escalate the situation in the region following the US action in Lebanon and so refused Nasser's request for more aid in 1958.[43] Khrushchev realised that the US action was taken to protect its oil interests in the region, which were extremely important to the West and not so important to the USSR.[44] However, Khrushchev was also not willing to desist from exploring further avenues for involvement in the MENA at a time when the Soviets were making progress in military and strategic parity with the United States.[45] Pressures on US policy were increased when in late 1957 US newspapers discovered and published the findings of a committee headed by H. Rowan Gaither Jr., of the Ford Foundation. The Gaither Report concluded that Soviet gross national product (GNP) was increasing at a much faster pace than that of the United States, that the Russians were spending as much on developing heavy industries and military forces as the United States and that by 1959 the Soviets might be able to launch an attack on the continental United States with over 100 ICBMs carrying megaton-sized nuclear weapons.[46] As a result of the growing pressures and concerns Eisenhower increased the US military presence in the MENA region. He dispersed strategic bombers and installed medium-range ballistic missiles (MRBMs) armed with nuclear warheads in Turkey.[47] These policies were further embedded by the 1967 Six Day War and the deepening relations between the USSR and Egypt, Syria and Iraq that followed.

In November 1976 Jimmy Carter narrowly defeated Gerald Ford to become the President of the United States. While the preceding decade of US foreign policy had been characterised by the realpolitik of Henry Kissinger and confrontational doctrines such as the Eisenhower Doctrine, Carter's foreign policy would initially be idealistic and Jeffersonian.[48] He did not regard Communism as the chief enemy and argued that the United States had become too fearful of the perceived Communist threat. Instead he argued that the United States had given too much support to corrupt and dictatorial right-wing governments around the world as a result of its policy of Containment.[49]

Idealism rather than the strategic imperative would be the core of Carter's US foreign policy. Carter represented a return to normative principles such as the protection of universal human rights and the right to self-determination and the respect of the rule of law, whether domestic or international. With regard to the MENA region this entailed settlement of the Arab–Israeli conflict through establishing a viable and secure Palestinian state, the conclusion of peace treaties between Israel and her neighbours, and a resolution of the Palestinian refugee crisis.[50] However, Carter was shaken when in December 1979 some 85,000 Soviet troops invaded Afghanistan to support the existing pro-Moscow government there which could not suppress a growing Muslim insurgency. Carter went as far as to declare that the Soviet invasion of Afghanistan constituted 'the most serious threat to world peace since the Second World War'.[51]

Fearful of a threat to Western oil supplies, Carter backed away from the SALT II talks, announced that the restrictions on CIA activity abroad would be lifted and declared a Carter Doctrine for South West Asia. Defining the Persian Gulf region as an area of vital importance to the United States, Carter announced that he would repel any Soviet assault there by any means necessary – meaning the use of military force, including nuclear weapons.[52] This stark contrast with the idealistic foreign policy Carter had intended to formulate and implement when he came to office was further influenced by other events taking place in the MENA region.

In an unexpected turn one of Carter's aims, that of securing peace in the MENA, became a real possibility. In December 1977 then Egyptian President Anwar Al-Sadat went to Israel to speak directly to the Israeli parliament. This was an act of great courage that was helped by Carter's efforts to mediate between the Israelis and the Arabs. Sadat also realised that Egypt could not afford another war with Israel and was incapable of removing the Israelis from the Sinai Peninsula by force.[53] In the fall of 1978, Carter invited Sadat and Israeli Prime Minister Menachin Begin to the Presidential retreat at Camp David. In almost two weeks of intensive discussions there were five issues on the table: Israeli withdrawal from the Sinai Peninsula, Golan Heights, West Bank of the Jordan River, and East Jerusalem and recognition of the PLO as the legitimate representation of the Palestinian people. In return Israel would receive recognition of the right to exist in peace and security from her Arab neighbours.[54] However, only the issue of Israeli withdrawal from Sinai and subsequent Egyptian guarantees of peace could be agreed upon and the talks reached an impasse. Undeterred, Carter made a sudden trip to the MENA in early 1979 during which he persuaded Sadat and Begin to sign a peace treaty resulting in a staged Israeli withdrawal from Sinai.[55]

Carter's idealism had paid off. However, it was the very conclusion of a peace treaty between Egypt and Israel that further solidified the lack of stability and peace in the remainder of the MENA and hindered the achievement of US policy goals there. The Arab states had been split into two camps and Israel's position strengthened as a result. The division rendered the Arab states unable to bargain and achieve at least some of their goals. Without achieving the necessary goals it would be impossible for the Arabs to negotiate peace with Israel.[56] Israel in the meantime was rewarded not only with peace with Egypt but also a massively improved negotiating position from which point they could engage in negotiations if it best suited them, or not if the likely outcomes of negotiations would be negligible.[57]

In the same year as the Egypt–Israel peace treaty, events farther to the east also shook the foundations of US foreign policy. Since 1953, the year in which the CIA was involved in a coup to restore the Shah to power in Iran, the United States had strongly supported Iran. Eisenhower was perhaps the most enthusiastic supporter of the Shah while Kissinger and Nixon viewed Iran as the United States' best friend in the Middle East, a principal partner in the containment of the Communist threat and the only reliable supplier of Middle Eastern oil.[58] However, what the US, especially the CIA, failed to realise was that the Iranian leader was despised at home as much as he was praised abroad and anti-US feeling was growing among Iranians. In late January 1979 the Ayatollah Khomeini – an exile living in Paris who had emerged as the leader of the Iranian opposition – returned to Iran while the Shah was on extended 'vacation'. Khomeini was greeted by hundreds of thousands of supporters, concluding a bloodless revolutionary coup moved by a religious and nationalistic zeal that the US administration had not imagined was possible.[59] The result was the loss of perhaps the most strategically important ally the United States had outside of Europe. Despite all the rhetoric of idealistic foreign policies – of which US support for the Iranian dictator was not an example – events in the Middle East had once again shown that strategic interests, not liberal ideals, had to dictate foreign policy. Furthermore, the three core policy goals the United States was pursuing there had to be pursued using force and coercion if necessary.

On 2 August 1990, Iraqi troops invaded and overran Kuwait. On the same day President George H.W. Bush condemned the invasion and asked world leaders to join him in action against Iraq. On the same day the UN Security Council condemned Iraq and demanded an immediate and full withdrawal from Kuwait on pain of mandatory sanctions.[60] Four days later a full economic embargo was placed on Iraq. This followed a joint statement issued by then US Secretary of State, James Baker III and the Soviet Foreign Minister Eduard

Shevardnadze, in Moscow calling for a worldwide embargo on arms to Iraq.[61] The Cold War had ended and Communism had ceased to be a major threat to the United States. The geopolitical environment had been greatly altered, so much so that many heralded the dawn of a 'new world order' in which the rule of law and multilateralism would be the key characteristics of international relations.[62] In this new environment the Persian Gulf Crisis of 1990–91 presented the first real test of both these characteristics as well as what US policy in the new world order would look like.

By 8 August 1990 President Bush had put in motion a defensive operation entitled Desert Shield in which he dispatched US paratroopers, an armoured brigade and fighter planes to Saudi Arabia where they were joined by forces from Syria, Egypt and Morocco. At the same time the UN was finally fulfilling its role. Since its foundation following the Second World War, the UN had been largely left paralysed by great power rivalry and the use of the veto in the Security Council. With the end of the Cold War came the end of much of this hostility and in the political vacuum created was space for greater UN effectiveness.[63] The six months following the invasion that started the crisis saw the United States actively pursuing the creation of an international military coalition that would eventually consist of over 30 states, empowered by a UN mandate to restore Kuwaiti sovereignty and punish Iraqi aggression. With regard to the invasion President Bush declared that 'this will not stand'. A veteran of the Second World War and head of an administration filled with other war veterans, Bush had seemingly learned the lessons of Munich in 1938.[64] Open aggression between members of the international community simply could not be accepted and collective action must be employed in order to preserve world peace.

It is important not to make the mistake of interpreting Bush's foreign policy in the early 1990s as being idealistic. At the same time as the Persian Gulf Crisis, events around the world perhaps demanded more multilateral humanitarian intervention. In the former Yugoslavia conflict was erupting between Serbs, Croats and Bosnians which was tearing the state apart. This conflict was characterised by massive civilian and material loss and ethnic cleansing.[65] However, President Bush, and indeed all of Western Europe, did little to intervene until the mid-1990s. Furthermore, US interest in the Persian Gulf was still dominated by strategic imperatives. While Bush had lived through the Second World War, he had also lived through the oil crisis of 1973–74 and fully understood the importance of the MENA to US interests and security. As such the overwhelming US response to the crisis can be seen more as a result of a US foreign policy constructed on realist interpretations of events than one founded on the concern for Kuwaiti civilians.[66] This is extremely important in terms of US policy towards the MENA region. Bush's response to the events of the summer of 1990 indicated that the United States, free from the constraints of Cold War considerations, was still inclined to pursue its key foreign policy goals there by force if needed.

When Bill Clinton took office in 1992 he inherited a US foreign policy framework that was unlike any previously seen. The United States remained militarily engaged around the world, and pivotal to the global economy. However, the United States that President Clinton would lead for the next eight years was the only superpower in a world relatively free from great power rivalries and characterised by an emerging pattern of multilateralism. Furthermore, with the collapse of the Soviet Union and international Communism (with the exception of North Korea, Cuba and China – in the last of which a slow process of economic liberalisation was taking place) the world was seen as embracing the very values that the United States was founded upon.[67] The rule of law, democracy and free market economics were interpreted as being in ascendancy around the world.[68] However, Clinton possessed no post-Cold War, post-Gulf War strategy which he would promote while in office. He did, however, have three broad policy goals which he intended to pursue. His administration would work firstly to modernise and restructure the US military and security capabilities; second, elevate the role of economics in international affairs; and third, promote democracy abroad. These three imprecise aims would shape US policy towards the MENA region for the next decade and more.

On the whole, though, Clinton had little interest in forging a new and grand relationship with the rest of the world with foreign and trade policies to complement it. In his first eight months in office he made only four foreign policy speeches and in general followed the implementation of his predecessor's policies.[69] By the end of his first year as President, Clinton began to realise the importance of a central foreign policy doctrine both for purposes of domestic appeasement and international stability.[70] The administration's public and much touted military blunders in Haiti and Somalia, along with right-wing rumour-mongering and severe criticism by foreign policy analysts, indicated the necessity for some form of foreign policy direction. For such a direction Clinton turned to his National Security Adviser, Anthony Lake, to construct some form of concept that would embrace his three main policy goals.[71] The result was 'democratic enlargement', a phrase which embodied the notion of expanding the international community of free market democracies. Working with Jeremy Rosner, a speechwriter for the National Security Council, Lake developed a blueprint that had four key components. First, 'strengthen the community of market democracies'; second, 'foster and consolidate new democracies and market economies where possible'; third, 'counter the aggression and support the liberalisation of states hostile to democracy'; and finally 'help democracies and market economies take root in regions of greatest humanitarian concern'.[72]

At first interpretation the doctrine of democratic enlargement can appear to be idealistic. Encouraging and facilitating the empowerment of the masses and supporting the accountability of those who govern in order to truly emancipate the individual is indeed a noble cause. However, Clinton categorically rejected the idealistic notion that the United States was duty bound to promote constitutional democracy and free market economics around the world.[73] Rather like his predecessors, he saw the protection of primary US strategic and economic interests as the core of US foreign policy. The interests the United States had in the MENA region were no exception. He simply needed a policy that would provide this protection, and the spread of democracy and economic freedom was seen as the surest way to international peace and cooperation.[74] At the heart of the Clinton Administration was an overwhelming concern with domestic renewal. The United States had by 1992 amassed a federal budgetary deficit of over $290 billion, the highest in US history. Clinton saw the fiscal imbalances he had inherited as the result of 12 years of Republican economics and an overemphasis on foreign policy as opposed to domestic management.[75] Nevertheless, by 1994 Clinton and his staff had begun to incorporate foreign policy with domestic renewal.

The realisation that the processes of globalisation had led to the rapid integration and interdependence of many of the world's states and in particular the most advanced and prosperous states, was reflected in one of the more important policy documents of the Clinton presidency: the *National Security Strategy of Engagement and Enlargement* (the so-called En-En document).[76] The document states that:

> the line between our domestic and foreign policies is disappearing – that we must revitalise our economy if we are able to sustain our military forces,

foreign initiatives, and global influence, and that we
must engage actively abroad if we are to open foreign
markets and create jobs for our people.[77]

Between the release of the first En-En document in 1994 and
a third in 1996, domestic renewal and democratic enlargement
had become intertwined to form the linchpin of US foreign
and trade policy. While Washington had for some years taken
the lead in trying to achieve peace in the Middle East, in
December 1993 Clinton was on the sidelines when representatives of the late Palestinian leader Yasser Arafat met
with the late Israeli Prime Minister Yitzhak Rabin in Oslo to
resolve political differences. The result of the Oslo process
was a Declaration of Principles between Palestinians and
Israelis which included a removal of Israeli soldiers from
Arab towns in the occupied West Bank and self-rule for the
Palestinian Authority (PA) by mid-1996.[78] The declaration was
signed in an elaborate ceremony held at the White House on
13 September 1993, but Clinton was more of a spectator than
an active participant. With a peace process under way that had
little to do with US foreign policy Clinton adjusted his focus
on the MENA region to economics. He organised a series of
economic summits with Israeli and Arab leaders, held in
Casablanca, Amman and Cairo. These summits, while not
providing any substantial agreements between the various
parties, did signal a major development in the normalisation
of relations between Israel and the Arab world. Furthermore,
Clinton's push for democratic enlargement relied first on
economic liberalisation and the adoption of free market
economic policies that would help integrate the MENA
region into the global economy.[79]

For the remainder of his time in office President Clinton
led his administration in foreign and trade policies that would
be determined in its pursuit of national interests. However,
this policy direction was implemented not by strategic brink-

manship, open hostility or the stockpiling of increasingly destructive weapons systems but by encouraging the spread of the liberal principles of democracy, the rule of law and free marketeering – in short, liberal international institutions. This approach to foreign policy construction and implementation would be to a certain extent inherited by Clinton's successor. As has constantly been the case in US foreign and trade policy, the junior Bush administration's policy approach differed from that of previous administrations. This was partly a result of changing international relations and partly a result of the individual peculiarities of those involved in the decision making process. Nevertheless, the legacy of democratic enlargement and the use of international institutions remained, albeit in an altered form and implemented through more overt means (such as the forced regime change in Iraq).

The terrorist attacks on the continental United States on 11 September 2001 marked the first time since the war of 1812 that the US mainland had been attacked by a foreign power. The severity of the attacks and the psychological ramifications they brought with them cannot be underestimated. A President who, much like his predecessor, had little interest in foreign policy when he took office was thrust into a major international crisis that necessitated a major US response at the international level.[80] When George W. Bush took office in 2000 he had given only one foreign policy address in his election campaign. This trend was followed for the first six months of his administration, which focused overwhelmingly on domestic issues such as education reform, faith based initiatives, energy sources and production, and tax relief.[81] As a consequence Bush was criticised not only for his lack of interest in foreign affairs but also for his seemingly dangerous lack of knowledge about the international realm. In comic humour, *The Economist* in 2000 showed a picture of a US astronaut on the moon with the caption: 'Mr. Bush goes to Europe'.[82] In no region of the world was the Bush Administration's lack of will and ability to engage felt more than in the MENA region.

During the 2000 presidential campaign Condoleezza Rice published a foreign policy manifesto which argued for a strict national interest standard for US foreign policy.[83] Rice criticised Clinton's failure to distinguish between areas of vital US interest and areas of trivial importance. She claimed that rather than concentrating on powers that had the ability to affect the global order, such as Russia and China, or on pivotal alliances such as in North East Asia, the Clinton Administration had dissipated US credibility and military prowess on issues and regions of a peripheral nature.[84] In this manifesto Rice only mentions the MENA region once. Furthermore, she argued against the pursuit of societal engineering on the vast scale envisioned in the doctrine of democratic enlargement. Rice's suggestions were evident in the foreign policy of the first nine months of the Bush Administration. The main foreign policies pursued focused on the US withdrawal from the 1972 Anti-Ballistic Missile Treaty, the deployment of ballistic missile defences and challenging emerging Chinese pretensions to regional hegemony.[85]

With regard to the most pressing issue in the politics of the MENA region, the Israeli–Palestinian conflict, it was clear that Bush had regarded the conflict as beyond effective US influence, in part because of the Al-Aqsa Intifada. The level of violence, distrust and political disagreement had seemingly unravelled previous advancements in the peace process and Washington had no desire to engage to the extent that Clinton had in 1999 – when the President made a spectacular last push for peace culminating in the Camp David summit between Israeli Prime Minister Ehud Barak and Yasser Arafat.[86]

The events of 11 September 2001 provided the 'hawks' in the administration, especially those who saw re-shaping the Arab world the best chance for securing US interests, with the opportunity to push their agenda.[87] Since 1945 the United States has had to interpret and react to threats and overtures of friendship emanating from the MENA region. Often these have not come from the Arab world as much as they have come from outside powers such as the Soviet Union. However, in the post-Cold War era the only threats perceived by the United States in the MENA region have come from the Arab world.[88] As a result of US interpretation of Arab threats over the past decade or so Washington has formulated policy initiatives that revolve around either accommodation of Arab interests or imposition of US interests – the latter of which has been the more common of the two and an example of which is the forced regime change in Iraq.[89]

US trade policy in the twenty-first century

According to John Rothgeb Jr., US trade with other states is a very significant element of both the global economy and the United States' international relations.[90] Furthermore, US trade policy has for the best part of the last century been a major constitutive element of overall US foreign policy.[91] Within the making of US foreign economic and trade policy there are two broad camps that can be identified. The first camp advocates free trade and the expansion of liberal international institutions to govern and protect free trade.[92] The second advocates protectionism and public–private partnership in order to achieve economic prosperity and maintain the United States' position in the world economy.[93] According to Carl Kress, the Regional Director for the MENA at the US Trade and Development Agency, within both of these camps exist two other schools of thought which cut across the divisions between free trade advocates and protectionists. These are those who view trade policy as a key component in broader US foreign policies and in essence synonymous with political policy, and those who place little emphasis on the importance of trade policy with respect to achieving policy goals.[94] Fred

Bergsten argues that the former school of thought is prevalent in contemporary decision-making circles in Washington.[95]

The utility of trade policy in achieving foreign policy goals is described as consisting of two elements. The first is punitive and is perhaps the better established of the two. Here, economic sanctions and trade embargoes have historically been employed in order to punish actions which are undesirable to the United States or which are classed as illegal under international law. Furthermore, this type of policy is employed to discourage further undesired actions on the part of the target state and to coerce alternative actions.[96] The second and more recent element dates back to the twentieth century in terms of US trade policy. Here the use of trade policy is more positive and seeks to either reward a course of action by another state, encourage interdependence between the United States and the target state, or both. In the case of the latter the assumption that institutions lead to trade liberalisation, which in turn leads to economic integration and inter-state cooperation, is key.

Contemporary US trade policy is dominated by the advocates of trade liberalisation and international institutions.[97] Furthermore, a paradigmatic shift has been witnessed in the past 20 years which has greatly transformed the directions of US trade policy. Through the early 1990s US trade policy centred on multilateralism and engagement with IOs and governing regimes. The Uruguay Round of trade negotiations under the GATT system, while long and tumultuous, signified a watershed in multilateral trade policy. The eventual conclusion of the round resulted in the creation of the WTO after the signing of the final agreement in Marrakech, Morocco in 1994 by 111 states. The WTO was designed to strengthen the GATT system of governance, to serve as a forum for the completion of future FTAs and strengthen the overall multilateral system of international institutions governing trade.[98]

The United States played an instrumental role in completing the Uruguay Round and creating the WTO. However, the encouragement of European states was perhaps more significant. The drift towards bilateral negotiations and initiatives that had begun to characterise US trade policy resulted in European states relaxing certain objections to greater multilateral trade liberalisation. These included various agricultural, textiles and clothing, and manufactured goods objections.[99] The enticement was enough to ensure US engagement and support for the completion of the negotiating round. While 1 January 1995 signified a strengthening of the multilateral trading regime, it did not signify that the United States was enduringly committed to multilateralism in its pursuit of foreign economic policy goals.

By the late 1990s a clear break with the reliance on multilateralism had emerged as the United States focused increasingly on the creation of bilateral international institutions. This move gathered pace following the 1994 implementation of the North America Free Trade Area (NAFTA) agreement which, while multilateral in the sense that it included three states, shared more characteristics with bilateral agreements. Furthermore, NAFTA in essence was counter to the broader multilateral processes of trade liberalisation through the GATT and then the WTO.[100] The move to bilateralism was solidified after 2000 with the completion of the JUSFTA and its subsequent ratification and the rapid increase in bilateral FTAs signed by the United States since. According to Jeff Schott, the US government has been very eager to encourage trade liberalisation and the expansion of various institutions such as respect for IPRs but has been unhappy with the slow pace of multilateral negotiations.[101] In short, the success and utility of trade liberalisation and international institutions governing trade for US policy interests depends on their implementation. If implementation is slow then the achievement of US policy goals will also be slow.

As discussed in Chapter 2, the JUSFTA was only the fourth bilateral FTA signed by the United States. Since 2000, however, the United States has signed and implemented a further six bilateral FTAs and is currently in negotiations with 13 states for future FTAs. Three of these are pending Congressional approval, two are pending implementation and three are still being negotiated. The bilateral FTAs already agreed and ratified are as follows: Singapore (2003), Chile (2004), The Dominican Republic (2004), Bahrain (2004), Australia (2005) and Morocco (2006). At the time of writing agreements with Colombia, Panama and the Republic of Korea are awaiting congressional approval, and agreements with Peru and Oman are awaiting implementation. The United States is currently negotiating FTAs with Malaysia, Thailand and the United Arab Emirates.[102]

In addition to bilateral FTAs the United States has also pursued regional FTAs with a small number of states. While these agreements are multilateral by definition there is a clear connection with the bilateral policies pursued. The United States is currently negotiating a regional FTA with Botswana, Lesotho, Namibia, South Africa and Swaziland – the five members of the Southern African Customs Union (SACU). The negotiations were launched in 2003 but the process has been somewhat slow and has often stalled on issues such as IPRs.[103] After only 12 months of negotiating, the United States agreed to an FTA with Costa Rica, El Salvador, Guatemala, Honduras and Nicaragua in 2003. The agreement, labelled the US–Central America Free Trade Area agreement (CAFTA), was coupled with the US–Dominican Republic FTA to become the US-DR-CAFTA. The United States is also negotiating a regional FTA with Colombia, Ecuador and Peru (US–Andean Community Agreement).[104] The one thing all of these agreements have in common is that the United States is negotiating on one side and the other states either already constitute a regional grouping of some kind (such as the SACU) or are negotiating with the United States as a group. The result is that they reflect the same processes as bilateral FTA negotiations.

The increase in bilateral FTAs in the MENA region from two in 2001 to a likely six by the end of 2008 and a further three or four (with preliminary talk of negotiations with Kuwait, Qatar, Saudi Arabia and Egypt)[105] by 2012 is highly significant. This represents not merely isolated occurrences of bilateral FTAs but instead a development of US policy to the region as a whole in pursuit of its core interests.

In comparison with other regions such as Europe, South America and South East Asia, US trade policy towards the MENA region has been fairly uncomplicated. Historically, the United States has pursued access to the region's markets and natural resources.[106] However, the latter of these two policy goals has received far more attention and rightly so. Discounting trade in natural resources, which means US imports of oil and gas from MENA producers, levels of trade between the United States and the MENA region have traditionally been very low.[107] In the latter half of the twentieth century, as discussed above, emphasis was placed upon creating and maintaining cooperation on the behalf of MENA states. Little emphasis was placed on broader economic integration. On the other hand, the proliferation of US–MENA bilateral FTAs, which now account for almost one-third of US bilateral FTAs either implemented or being negotiated, is very significant – which reflects the growing frustration of the US government with slow multilateral processes, the Doha Round and the WTO dispute mechanisms. This is a key indicator of a shift in policy focus to the region. One would assume that if trade liberalisation leads to greater trade and economic growth then the United States would pursue more vigorously FTAs with major trading partners. Or at least one would assume that the United States would pursue FTAs with states and regions which constitute important trading partners. The MENA region does not fall into this category.

The comparison between the levels of trade between the United States and the MENA region (when discounting oil and gas) and US trade with other regions is clear: trade between the United States and the MENA region is far below trade with other regions. Regardless of the traditional low levels of US–MENA trade, and US–Jordan trade in particular as discussed in the previous chapter, the United States has developed an initiative to create bilateral FTAs with regional states (starting with Israel in 1984 then Jordan) which will lead to an eventual US–MENA FTA (the MEFTA initiative).[108] The policy direction is clear and needs little further analysis: contemporary United States trade policy to the MENA region (obviously including Jordan) is to liberalise trade through bilateral FTAs followed by a region-wide FTA. It must be noted here that a number of states in the region are excluded from these policies (Syria, Iran and Sudan). However, the demands and constraints which have led to these policies and the policy goals are less clear. As discussed above there are three core policy interests in the MENA region for the United States, yet most analyses (as discussed in Chapter 1) examine how these are pursued through conflict or hard power. A discussion here is necessary on interpreting how US trade policy may be aimed at achieving its main interests in the region.

Former Secretary of Defence Donald Rumsfeld defined the Bush administrations' approaches to the MENA region as being aimed at combating instability, terrorism and non-cooperation by states in the region.[109] Military action such as that taken in Afghanistan in 2001 and the ongoing occupation there along with the invasion, occupation and counter-insurgency in Iraq, is but one type of component in this approach. A second more subtle but perhaps more intense component of the United States' approach to achieving its goals in the region is to address the structural and systemic factors which hinder greater inter-state cooperation. Most answers to such an endeavour focus on political or cultural explanations. The unresolved Arab–Israeli conflict is often cited as the root of all the region's problems.[110] Culturalists such as Bernard Lewis argue that cultural and historical resentments of colonialism and religious grievances are the root cause.[111]

If these factors (or either one of them) are the roots of the MENA's region's disillusionment then there is little that can be done. The Arab–Israeli dispute is one of the world's longest-running conflicts and has proven very difficult to resolve. Colonialism is a past phenomenon that cannot be changed. However, we can identify a third possible cause that is centred on economics. South America, East Asia and South Asia all have deep-rooted ethnic and religious conflicts and colonial legacies; however, they are arguably less prone to instability as the MENA region when US interests are concerned.[112] The most evident difference between these regions is that the economy of the MENA region remains relatively divided and isolated at the regional and global levels. Perhaps the very lack of trade between the United States and the region is a cause of instability and hinders US–MENA cooperation. The United States seems to have adopted this interpretation and developed a policy framework which is aimed at increasing economic integration through trade.[113]

Furthermore, policy-makers in the second Bush Administration highlighted the fact that the lack of political modernity in the MENA region has become increasingly evident since the 'second wave' of democracy in the 1960s and 1970s.[114] In the MENA region, democracy, full respect for human rights, freedom of speech and transparent and accountable governance are all relatively rare. According to Freedom House's *Global Survey of Political Rights and Civil Liberties*, the region suffers from 'a democracy gap'.[115] Although three quarters of non-Muslim countries around the world are democracies and have been rated as 'free' by Freedom House, no Arab state has been rated as 'free'.[116] Also highlighted is the fact that economic growth in the Arab world has been disappointing and has struggled to keep pace with demographic growth.[117] Since the 1980s the MENA region (excluding the GCC states) has been one of the slowest growing regions.[118] According to some observers the US government seems to have pursued liberalising trade through international institutions in order to encourage economic integration and inter-state cooperation with the region.

In a speech given at the 20th anniversary of the National Endowment for Democracy at the US Chamber of Commerce on 6 November 2003, President Bush outlined his administration's underlying approach to the MENA region. In this speech Bush described the emergence of an approach that would foster and support economic growth and integration as well as democracy and economic freedom in order to assist the region in realising its economic and social potential.[119] The President somewhat boldly highlighted that:

> Sixty years of Western nations excusing and accommodating the lack of freedom in the Middle East did nothing to make us safe – because in the long run, stability cannot be purchased at the expense of liberty. As long as the Middle East remains a place where freedom does not flourish, it will remain a place of stagnation, resentment, and violence ready for export. And with the spread of weapons that can bring catastrophic harm to our country and to our friends, it would be reckless to accept the status quo.[120]

The Bush Administration pushed forward an agenda that adopts strategic considerations as its core. It also adopted the Doctrine of Democratic Enlargement through international institutions and economic integration as a means of securing inter-state cooperation and thus US interests. The JUSFTA was, as has been discussed above, the first bilateral FTA with an Arab state and only the second in the MENA region after the 1984 US–Israel FTA. The US–Jordan agreement was perhaps the logical first step in proliferating bilateral US–MENA FTAs for a number of reasons. First, Jordan–US trade had already been to a certain extent liberalised following the establishment of the qualifying industrial zones (QIZs) initiative (see Chapter 2). Second, Jordan–US trade levels prior to 2001 were among the smallest between a MENA state and the United States; thus the impact of the FTA would not be significant on the US economy – allowing it to pass through Congress easily. Third, the relatively stable and high levels of cooperation between the United States and Jordan at the state level made the JUSFTA a good test (and even model to emulate) for further US–MENA FTAs. In short the JUSFTA can be seen as the first step on the path to a broader US–MENA FTA and a test for the impacts of trade liberalisation between the United States and a MENA state (excluding Israel).

This chapter has discussed US interests in the MENA region as a whole and has outlined contemporary US trade policy to the region. It has also discussed the context for the more detailed discussion in the study, as well as exploring some of the main forces and factors at work in US policy-making towards the MENA region. The United States has traditionally held three core policy interests in the MENA region which have shaped and held primacy over all other interests. These core interests developed over the past century or so in stages, with the first interest emerging in the late nineteenth century. This interest was the securing of access to the region's markets both as sources of imports – not oil or gas at that stage – and markets to export to. The second core interest emerged in the 1930s and was securing access to the region's oil and gas resources. It must be highlighted again that the United States has sought access to the region's resources for itself but also for the global economy as a whole. The third core interest has been the establishment and maintenance of stable relations with governments of the region in order to ensure inter-state cooperation on the part of MENA states. This interest developed and intensified through the 1950s as European powers withdrew from the region and Soviet power grew.

Jordan, while a small state with no natural resources of significance, has become a key state in the region for the United States in its pursuit of its interests there. The traditionally cooperative relationship between the two states, the strategic location of Jordan (neighbouring Palestine, Israel, Syria, Iraq and Saudi Arabia) have been magnified by worsening relations between the United States and some of Jordan's neighbours. Increasing instability at times in some of these states and stability within Jordan have further enhanced the kingdom's importance to the United States.

The United States' pursuit of its policy goals over the past six decades or so have been characterised by two key trends. The first is the employment of hard power in the form of military power and coercion. This trend dominated the 1950s and 1960s as the United States endeavoured to contain the Soviet Union's influence in the region and support its allies in regional wars. The use of hard power remains a key policy direction, as the 1990–91 Gulf Crisis and War as well as the 2003 Third Gulf War have shown. However, a second policy trend can also be identified: this is the employment of soft power through international institutions and economic tools. This second policy direction gained in importance in the 1970s in the early Carter Administration and again in the 1990s under the Clinton administrations and the doctrine of Democratic Enlargement. Both policy trends, however, are aimed at achieving the three core interests.

Contemporary US trade policy as a whole and to the MENA region in particular is characterised by a shift from multilateralism to bilateralism. In the case of US trade policy as a whole, the mid-1990s saw a move away from focusing on multilateral trade liberalisation through IOs such as the WTO and the creation of global trade regimes such as the trade-related aspects of IPRs (TRIPs) agreement. Rather US trade policy began to become more bilateral in nature and reliant on the engagement with international institutions on a smaller scale. The belief in the utility of international institutions and trade liberalisation in achieving US policy interests is key here. The slow pace of multilateral liberalisation was addressed by pursuing bilateral and small-scale regional FTAs and expanding the scope of trade regimes on a case-by-case basis. Trade policy towards the MENA region has not been an exception to this policy direction.

Following the implementation of the JUSFTA, which as previously discussed was only the fourth bilateral FTA the United States had signed, the United States has embarked upon a relatively rapid process of creating bilateral FTAs. A number of FTAs have been implemented and a large number of others are in the process of being negotiated or ratified. Significantly approximately one-third of these bilateral FTAs are with states in the MENA region. When considering that US–MENA trade has historically been among the lowest of US trade with any region this is a somewhat perplexing policy focus. Significantly, the bilateral FTAs which have been pursued have not included the major oil and gas suppliers besides the UAE. The overall aim of US–MENA trade policy is the creation of a region-wide US–MEFTA and this is being pursued by completing bilateral FTAs and encouraging the process of intra-region trade liberalisation.

The JUSTA was, therefore, the initial step (not including the 1984 Israel–US FTA) and can be seen as a model and test case for the completion of further FTAs with the region. It is possible to argue that due to the close relationship between the United States and Jordan, the partially liberalised trade between them (that existed as a result of previous engagement in international institutions) as well as the Jordanian commitment to trade liberalisation in general that a Jordan–US FTA was the logical initial step. Thus US interests in the region, the pursuit of these interests and broader trends in US trade policy have combined to lead to trade facilitation with Jordan through international institutions.

4

BILATERAL TRADE IN TEXTILES AND CLOTHING

Thus far the study has considered contemporary issues relating to the advancement of the discipline of IPE and the study of US–Jordan trade relations in particular. An analysis has also been presented of state facilitation of trade between the United States and Jordan and the advancement of a liberal economic agenda through the agency of state actors. What follows in this third section of the study is an analysis of the agency of non-state actors and how state agency interacts with that of non-state actors to form contemporary trade relations between the United States and Jordan. The importance of Jordanian–US trade is highlighted in this and the following two chapters by showing the uniqueness of *how* trade has developed on the ground. The wider implications of Jordanian US trade relations as a model of economic cooperation and growth are also considered.

The purpose of this chapter is to expand on the discussion of state-level facilitation of trade by examining bilateral trade in textile and clothing (T&C) goods.

In so doing it will also be possible to begin to determine how non-state actors in the two markets are interacting in the post-FTA regulatory environment.

The Jordanian economy is a developing economy and one which has had limited success in industrialising over the past six decades. In view of this it is no surprise that the production and export of low value-added, often labour intensive goods forms a large part of the kingdom's exports. Recently the production and export of T&C goods has become one of the leading sectors in Jordanian exports to the US market since 2001 as well as to the MENA and global markets. Exports of low value-added goods from the US market to the Jordanian market are not a major characteristic of contemporary bilateral trade. Therefore, while this chapter concerns bilateral trade in T&C goods, the discussion is focused largely on Jordanian exports of T&C goods to the US market in order to exemplify the development of Jordanian–US trade.

In this chapter the plurality of actors in the relationship between Jordan and the United States and trade between them is a key principle. The link between these actors and their interests at the domestic level is linked to the international level through a discussion of the broader global market in T&C goods and through international institutions which govern this sector. A key premise of this chapter is that bilateral trade in T&C goods between Jordan and the United States is largely a zero-sum game in that Jordanian gains are significant while the United States gains very little if anything at all from trade in these goods.

In order to develop the analysis in the preceding chapters and engage with the core research questions established in the introduction and developed in Chapter 1, it is necessary to examine the main characteristics of the Jordanian T&C sector. Any consideration of Jordanian exports in T&C goods to the US market must begin with a (largely) empirical description of the emergence of this sector as a significant and relatively new component in the Jordanian economy. A description of bilateral T&C trade flows between Jordan and the EU precedes a discussion of Jordan–US trade. The following sections of the chapter then discuss the mechanisms which have made this growth possible and the limitations to it. Section four therefore considers the Jordanian QIZs and industrial estates introduced in chapter two in more detail. Section five considers public–private coordination in the sector and analyses the agency of non-state actors in the Jordanian T&C sector. This section highlights how activity in the T&C sector in Jordan is to some extent directed and supported by the government. The analysis here develops the concept of a public–private developmental partnership. This is followed by a section examining patterns of domestic investment and FDI in the T&C sector.

Section seven considers the multilateral labour force involved in the Jordanian T&C industry and how, through mechanisms in the JUSFTA regarding labour rights, labour issues have acted as a limitation to bilateral trade in T&C goods. Any understanding of the development of this sector in Jordanian-US trade cannot be fully understood without including an analysis of the market for which these goods are destined. The eighth section thus addresses developments and preferences in the US market for T&C goods since the mid-1990s and in the post-Multi-Fibre Agreement (MFA) era. A concluding section summarises the main points and arguments of this chapter and further develops the answers to the core research questions.

The growth of the T&C sector in the Jordanian economy
The T&C industry in Jordan is relatively young. Prior to 1997 the sector was largely inactive and what activity existed was geared towards the domestic market as opposed to export markets.[1] The principal reason for the emergence of the sector in the Jordanian economy was a decision made by the

Jordanian and US governments to further develop bilateral trade relations. The desire to deepen trade between the two economies came as result of the 1994 Treaty of Peace between Jordan and Israel and took the QIZs as the cornerstone.[2] The initiative to develop QIZs in Jordan had three main aims: firstly, the QIZs would require joint commercial activity between Jordan and Israel – thus helping to 'normalise' relations between the two and promote economic cooperation between them; secondly, to provide a catalyst for job creation and FDI within Jordan; and finally, to provide certain sectors of the Jordanian economy with unfettered access to the US market – in effect as a peace dividend.[3] The QIZs and the joint US–Jordanian agencies which regulate trade in goods produced in both countries along with the regulatory legislation agreed upon by both states represent a key set of institutions.

The QIZs give Jordanian goods manufactured within them duty- and quota-free access to the US market. Out of this opportunity has emerged the Jordanian T&C industry which as stated above and as shown below was largely irrelevant in 1997, accounting for a mere 1 per cent of GDP ($71 million). Following the initial establishment of QIZs in Jordan the government, through the Ministry of Industry and Trade, completed a number of studies on how best to benefit from the project.[4] Jordanian manufactures in the mid-1990s were largely uncompetitive internationally and domestically and were grossly inadequate to make full use of the QIZ project. The development of the T&C industry relied heavily on the comparative advantages inherent in the Jordanian economy. These were: access to cheap semi-skilled and skilled labour, relatively well developed infrastructure including above regional-standard road and transport networks, and a supportive government. According to Yousef Al-Shamali, Deputy Director of the Department of Foreign Trade Policy at The Ministry of Industry and Trade, '[e]tablishing the T&C industry in the QIZs was the only really viable option. There would not have been any other industrial sector which would have been able to establish itself and compete successfully in the US market – even with (the) free access.'[5] The decision to use the QIZs to develop the T&C export industry within Jordan has thus far proved to be highly successful.

In comparison to the early levels of growth and the limited relevance to the Jordanian economy as a whole, by 2009 the sector was contributing significantly to export revenues, job creation, overall employment and overall GDP. In 2006 the T&C sector accounted for 9.4 per cent of overall GDP in Jordan and 20 per cent of overall industrial value-added.[6] To provide some measure of how important these figures are it is useful to compare the Jordanian T&C industry with similar industries in other states. Here it is most useful to examine Jordan's main competitors in the T&C export industry. These are the three major Arab T&C exporting economies Tunisia, Morocco and Egypt (along with Jordan referred to here as the MENA 4). In Tunisia, Morocco and Egypt the percentage contribution to GDP of their respective T&C sectors in 2006 were 5.6 per cent, 5.1 per cent and 3 per cent respectively.[7] The T&C industries in these states are well established and were among the first sectors to develop as their modern economies emerged after independence from their former European patrons.[8] In Egypt, the T&C industry dates back many centuries, yet in comparison to the Jordanian T&C industry it is playing a far smaller role in the modern Egyptian economy. At the same time, contributions to industrial value-added of the T&C industries in two of these three states are much higher than in Jordan; 42 per cent and 30 per cent for Tunisia and Egypt respectively but slightly lower for Morocco at 17 per cent. This suggests that while there has been rapid growth of the T&C industry in Jordan the relative value-added in comparison to other industrial sectors, such as the pharmaceutical sector, is low. In Egypt and Tunisia the opposite is true.

The contribution to employment of the T&C sector is also extremely important in the MENA 4 economies. Employing low-skilled and semi-skilled workers the T&C sector accounts for as much as one-third of the industrial labour force in Egypt (approximately one million employees) and over 200,000 in both Morocco and Tunisia. In Jordan this figure is much lower (expected in the comparison to Egypt due to the immense difference in the sizes of the industrial labour forces in the two states) at approximately 80,000 employees.[9] However, the industry is relatively young and has only been growing with consistency since 2001.

While the importance of the T&C sector in Jordan has grown in terms of contribution to overall GDP and employment, it is in the sector's utility as a source of foreign exchange that its real significance is found. Between 1997 and 2006 exports of T&C manufactures grew from 1 per cent to 32 per cent of total exports in value terms.[10] Again, it is worth comparing this figure to the other MENA 4 economies as they provide a benchmark for sector utility in foreign exchange as their T&C industries are well established and have well established links to international markets. In 2006 Tunisian T&C exports accounted for a massive 58 per cent of total non-oil exports, while in Egypt and Morocco the figures were slightly lower at 52 per cent and 42 per cent respectively.[11] No other MENA T&C industry or in fact any other MENA industrial sector has experienced such a dramatic growth in the same period as the Jordanian T&C sector.

Importantly, the composition of Jordanian T&C exports is relatively more diverse than the other major Arab T&C exporters.[12] In Tunisia for example, suits (for men, women, boys and girls) represent 47 per cent of total T&C export revenues. At the same time, the T&C exports in Jordan with the highest share of export revenues are jerseys, pullovers and cardigans, which make up only 28 per cent of total T&C export earnings. Women's and girl's suits make up the next largest share at 20 per cent of export earnings.[13] While Morocco exemplifies a similar pattern to Tunisia (with women's and girl's suits alone comprising 31 per cent of overall T&C export revenue), Egypt has a relatively diversified T&C industry with no single group of products surpassing 17 per cent of total export earnings (men's and boy's suits).[14]

The performance of Jordanian T&C exports in the EU and US markets

As is the case for many developing economies and most industrial sectors, the global export market for Jordanian T&C products is largely confined to the EU and US markets. However, the reliance on these two markets is not evenly balanced. Jordanian T&C exports since 1997 have had very little success in the EU market and this difficulty has only been magnified by the end of the MFA in 2005 (discussed below). In 2006 Jordanian T&C exports to the EU market totalled only $15.3 million. This was an actual drop from the 1997 figure of $23 million and represented only 0.02 per cent of the EU market share – compared to 0.05 per cent in 1997.[15] In 2006 Tunisia and Morocco, on the other hand, exported $3.7 billion and $3.4 billion worth of T&C goods to the EU, accounting for 5.1 per cent and 4.8 per cent of the market share respectively.[16] The largest 2006 market share went to China which exported a staggering $25.4 billion worth of T&C goods to the EU, representing 26.9 per cent of the market share.[17] This level was an increase on the 1997 figure of $13.5 billion (23.3 per cent of market share).

Even on the back of the JEUAA signed with the EU in 1997, Jordanian T&C exports have proven to be uncompetitive with both regional T&C exporters such as Morocco, Tunisia and Egypt – which all have AAs with the EU and longer trading relationships in T&C goods – as well as global competitors such as China and other South East Asian producers. The comparative advantages Jordan enjoys, such as having access to cheaper labour than regional competitors and closer geographical proximity to the EU market than South East Asian competitors,[18] have gone largely unexploited.

The main factor which has hindered Jordanian access to the EU market is the relative insignificance the JEUAA has had on all Jordanian exports to the EU market. In theory the JEUAA should have led to greater bilateral trade levels between Jordan and the EU.[19] This has not happened. Rather, imports from the EU have increased significantly but exports to the world's largest market have struggled and in some sectors, such as the T&C sector, have decreased. The primary causes of this have been the increase in import demands in Jordan due to rising levels of consumer prosperity and industrial growth, and the signing of AAs and broader liberalisation of EU trade with other states.

The US market for T&C goods, especially manufactured clothing, has been growing steadily over the past 15 years, resulting in expanding opportunities for T&C exporters. Although Jordan is a small producer of T&C goods, according to Halim Abu-Rahmeh, the CEO of the Jordan Exporters Association, it has not missed this opportunity.[20] However, unlike the EU market with its diversified sources of T&C goods, the United States has traditionally imported the vast majority of its T&C goods from Mexico, China and the Central American Free Trade Area (CAFTA) member states. In total these three main sources accounted for 48 per cent of total market share in 2006.[21] MENA exporters have fared much worse. Tunisia, Morocco and Egypt, for example, while being relatively important sources for the EU market, only accounted for 0.83 per cent of US imports of T&C goods in 2006.[22] Jordan on the other hand ranks as one of the more important sources of US T&C imports, accounting for a market share value of 1.5 per cent in 2006.[23] While at first impression this is a small figure, in the context of global US

T&C market import shares the young and relatively small Jordanian T&C export industry has achieved a relatively large share of the US market in a very short period of time (1997–2008).

Table 4.1: Market share among major suppliers to the US T&C market, 1997 and 2006, in US$ million[24]

Exporting state or region	1997		2006	
	Export	Market share %	Export	Market share %
Greater China	14,613	21.5	24,856	23
CAFTA-DR	7,247	16.4	9,984	14.7
Mexico	6,541	14.8	8,701	10
South Asia-4	6,813	10.5	11,124	10.5
Jordan	4.2	0.01	1,250	1.48
Egypt	410	0.72	601	0.65
Morocco	56	0.12	80	0.11
Tunisia	15	0.03	50	0.07

The experience of the Jordanian T&C export sector has been based largely on the combination of comparative advantages within the Jordanian economy and government facilitation of trade. Unlike the experience of exports to the EU market, advantages bestowed upon the Jordanian economy have allowed T&C exports to penetrate the US market in a sustainable manner. These advantages include access to large pools of unskilled, semi-skilled and skilled labour, as well as economic and political support from the government.[25] Jordan does not possess the advantage of close geographic proximity to the US market, as it does with the EU market, and is therefore disadvantaged in this way. It would not, therefore, be surprising if Jordanian T&C exports enjoyed greater success in the EU market than in the US market. However, as has been mentioned above there are certain disadvantages the T&C sector has encountered in competing in the EU market. These disadvantages also exist in the relationship with the US market; however, the mechanisms by which they are overcome vary greatly.

The United States has completed a large number of international agreements aimed at providing access to its market for international exporters. The US market is, indeed, more open than that of the EU when T&C imports are concerned.[26] There are other similarities between the two markets: the US market has integrated with those of Mexico and Canada through the mechanisms included in the North American Free Trade Area (NAFTA) agreement; the US market has witnessed rapidly increasing imports of T&C goods from China and South East Asia;[27] and trade has been promoted with the United States' closest neighbours and T&C sources in South America.[28] This latter point is shadowed by the increased integration of the EU with its neighbours in the southern Mediterranean. In the case of T&C exports to the EU, the Jordanian experience has been one of decline and stagnation. Faced with similar market access circumstances in the US market since 1997, the Jordanian T&C export sector has been one of dynamism and growth.[29] This is due to one simple difference in the mechanisms of trade facilitation provided for by cooperation between the governments of Jordan and the United States that does not exist between the government of Jordan and the EU. This difference is grounded in the seemingly urgent and highly solidified government commitment to promoting US–Jordanian trade in general, as discussed in the previous two chapters.

Chapter 3 analysed the nature of US trade policy towards the MENA region in general and to Jordan in particular. The conclusion was that US–Jordanian trade has increased in significance in the past decade (due to economic, political and strategic considerations) and now acts as a model of US trade policy with the MENA region as a whole. Much the same was found in the analysis presented in Chapter 2, where Jordanian trade policy was assessed: here it was determined that the political and economic reforms embarked upon by the government of Jordan since 1999 are supported by the success of Jordanian–US trade. This dual urgency in promoting trade between the two states has led to the mechanisms of special economic zones and the FTA.

The Qualifying Industrial Zones and Industrial Estates

The QIZs in Jordan were initially established following the signing of the Treaty of Peace between Jordan and Israel in 1994. Within the treaty there are a number of articles demanding the implementation of joint projects between the two states.[30] The creation of a number of QIZs which would act as economic bridges between the two markets was one of these requirements. In brief, the QIZs were established as designated industrial estates where all goods therein produced would receive duty- and quota-free access to the US market. The conditions set upon the production of these goods concern the rules of origin and percentage value-added. In order to receive unrestricted access to the US market any goods produced in the QIZs would have to have a certified amount of material input of a minimum level from the Israeli economy (8 per cent) and a minimum value-added from the Jordanian economy (35 per cent).[31] Certification of these requirements is issued by a joint commission consisting of Jordanian and Israeli representatives and government bodies.[32]

Initially the QIZs witnessed little growth, mostly due to the lack of government support by the Jordanian and Israeli regimes as well as a fundamental lack of manufacturing capacity. However, the utility of the QIZs as a means to increase exports was realised following further growth in exports to the US market. An increase in FDI, which reached over $500 million by 2005, was also a key factor in the government's decision to promote the QIZs and expand export oriented industrial sectors.[33] In 1997 QIZ exports to the US totalled a mere $6.9 million but by 2007 this figure had grown to well over $1 billion. According to Mohamed Atmeh, the Deputy CEO of the Jordan Industrial Estates Corporation (JIEC) – one of several corporations with close links to the Jordanian government involved in establishing and running industrial estates and QIZs – the QIZs were not initially set up as part of the government's trade regime. Rather they were 'a unique project, which were running more as an anomaly (as) opposed to in conjunction with our economic strategies of the late 1990s'.[34]

The QIZ projects were not the central tenet of economic policy and export activity in Jordan in their first three years. Nevertheless, with increasing exports from the zones, and previously unseen levels of FDI flowing in to them, the new impetus placed on economic reform and export-led growth which King Abdullah II's rule introduced in 1999–2000, the QIZs became more important. According to Mohamed Atmeh by 2000 it was believed that there were two main benefits from the QIZs. The first was the potential for job creation within them and in the economy as a whole as a result of greater activity in sectors pivotal to the operation of the QIZs (such as transport and services). The second Atmeh described as 'the very tempting access to the US market for foreign investors'. He continued to clarify that:

> The government realised that vast potential for short- to medium-term investment existed. It was believed that this investment would be focused on the setting up of short- to medium-term projects to gain quick access to the US market for a limited period of time. By this I mean in sectors like clothes and other textiles, where quick production could be established with limited capital requirements and limited capital gains and risk.[35]

As indicated above, the Jordanian government's initial assessment of how to utilise the QIZs resulted in the decision to foster the growth of a T&C export sector.[36] By the turn of the century this was coupled with the private sector's interest and growing investment in the T&C sector within the QIZs. The result has been the overarching dominance of the QIZs by the T&C sector – which accounts for approximately 90 per cent of QIZ exports to the United States – and the sector's expansion in the Jordanian economy as a whole through specially constructed industrial estates. It is important to note that industrial estates in Jordan are not QIZs. However, the 2001 implementation of the JUSFTA has largely negated this fact as all T&C goods now enjoy duty- and quota-free access to the US market.[37]

The first industrial estates were established in Jordan in the early 1960s. Prominent among them was the special economic zone established in Aqaba in 1963.[38] However, slow economic growth and industrialisation through the 1980s meant that the growth of industrial estates was negligible over this period. Furthermore, the government's concentration on structural policies aimed at import substitution rather than export-led growth hindered investment in the industrial estates which had been established.[39] Fuelled by the success of the QIZs after 2001 when the FTA was implemented and the shift of government economic policy to export-led growth and trade liberalisation, the past few years have seen a flurry of economic activity. Key among the developments of this period was the establishment of more industrial estates and the expansion of existing ones.[40] Other important developments have been the creation and growth of a number of corporations tasked with constructing and managing industrial estates;[41] corporations oriented towards the promotion of Jordan's industrial estates abroad in order to attract FDI;[42] and the deepening of the public–private relationship – albeit discreetly, as is discussed below.

There are currently just over 300 T&C manufacturers operating in Jordan. Of these 92 operate within the QIZs and the majority of the rest are located within industrial estates.[43] While the dominance of the T&C manufacturers in terms of overall numbers lies with the industrial estates, dominance in terms of value is still firmly in the QIZs. In 2006 T&C exports from the QIZs (only to the US market) totalled $1.06 billion whereas T&C exports form the industrial estates to the US market only totalled approximately $200 million.[44] The difference in value of exports is attributable to two key factors. Firstly, the main T&C manufacturers have been operating in the QIZs for much longer than the T&C manufacturers in the industrial estates. The infrastructure and operations were established in the QIZs from 1997 whereas in the industrial estates this only happened several years later.[45] Secondly, growth of the T&C sector has slowed down in the past few years, meaning further growth in the industrial estates has been limited.[46] The main advantage the industrial estates do have over the QIZs is the continued strengthening of the relationship between public and private actors. This relationship is likely to continue, promoting activity in the industrial estates in general including the T&C sector.

Public–private partnership

Governmental involvement in the Jordanian economy has a long history. As was outlined in Chapter 2, through much of the kingdom's history the government has played a central role in guiding economic activity and determining macroeconomic structures.[47] The result of this link between state and market was limited economic growth and industrial development followed by unsustainability in the late 1980s, culminating in the 1989 financial crisis. What has been seen in Jordan since 1989 is a period of economic reform through structural adjustment, privatisation and trade liberalisation (see discussion in Chapter 2).[48] However, clearly government involvement in the economy has not been fully withdrawn. Government involvement in the economy has been transformed, but it still exists. This transformation has led to a shift in the balance between state and market actors in the economy and the emergence of a public–private partnership. This partnership is characterised by the government having a regulationist role by forming policies and controlling macro economic decisions and market actors implementing these policies, and by micro-managing economic activity. The sustainability of this relationship is perpetuated by the fact that both state and market actors achieve their goals through this partnership. On the one hand the economy is made 'business friendly' and conducive to the needs of private enterprise and on the other the government achieves economic growth and industrial development.

This partnership operates through a number of key organisations which act as a bridge between the public and private sectors. Of these organisations there are three identifiable types. The first type of organisation is the traditional public–private agency that is oriented towards economic affairs, such as the Amman Chamber of Commerce, the Amman Chamber of Industry and the American Chamber of Commerce in Jordan. The second type of organisation operating in Jordan is the 'developmental corporation', such as the Jordan Enterprise and Development Corporation (JEDCO), the Jordan Industrial Estates Corporation (JIEC) and the Jordan Investment Board (JIB), whose purpose is to provide services to private enterprise and who generally claim to have autonomy and independence from the government. These actors do in fact have close links to government. The third type of organisation or actor is the private enterprise. These are wholly private actors such as MNCs and domestic businesses which work in a symbiotic relationship with the government to further their own interests.[49]

The Amman Chamber of Commerce is a good example

of the first type of actor involved in promoting the public–private partnership in Jordan. According to Sabri Al-Khassib, the Director of Research at the chamber, 'the main aim [of the institution] is to meet economic development goals'. He continued '[W]e do this by helping the governmental decision making bodies use the expertise and advice of private actors. This task [is] done by registering private corporations, setting up joint committees and conducting micro-economic research.'[50] The Amman Chamber of Commerce, much like the Amman Chamber of Industry and the American Chamber of Commerce in Jordan, is a joint public–private entity. The board consists of 12 board members who are all elected from the private sector. However, a large part of the chamber's budget and in fact much of its infrastructure (such as the head office) are government owned or supplied.

There are currently over 32,000 trade and commerce related bodies registered with the chamber which operate in Amman and in the surrounding areas. Al-Khassib stated that this number increased from 4,000 new registrations in 2001 to just under 9,000 in 2006. The vast majority of these new registrations were 'involved in trade and commerce with the United States, Saudi Arabia and India'.[51] Approximately 30 per cent of the registrations in 2006 were for corporations involved in the T&C export industry. This signifies a drop of 7 per cent on the 2005 figure and is indicative of the overall slowdown in growth of the T&C sector.[52]

The case of JEDCO is more exemplary of how the public–private relationship has developed in the post JUSFTA era. According to Khawla Al-Badri, the Managing Director of JEDCO, the corporation's 'main aim is to help Jordanian companies involved in exports to establish themselves, then promote them and help their development'.[53] Al-Badri explains the transformation in JEDCO's role since the late 1990s as '[because] under agreements signed with international partners such as the EU and the US, and especially following WTO accession the government could not offer this support to businesses wishing to export to other markets, there was a niche in the market for people like us'. JEDCO was established in 1972 as a public–private corporation, owned jointly by the Jordanian government and the Amman Chamber of Commerce as well as the private sector. It had its own budget and own Board of Directors but was located within the Ministry of Industry and Trade. The head office is now located in an independent commercial high rise building, but is only a stone's throw from the Ministry of Industry and Trade. The Board of Directors is still split equally between public and private members but the director is the Minister of Industry and Trade.

While JEDCO operates as a private actor in terms of micro-planning and implementation, it is increasingly controlled by the government. When questioned about the annual budget of JEDCO, Al-Badri admitted that 'we used to have more of our own budget, half from the private sector and half from the government, now the government accounts for our entire budget'.[54] Even more important is the fact that by 2005 the government accounted for full ownership of JEDCO as opposed to its previous ownership of one-third.

Though JEDCO has seemingly become a wholly government body, supporting Jordanian export businesses, to some extent in contradiction to a number of international agreements signed with other states, a closer examination suggests otherwise. The process of government macro-decision making and private sector implementation is very much embodied in the structure of JEDCO. According to Al-Badri, JEDCO operates independently of the government. She claims that 'the government made the decision that Jordanian exports should be promoted and supported so that economic growth can be led by exports. What we do here is provide this support through the private sector.'[55] It is worth noting that while JEDCO's budget is supplied by the government, its staff (apart from half of the Board of Directors) is sourced entirely from the private sector. Furthermore, the management and allocation of the budgetary funds are under the control of JEDCO staff, not the government. Al-Badri explained that the government entrusts JEDCO and other such corporations with promoting and developing Jordanian export related corporations, supplying the means to complete this task but then relying on expertise from the private sector. 'People realised after 1989 that the government was not capable of directing the economy successfully. Governments, especially the one under Ali Abul Ragheb moved to use the private sector in a productive way.' Al-Badri continued to describe the now dominant belief within government that the private sector can promote the Jordanian economy more efficiently than the government.[56]

While JEDCO's budget has been increasing over recent years it is still insufficient to promote and help develop all sectors within the economy. Rather JEDCO (and not the government) has taken the decision to focus on the most beneficial sectors – among them the T&C export sector. Support is provided by JEDCO to T&C export-oriented corporations operating within Jordan in a number of ways. In the autumn of 2006, for example, JEDCO organised a trade mission to Italy in order to showcase Jordanian T&C goods. T&C corporations were invited to join the trade mission and prepare marketing and study material along with actual goods to promote abroad. JEDCO supplied the funds, arranged the venues, organised all bureaucratic matters relating to visas and so on.[57] In short JEDCO acts as a middle man between Jordanian suppliers and potential destination markets. However, the operations of JEDCO do not benefit only Jordanian corporations. Rather JEDCO also promotes other actors within the T&C sector (among other sectors) through trade missions as mentioned above as well as providing technical support to corporations, conducting market, financial and consultancy studies and promoting the Jordanian T&C sector abroad.[58] Perhaps the most fitting way to understand the operations of JEDCO are as Al-Badri has described them: 'Jordan in general has a centralized decision-making system, but there is an agenda and many actors involved with some autonomy and influence in the implementation of decisions'.[59]

JIEC is one of a number of private sector entities which create, promote and maintain industrial estates and QIZs within Jordan. JIEC is perhaps one of the more useful examples when trying to understand how the public–private relationship impacts economic activity 'on the ground', especially with regard to the T&C sector. At the time of writing JIEC operates five industrial estates including three QIZs[60] and is planning the construction of four more.[61] It is an independent, autonomous corporation that has its own budget, but has close links to the government. Key among these links is that the Head of the Board of Directors is the Minister of Industry and Trade (as is the case with JEDCO) and 67 per cent of the capital comes from the government.[62] Again, similar to JEDCO, the remainder of the Board of Directors (the board has 13 members in all) come from the private sector and have no role in government. Another similarity with JEDCO is that JIEC was established by the government in 1984 but later developed into an autonomously operating corporation. In an interview conducted with Mohammed Atmeh, the Deputy CEO of JIEC, in December 2006 JIEC was described as 'a profit oriented corporation, but (it is) also oriented towards the development of the nation'.[63]

Atmeh outlined four main contributions to the national economy which JIEC focuses on. The first he described as inward capital flow or FDI. The very nature of the Jordanian trade regime is oriented toward making the Jordanian economy appealing to foreign capital for both medium- and long-term investment. In short, the activity of actors such as JIEC is intended not only to make profits but also to make Jordan 'business friendly'. By creating industrial estates and QIZs, JIEC attracts foreign corporations and capital to expand their operations or relocate to Jordan. Here duty- and quota-free access to the US T&C market, as well as increasingly liberal access to MENA T&C markets and the EU market, are 'very tempting and very profitable'.[64] Furthermore, the majority of industrial estates in Jordan, including JIEC industrial estates, offer a number of key incentives. The JIEC-owned Al-Hassan (Irbid) industrial estate, for example, offers comprehensive custom-built infrastructure which investing entities can buy or rent. Other incentives include free amenities and services including free electricity, water and communication and all inclusive customer services.

Working in correlation with the JIB (discussed below), JIEC also offers foreign investors 12 years of tax free operations – JIB offers ten years tax free operations as standard to all non-Jordanian investors while JIEC offers an additional two years.[65] This is extremely attractive to foreign investors and MNCs that operate in the T&C sector but are likely to maintain only medium-term investment activities in Jordan. In recent these incentives, among others, have had the desired effect and according to Atmeh 'inward capital flow to [our] industrial estates and QIZs has been increasing very rapidly, and so [our] intention [is] to build five more estates in the near future'.[66]

Other key objectives which Atmeh highlighted as being at the heart of JIEC's operations include horizontal capital flow. Here, the industrial estates and QIZs are seen as central locations of economic activity which act as distribution points for capital at the local level. The wages of the employees of the factories located in the industrial estates, for example, add purchasing power to the local economy. Food, clothing, entertainment and transport all have to be provided in some measure to the employees and through this mechanism further economic activity is generated.[67] With this in mind, JIEC industrial estates and QIZs (much the same as virtually all industrial estates and QIZs in Jordan) are distributed around the kingdom, often according to where the government says they should be. Areas of low or lower economic development, such as Muagar (the location of one of JIEC's planned new industrial estates) have been the site of the development of industrial estates and QIZs. According to Atmeh:

> [t]his is because, from the business point of view, there is a large source of cheap labour, plenty of open land for development and good transport links. From a societal point of view, we can provide jobs for local residents both directly and indirectly through economic spread. We can benefit the nation as well as ourselves (...) in this relationship it is a partnership.[68]

In terms of sector development, the majority of industrial estates and QIZs are dominated by T&C manufacturers. The operations of JIEC are no exception to this. Of the existing two industrial estates and three QIZs which JIEC owns, only one is not dominated by T&C. This is the Ma'an estate where activity is more evenly spread between T&C and glass manufacture. There are two reasons why T&C dominate JIEC's industrial estates and QIZs: the first is that studies conducted prior to their creation concluded that focusing on T&C would be most beneficial. According to Atmeh these benefits are, firstly, that the US market for T&C manufactures is large and therefore offers greater profitability than other sectors. Secondly, focusing on T&C manufactures is a fast way to make money. This point is relevant to both public and private interests. Finally, in compliance with existing company policies, and in coordination with the ministries of Industry and Trade, and Labour, JIEC would be able to offer greater employment opportunities by promoting labour-intensive manufacturing.

The second reason why the industrial estates and QIZs are dominated by T&C is a result of other market forces. A common mistake in much trade literature is that government policy in developing states dictates the form of activity, such as the nature of industrial estate production.[69] However, in the case of the JIEC-run industrial estates and QIZs private sector actors seem to have been attracted by purely economic reasons; for example, duty- and quota-free access to the US market and the natural comparative advantages offered.[70]

The growth of JIB is exemplary of the increasing importance of market forces and private sector actors in the development of the T&C sector. JIB was established in 1990 as a department within the Ministry of Industry and Trade. Its primary objective was to attract FDI into Jordan.[71] Its original budget was low, as was its number of staff. However, following a number of key amendments to national laws governing trade and capital flows in the mid-1990s such as the 1995 Investment Promotion Law, JIB has been promoted as a key actor. The result was the detachment of the organisation from the government and its development as an independent and autonomous entity. The majority of its 75 employees are recruited directly from the private sector and not from government, as is common with many similar bodies.[72]

JIB's importance continues to grow and its participation in the Jordanian economy is becoming increasingly diverse. In 2006 the organisation's overall budget was $1.3 million. This figure rose to over $6.3 million in 2007 on the back of greater FDI and government revenues.[73] At the time of writing JIB has three main offices in Jordan – the head office in Amman, a regional head office in Aqaba and one at Queen Alia International Airport. Along with the increase in its budget, JIB is also opening new offices abroad to further enhance its role in promoting investment opportunities in Jordan. Offices which opened in 2007 are located by region as follows: in the

Persian Gulf – Qatar, Kuwait, Abu Dhabi and Riyadh; in the Far East – China; and in the EU – Spain, Greece and Italy.[74]

The focus of JIB's purpose and operations is on promoting Jordan as an investment market abroad. This is done in a number of ways and for multiple sectors. According to Elias Farraj, the Chief Advisor to the CEO of JIB, Jordan has seen a large increase in FDI since 11 September 2001. This is discussed in greater detail below, but it is useful to briefly assess the impact of JIB on investment in the T&C sector. 'The majority of FDI coming into Jordan in the past five years has come from the Gulf states.'[75] Farraj described this as being the result of two sets of processes. First, the withdrawal of GCC investment capital from the US market post-9/11 and the subsequent desire to re-invest in other markets – largely in the EU but also significant amounts in the MENA region. The second set of processes relate to political and economic instability in neighbouring regional states and the relative stability of Jordan as an investment market.[76] The construction and housing sector has witnessed the greatest increase in investment since 2002 and this is where GCC investment is mostly used. However, JIB does not promote this sector.

One of the sectors that JIB does promote is T&C manufactures. This sector is promoted in the Jordanian investment market and abroad. One of the main activities of JIB in promoting T&C manufactures is the organising and implementation of targeted trade missions. Here JIB staff conduct market studies to ascertain which location or market is most suitable for exploitation of opportunities. According to Farraj this could be a region, city or even a corporation. Once the target has been identified a trade mission is arranged and includes JIB staff along with representatives of T&C manufacturers operating in Jordan as well as representatives of other Jordanian corporations such as JIEC and JEDCO.[77]

The involvement of JIB does not, however, stop after the completion of any trade mission. If corporations wish to set up operations in Jordan or invest in existing ones JIB is the primary contact. The 'One-Stop-Shop' is the flagship operation provided by JIB and was established in 2003. Its purpose is to help private sector actors to establish their operations in Jordan as quickly and easily as possible. The rationale is that: 'the quicker [investors or corporations] get set up, the quicker we get economic activity in Jordan. Also, it is another incentive for foreign organisations wishing to invest and operate to make quick profits.'[78] There are ten different government departments responsible for investment. These are as follows: the ministries of Industry and Trade, Labour, and Interior; the Department of Health; the Department of Tourism; the Greater Amman Municipality and other municipalities – depending on location; the Department of Land; the Department of the Environment; and the Customs Department. These all now have offices within the JIB offices around the kingdom. Each of these ten departments has cut down red tape and continues to do so. The pre-2003 average period for registration of investment or a new corporation was 90 days. This has subsequently been reduced to 30 days and the target by late 2008 was 14 days.[79]

Once a private sector actor has registered with the One-Stop-Shop it can apply for registration with JIB. If the application is accepted – and according to Farraj every application as of 2007 had been accepted, although some with minor amendments – JIB provides support with all dealings with government and other private sector actors. The result of JIB's development and support of the T&C manufacturing sector as well as others has been the registration of over 3,500 projects worth over $6 billion since 1997. Approximately half of this figure has been in the T&C sector.

As mentioned above, investment in Jordan has been increasing since the mid-1990s and has witnessed unprecedented growth since 2003. Significant amounts of this investtment have gone to the T&C sector. In 1996 total investment in flows to the Jordanian economy amounted to $301 million. In 2000 this figure had risen to $754 million and by 2006 total investment amounted to over $4 billion. Investment in 2006 was split relatively unevenly between domestic investment and FDI – with FDI accounting for slightly over $3 billion. Significantly, 2006 was the first year that FDI in Jordan exceeded domestic investment.

The trend in total investments in Jordan has been slightly irregular in the years since 1996. According to JIB Chief Executive Officer Maen Nsour, the kingdom's economic and political reforms, including structural adjustment and trade liberalisation since the mid-1990s, have created a more attractive investment climate.[80] The improving climate resulted in steady increases in investment from 1996 to 2001. However, increasing tensions between Iraq and the international community and the intensifying Al-Aqsa Intifada led to a dip in investor confidence in Jordan from 2001 to 2004. A sharp drop of $498 million followed as overall investment decreased to $502 million in 2002. As the war in Iraq materialised in 2003 and the insurgency began to emerge, investments decreased even further to $303 million in that year – a fraction above the 1996 level before the major investment-friendly policy changes took effect. However, 2004 and 2005 witnessed rebounding confidence in the Jordanian economy. This was helped by the influx of (mostly wealthy) Iraqis wishing to avoid strife in Iraq and the emergence of Jordan as an entry point and base of operations for many private and government actors operating in Iraq.[81] By 2006 the investment climate had made a complete recovery and new levels of investment were being witnessed. This increase in investment has not followed the sectoral pattern in the 1997–2003 period. Instead, while some sectors such as construction have increased their share of total investment, others such as mining have actually seen their share decrease as investment figures have recovered.[82] After the construction sector the T&C sec-

tor has witnessed the strongest growth in investments. Overall levels of investment in the T&C sector increased from
$392 million in the 1997 to 2002 period to $1.06 billion in the
2003 to 2006 period.[83]

Traditionally the majority of investment in most sectors
has come from domestic sources. However, as a result of
greater economic liberalisation and the activity of organisations such as JIB and the Ministry of Industry and Trade,
FDI has become increasingly important. As stated above FDI
now comprises over half of all investment annually and accounts
for most of the rapid increase in investment levels seen since
2006. In relation to the T&C sector, FDI has counted for the
bulk of total investment since the sector first began to emerge
in the mid-1990s. This is partly due to the fact that the sector
was established and promoted as primarily export-oriented,
taking advantage of free access to the US market.[84] Farraj has
highlighted the fact that the Jordanian market offers only limited profitability. With a population of approximately five and
a half million in 2008 and GDP per capita of $1,960 (or
$4,900 Purchasing Power Parity method) the Jordanian con-
sumer market is limited.[85] Investors are attracted to Jordan
because the Jordanian economy as a whole has 'free access to
a market size of over 1.3 billion people'.[86] This is the combined population total of all the markets to which Jordan has
duty- and quota-free access following the signing of the various agreements outlined in Chapter 2.

As highlighted above, the T&C manufacturing sector in
Jordan is a labour-intensive sector. A characteristic of the
sector is that the labour force employed is generally semi
skilled. Furthermore, T&C is a low value-added sector – albeit
profitable to a certain extent. These three characteristics when
combined with the average income for semi-skilled labourers
in Jordan (approximately $900 per annum) results in a low
salary for employees of the T&C sector, which is estimated to
be $700 per annum.[87] By international and domestic standards

this is not necessarily an extremely low figure. However, when coupled with two other dynamics of labour in the T&C sector the issue of labour rights emerges. These two dynamics are the multinational characteristics of the workforce, and employee representation.[88]

First let us examine the multinational nature of the work-force. The Ministry of Labour in Jordan has estimated that there are over 36,000 expatriate workers employed by T&C manufacturing corporations operating in Jordan.[89] The remainder of the approximately 80,000 employees in the T&C sector come from the local population. Of the expatriate employees there are four main nationalities: Bangladeshi (25 per cent), Chinese (18 per cent), Sri Lankan (17 per cent) and Indian (7 per cent).[90] The vast majority of the expatriate work-force enters Jordan through international employment agencies. The average employment period for these expatriates working in Jordan is estimated by the Ministry of Labour at between two and a half and three years.[91]

In early 2006 international and domestic media attention began to focus on the conditions and rights of T&C sector employees. Concerns emerged about the number of hours employees were made to work, the salaries paid to them, human rights abuses and representation issues.[92] As stories of worker abuse and mismanagement increased in frequency a number of US-based and international human rights organi-sations began to call for government intervention. On 21 September 2006 the American Federation of Labour and Congress of Industrial Organisations (AFL-CIO) and the National Textile Association (NTA) – both US-based organi-sations – asked the US government to invoke chapter 17 (the dispute mechanism) of the JUSFTA, citing violations of labour rights.[93] The JUSFTA, which, as highlighted in Chapter 2, now forms the backbone of US–Jordan trade relations, included an unprecedented chapter regarding labour rights (Article 6). This chapter requires both states to comply with

internationally recognised labour rights and to enforce their
respective labour laws.[94]

The problem of labour abuses in Jordan's T&C sector
stems from two main factors which have allowed labour
abuse to occur. The first is related to the nature of the global
T&C industry and the T&C sector in Jordan. As outlined
above the semi-skilled, multinational and low-paid labour
required by this sector means that labour is sourced from peripheral labour pools.[95] The second factor is that Jordan's
labour code and related laws have serious deficiencies that
allow for the weakening of labour rights. In short there is a
naturally vulnerable workforce operating with limited protection from private capital interests.

There are a large number of key deficiencies in the
Jordanian labour code and laws. Firstly, and extremely important in relation to the rights of the T&C labour force, union
membership is restricted to Jordanian nationals – no expatriate workers can be involved in any way in any trade or labour
unions.[96] Second, union membership for Jordanians is also
restricted by age, occupation and criminal background. Any
Jordanian seeking union membership must be 25 years old or
more, have no criminal convictions and can only be involved
in a union of his or her profession.[97] A third major deficiency
is that the government controls union representation by
industry, allowing only one union per industry (of which only
17 have been defined as eligible). Furthermore, the government's labour code and laws demand that any union has to
have at least 50 members when first established.[98] A fourth
issue is that the government's labour code gives the Minister
of Labour control over the governing documents and charters
of any union. This means that the minister must be consulted
and his consent given before any union can be formalised – in
effect allowing the government to determine what the union's
purpose is. The final issue is that the government of Jordan
requests a minimum of 14 or 28 days notice prior to a general

strike for the non-public service and the public service sectors respectively.[99] In practice this means that unions are required to obtain permission from the government to strike. When combined, these five deficiencies in labour code and laws means that labour rights in Jordan are limited, thus weakening the position of the labour force in relation to both government and business.

Several days after the AFL-CIO and NTA request to the US government, the Jordanian government issued a statement declaring '[R]egrettably the AFL-CIO and the NTA decided to file their case just days after labour conditions in Jordan were vigorously scrutinised and further remedial steps were agreed upon'.[100] The 'remedial steps' referred to in this statement were declared a number of weeks prior to the AFL-CIO and NTA action. The then Minister of Industry and Trade, Salem Khazala, acknowledged in June 2006 that the government had failed to enforce its own laws regulating labour and had failed to protect expatriate workers.[101] It was also announced that a number of factories in the kingdom's industrial estates and QIZs where violations had been reported would be closed until investigations could be completed. By January 2007 four factories had been closed, three of which remained closed through 2007.

In an interview with Maha Ali, the Director of the Department of Foreign Trade Policy in the Ministry of Industry and Trade, conducted in December 2006, the issue of labour rights in Jordan were highlighted. According to Ali the development of trade relations with the United States has been good for labour rights in Jordan. It is worth quoting her at length here:

The JUSFTA was an historic agreement with relation to labour rights. No previous bilateral free trade agreement had included a chapter on labour. Here we do take seriously the condition of employees in

the industrial estates [and QIZs] and enforcement
of Article 6 of JUSFTA has become a priority.
Before the JUSFTA was signed, we would not have
any action on labour abuses so in that way the
agreement is progressive.[102]

The US market and Jordanian T&C exports

The US T&C market is the largest in the world. It accounts
for approximately 24 per cent of global T&C imports
(approximately 37 per cent for apparel).[103] Over the past
decade the US market has witnessed sustained growth in imports.[104] Foreign imports of T&C goods now supply over
two-thirds of the US market. This figure has been increasing
consistently in recent years as US T&C firms continue to
source goods directly from developing states. The US T&C
manufacturing sector has seen production decline to $53
billion in annual exports – a decline of over 15 per cent in the
1999–2006 period.[105]

At the same time that US T&C production has been decreasing the overall market size has been increasing. The
difference in domestic supply and demand has been met by
foreign imports, which have increased rapidly due to freer
trade. Since 2001 the United States has signed a number of
FTAs and Trade Promotion Acts (TPAs)[106] and the MFA
came to an end in 2005. The result has been greater access to
the US market for overseas T&C producers and greater potential for outsourcing by domestic producers. The introduction
of the MFA in 1974 controlled the amount of T&C goods
exported by developing producers and so protected the US
T&C sector somewhat. The ending of the MFA on 1 January
2005 saw the EU and US markets flooded with developing
states' exports of T&C goods. Most of the increase in imports
came from China and India, which increased their exports to
the US market by approximately 55 per cent and 26 per cent
respectively in the first five months of 2005. In response the

US and EU re-imposed quota limits on Chinese imports. In the case of the United States a unilateral imposition of a 7.5 per cent growth quota was implemented in June 2005.[107]

The effect on Jordanian T&C exports to the US market was minimal in comparison to the effects on other states: such as Moroccan exports to the EU. T&C exports from Jordan increased by 13 per cent in 2008, down from the 19 per cent increase seen in 2004, but nonetheless still one of the more impressive postings after China, India, Cambodia, Bangladesh and Indonesia. While the US market became more competitive with the end of the MFA, some states which had previously been supplying the US with large quantities of T&C goods maintained a competitive edge. Jordan was one of those states and the T&C export sector remained strong in the US market. This is in part a result of the near-total orientation of the Jordanian T&C sector to the US market as well as lower labour costs than most competitors and quicker production times despite the greater distance to the US market in relation to some producers.[108]

One advantage that Jordan enjoys over the majority of other T&C competitors in the US market comes from the JUSFTA. While other states now have duty- and quota-free access to the US market, stringent rules of origin lower efficiency and profitability. Article 14 and annex 2.2 of the JUSFTA allow Jordan to source material from anywhere in the world and still have free access to the US market. This is an unprecedented measure and one that has not been replicated in any other agreement between the US and another state.[109] According to Maha Ali this provision was granted to Jordan in part as a peace dividend for the peace agreement with Israel and partly because the United States wants the Jordanian economy to thrive.[110] This latter point cannot be over-emphasised. 'Jordan–US trade is an important model of bilateral cooperation for the United States in the Middle East [and North Africa], one that the Bush Administration wants to see work.'[111]

The quota restrictions re-imposed on China by the United States came to an end in 2008. It is anticipated by many that Chinese T&C exports will again increase exponentially and thus so will competition in the US T&C market.[112] The forecast decline in the US T&C production sector will offset some of this increased competition, as will continued growth of the market. Nevertheless, the Jordanian T&C sector will face increased competition in the future. However, it is likely that the three main advantages the Jordanian T&C sector enjoys over other states – relaxed rules of origin, being oriented to the US market and favoured support from the US government – will remain and allow exports to continue to post steady yearly increases.

The growth of the T&C sector within Jordan can be seen as being linked directly to the transformation of the government's macro-economic policy as well as to the establishment of the QIZs and their related bilateral institutions. In particular, changes in foreign trade policy and engagement with institutions involved in trade since the mid-1990s have had a significant impact. The pursuit of greater economic integration with international markets through trade liberalisation and bilateral agreements with the United States and others has provided the opportunity for the T&C sector to expand. Gaining duty- and quota-free access to the US market was taken advantage of by promoting certain export-oriented manufacturing sectors within the Jordanian economy from 1997 onwards, and the implementation of the JUSFTA in 2001 furthered these processes. In the subsequent years the Jordanian government has worked in conjunction with private sector actors and semi-governmental organisations to support and promote the T&C sector both at home and abroad.

Since 2001 inward investment to the T&C sector has seen exponential growth. The build-up to and materialisation of the US-led invasion of Iraq temporarily disrupted investment flows but levels of FDI and domestic investment have since reached record levels. Continued growth in exports to the US market is expected over the coming years as Jordanian exports compete in an increasingly aggressive market in the post-MFA era. The overall partnership between the Jordanian government and private sector actors – largely from abroad – and the relatively strong position of Jordanian T&C manufactures in the US market should lead to a further entrenchment of US–Jordan trade relations. In turn this will likely serve to compel the Jordanian government to maintain the current 'business friendly' environment within the kingdom and potentially further liberalise the economy. In turn T&C exports to the US market likely will continue to grow in the short to medium term.

The analysis presented in this chapter suggests that the engagement with multilateral and bilateral institutions in the forms of IOs such as the WTO, trade regimes such as the MFA and key agreements such as the JUSFTA have had a significant impact upon trade liberalisation. Furthermore, trade levels between Jordan and the United States have also been impacted. In the first instance trade liberalisation has occurred to a great extent between Jordan and the United States so that at the time of writing all trade in goods is fully liberalised. In the second instance trade levels in T&C goods have grown rapidly, albeit in a bilateral manner as exports from Jordan to the US market account for practically all trade in T&C goods. The economic growth of this sector in Jordan is highly significant and has been relatively rapid, adding to the overall Jordanian economy and GDP through increased exports, investment and horizontal economic spread. This suggests that Jordanian governmental facilitation of trade with both the United States and other markets through engagement with international institutions and domestic reform is achieving the aim of economic growth. However, this analysis is only of one economic sector. Furthermore, it is a low value added, labour-intensive sector which is not necessarily representative of the Jordanian economy as a whole.

The issue of state-actor involvement in international institutions as a means to increasing economic integration is important to the analysis in this chapter. However, the role of non-state actors also is pivotal. Here, the roles of organisations such as JIEC, JEDCO and the JIB have been instrumental in the increasing levels of bilateral trade in T&C goods. The support that these actors have given to T&C manufacturers has been very important in allowing these corporations to operate in Jordan and export competitively to the US market. The T&C manufacturing corporations operating in Jordan have been buoyed by rising levels of international investment. This has allowed them to exploit the opportunities provided by the JUSFTA and export to the US market. In short, if it were not for the agency of these actors the impact of international institutions on their own would not have the significant impact on bilateral economic integration that has been witnessed.

With regard to the United States, as discussed in Chapter 3, economic growth has not been the key interest that has compelled the United States to pursue greater cooperation with Jordan through international institutions and subsequent bilateral trade liberalisation. Rather, broader interests relating to inter-state cooperation at the international level and in the political and security spheres seem to have been more important. In this study there is evidence of greater market integration, or possibly the creation of market dependence, where the Jordanian T&C sector has become dependent upon access to the US market. There is also evidence of the utility of international institutions in facilitating trade and encouraging non-state actor cooperation across markets. However, there is little evidence, beyond speculation, in the analysis of trade in T&C goods that suggests that greater state-level integration and cooperation between Jordan and the United States has followed.

The issue of labour rights in Jordan, which is embodied in the JUSFTA and which forms a key element of the regulatory regime of trade between the two states, offers some insights here. The linkage of a domestic non-state actor economic matter in Jordan to state actor cooperation and regulation at the international level through international institutions is certainly important. The AFL-CIO request to the US government regarding non-state actor management of labour issues in Jordan, as discussed above, and subsequent state-level coordination is an example of state-level cooperation and integration. However, how far this form of cooperation permeates other state relations is unanswerable at this stage. Simply assessing one economic sector and one form of trade is not sufficient to answer the main questions in this study and so two more economic sectors and forms of trade are analysed in the following chapters in order to shed more light on the topic.

5

BILATERAL TRADE IN PHARMACEUTICAL PRODUCTS

The purpose of this chapter is to assess the nature and level of trade in pharmaceutical goods between the United States and Jordan, and to examine how the regulatory framework within which this trade takes place has begun to reshape the interaction of the two sectors. The assessment of the political economy of trade relations between Jordan and the United States is furthered by analysing what can be termed a 'second form' of trade activity – trade in high value-added, capital intensive goods. This type of trade is characterised by relatively equal levels of trade in terms of total value and quantity as well as by a more important role for the United States in creating the framework within which bilateral trade occurs.

Analysis of bilateral trade in pharmaceutical goods between Jordan and the United States poses a number of problems as well as useful insights when assessing the political economy of trade between the two states. Problems are posed due to the relatively insignificant levels of trade in pharmaceutical goods in overall monetary terms. Jordanian exports of such products to the US market, for example, constitute a mere 2–3 per cent of total exports. US pharmaceutical exports to the Jordanian market are also small in relation to total exports and in relation to US exports to other markets in the MENA region. However, the pharmaceutical sector constituted a major element of the JUSFTA and a deeper analysis of both the Jordanian and the US pharmaceutical industries and how they are interacting presents some interesting conclusions. In relation to bilateral trade in T&C the interaction of the two pharmaceutical markets highlights a very different side to bilateral relations. While trade in T&C goods is heavily one-sided, in that Jordanian exports constitute the majority of trade flows, trade in pharmaceutical goods is more even, but with US exports constituting the larger part of trade levels. More important than the actual levels of trade in goods is the institutional framework within which pharmaceutical trade takes place. This structure has been reshaping the relationship between the two pharmaceutical markets since 2001.

Once again the following analysis will draw upon the key principles of the critical liberal institutionalist approach used in this study to examine the ways in which the international institutions engaged with by Jordan and the United States have liberalised and facilitated trade between the two. Also, this chapter will study a plurality of actors and their relationships at the domestic and international levels to analyse what the effects of trade liberalisation have been. A key question in this and the preceding chapter is whether or not state actor interests are being achieved or not.

To develop the analysis presented here it is necessary to first outline the global environment in pharmaceutical trade and the key institutions which govern it, of which the United States and Jordan are a part and so which largely determine this form of bilateral trade. The first section of this chapter thus addresses the impacts of the WTO-negotiated TRIPs agreement and how both the United States and Jordan have complied with this agreement. Following on from this first section is an assessment of the provisions of the JUSFTA relating to international IPRs and thus how trade in pharmaceutical goods is managed under the agreement.

The third section provides an overview of the Jordanian pharmaceutical industry and how it has developed over the past decade and a half. Here the growth of the sector to become the second leading export earner in the Jordanian economy is described followed by an analysis of the main actors operating in the sector. The importance of investment and technology flows are highlighted as these two issues have formed the backbone of activity in the sector since the mid 1990s. The relationship between domestic and external private sector actors is also briefly analysed.

A detailed assessment of the US pharmaceutical sector in this study would be overly complex and time consuming and is not necessary for the purpose of this chapter. However, a brief assessment is offered, followed by an assessment of pharmaceutical trade in relation to contemporary US trade policy and bilateral FTAs. A review of the main US actors either exporting to or operating in the Jordanian sector is then presented. A final section summarises the main points and arguments presented in this chapter and offers a conclusion on the complex nature of trade in pharmaceutical goods between Jordan and the United States.

TRIPs and pharmaceutical production in Jordan and the United States

At the time of writing there is no single legal international regime which governs IPRs with absolute jurisdiction. Copyright, patent or trademark for any product or process for which these rights are eligible can only be provided by national governments in the territorial entity for which such rights are required.[1] In many cases national legislation for the provision of these protective rights differs and in some cases does not exist in any recognisable form. However, attempts to manage the international issue of IPRs have been underway since the nineteenth century,[2] and a number of international agreements do exist. The most important of these is the WTO agreement on TRIPs established at the end of the Uruguay Round of Negotiations of the GATT treaty in 1994. As both the United States (1995) and Jordan (2000) are members of the WTO and therefore signatories to the TRIPs agreement their pharmaceutical industries and trade in pharmaceutical products are shaped by the rules governing international IPRs through these institutions.

The World Intellectual Property Organisation (WIPO) defines intellectual property as 'creations of the mind: inventions, literary and artistic works, as well as symbols, names, images, and designs used in commerce'.[3] In relation to the pharmaceutical industry this includes both products, such as a new drug or medicine, and processes by which pharmaceutical products are created.[4] The TRIPs agreement covers a broad range of IPRs, including patents, trademarks, copyright and trade secrets. Within each of these areas the agreement establishes the minimum standard of protection which all WTO members and signatories to TRIPs must abide by. Also included in the agreement are enforcement provisions and a dispute mechanism whereby any dispute is reported to the WTO's Dispute Settlement Body (DSB). If one member state believes that a second is in violation of the TRIPs agreement then these states may conduct dialogues through the DSB, following which, if no settlement is made, the DSB will convene a panel to rule on the dispute.[5]

The agreement includes the provisions of earlier treaties on copyrights, patents and trademarks. These are the Berne Convention in the case of the former and the Paris Convention in the case of the latter.[6] With regard to copyrights the TRIPs agreement obligates the member states to each provide protection from the time of registration up to a minimum of 50 years of protection from the death of the author or creator.[7] In relation to pharmaceutical goods this is not as relevant a provision as that pertaining to patents. Here member states agree to give the patentees the exclusive rights to exclude other actors from producing, using, selling or importing the patented good.[8] There are exceptions under certain circumstances, such as in situations deemed emergencies,[9] and the control of products/processes which is viewed as in violation of the *public or morality order*. Patents are given a minimum of 20 years' protection from the filing date under the agreement, after which time they would be off-patent unless otherwise negotiated. It is worth noting at this point that each bilateral FTA signed by the United States since 2000, including the JUSFTA, has addressed this provision in some manner. Under US law, patents are given a minimum of 20 years' protection from the date of issuance of the patent. The US concern here is that intentional delaying of the registration process could significantly reduce the period of actual patent protection once patentability has been issued under WTO rules.[10]

For many developing states, as has been the case for Jordan, signing up to the TRIPs agreement has resulted in major structural adjustments in their pharmaceutical Industries.[11] Prior to Jordan becoming the 136th member of the WTO and having to abide by the provisions in the TRIPs agreement, Jordanian pharmaceutical production consisted of about 10 per cent unlicensed in-patent products.[12] Under the agreement this would no longer be possible following the offered adjustment period (discussed below). In order for Jordanian pharmaceutical manufacturers to continue to produce in-patent products they had to either register these products with the government of Jordan by gaining a licence from the patentee to do so, or be issued a temporary licence by the government (usually in exceptional or emergency circumstances).[13] Under the TRIPs agreement the issuance of compulsory licences is allowed, although severely restricted. According to Article 31, compulsory licences can be issued if the proposed user has:

> made efforts to obtain authorisation from the patent owner on reasonable commercial terms and conditions and must demonstrate that such efforts have not been successful within a reasonable period of time. However, this requirement may be waived in the case of a national emergency or other circumstance of extreme urgency.[14]

Furthermore, the issuance of such a licence by a national government is revocable at any time, must result in remuneration of the patent holder and will be subject to bi-annual independent WTO review.[15] Under these strict controls the Jordanian government has not issued a compulsory licence for a patented pharmaceutical product.

In the case of Jordanian pharmaceutical manufacturers, a set time limit was given for abiding by all TRIPs agreement rules. WTO member states are given a transition period from membership to the TRIPs agreement in which to adjust and implement all necessary measures to comply with the stipulated rules.[16] This period is one year for developed states, five years for underdeveloped states and ten years for the least developed states until 2010, with the latter extended to 2013. Jordan became a member of the WTO in 1999 and had to accept TRIPs provisions immediately. However, rather than accepting the five-year transition period on offer the Jordanian government immediately upon becoming a WTO member fully implemented the TRIPs agreement.[17] Patent Law No. 32 was drafted in 1999 to supersede the Patent and Industrial Design Law No. 22/1953. The new legislation offered full compliance with TRIPs regulation, and includes the following features:

1) It allows the grant of patents in all fields of technology, whether it is a product or a process invention, provided that the conditions are met of novelty, inventive step and capability of industrial application. However, the only exceptions which pertain to the subject-matter is based on Article 27.3 of the TRIPs Agreement.

2) The patent owner's rights are covered in the Jordanian law in conformity with Article 28 of the TRIPs Agreement.

3) The law established a mechanism for issuing a compulsory licence and limited it to three situations only. Moreover, the Jordanian law adopted provisions similar, not identical, to the provisions of Article 31(a) to (k) of the TRIPs Agreement.

4) The Jordanian Patent Law has introduced a unique provision in order to encourage inventors to register their patents in Jordan and this is through Article 4(f), which extended the novelty term from twelve months from the first application to eighteen months after filing an application anywhere outside Jordan.

5) The Jordanian Patent Law has introduced a provision where, in the case of an infringement of a process patent, the burden of proof must be reversed, so that a defendant must prove that an identical product has been produced without infringing the rights of the patent owner, consistent with Article 34 of the TRIPs Agreement.[18]

As a founding member of the WTO and leading advocate of the TRIPs agreement, the United States was in compliance with all provisions of the agreement at its inception on 1 January 1995. The United States has been the leading advocate of respect for and implementation of protection for IPRs over the past three decades.[19] Furthermore, the United States government has consistently linked bilateral trade policy to IPRs since the early 1980s.[20] As mentioned above, US bilateral FTAs have addressed IPRs in detail and in most cases have strengthened further compliance with international IPRs.[21]

Protection of intellectual property rights and the JUSFTA
The provisions of the JUSFTA pertaining to IPRs were largely designed by the United States and were included in the agreement at the insistence of the US government.[22] There is no evidence that the Jordanian government actually resisted the inclusion of these provisions. However, likewise there is limited evidence that suggests that during the negotiating process the Jordanian government proactively pursued the inclusion of agreements on IPR-related issues. Rather the JUSFTA further strengthens the IPRs regime within which Jordanian pharmaceutical manufacturers must operate. Article 4 of the JUSFTA deals with IPRs by specifying provisions on ratifying previous international agreements, including the Joint Recommendation Concerning Provisions on the Protection of Well-Known Marks[23] and the Patent Cooperation Treaty.[24] It is important to note that these provisions were in relation to Jordan and not the United States. This is because Jordan was not a signatory to the previous agreements included, while the United States was.

The FTA also addresses trademarks (Article 4, 6–9), copyright and related rights (Article 4, 10–16), patents (Article 4, 17–21), measures related to certain regulated products (Article 4, 22–23), enforcement of IPRs (Article 4, 24–28) and transition periods (Article 4, 29). With regard to the provisions on patents the JUSFTA has slightly stricter rules than the

TRIPs agreement. The process of registering a patent is more demanding and the issuance of a patent right is made for a minimum of 20 years after the patent registration process has been completed.[25] Furthermore, the JUSFTA commits both states to ensure that their statutory punishments for infringements on IPRs are severe enough to deter any such infringements. United States legislation already ensures a very high level of protection for IPRs. In Jordan, prior to 2001 and the implementation of the FTA, legislation was not as stringent. Thus, again these provisions were largely aimed at strengthening such rights in Jordan.[26] Transition periods for meeting the provisions in Article 4 varied from immediate implementation to three years for the different requirements. Jordanian ratification of the World Copyright Treaty and WPPT, for example, was two years from the entry into force of the FTA, while abiding by rules on pharmaceutical patents would take effect immediately.[27] This is in comparison to the five-year adjustment period offered by the WTO in relation to the TRIPs agreement. As Hamed El-Said and Mohammed El-Said have noted, there exists a significant difference between TRIPs regulations and what has been termed TRIPs-Plus agreements as embodied in bilateral and multilateral FTAs.[28] Here, the provisions of FTAs relating to the protection of IPRs can be seen to be much more stringent than the WTO-negotiated TRIPs agreement.

The Jordanian pharmaceutical sector

Pharmaceutical manufacturing as a component of the Jordanian economy is one of the more dynamic sectors and over the past decade has been rapidly emerging as a leading contributor to GDP. While pharmaceutical manufacturers have been operating in Jordan since the 1960s their activity was limited and growth was not dynamic.[29] However, by 1990 increasing exports to regional markets in the MENA began to propel the sector forward. The domestic market is relatively small, with a current population of approximately 5.8 million, and was even smaller in 1990 with a total population estimated at only 3.5 million. Furthermore, European pharmaceutical manufacturers have traditionally captured a large share of the Jordanian market, leaving a smaller share for domestic producers. According to the Export and Finance Bank in Jordan, European corporations traditionally have supplied about two-thirds of the Jordanian market while the remaining one-third is accounted by Jordanian producers.[30]

Under these conditions domestic producers embarked upon export drives to neighbouring markets through the 1990s. As a result, Jordanian pharmaceutical producers have become the leading MENA region exporters to the Lebanese, Iraqi, Saudi Arabian and UAE markets. The Jordanian pharmaceutical sector is widely seen as the leading such sector in the MENA region outside of Israel. Production facilities, staff, market access and quality have all received a better rating than pharmaceutical sectors in other MENA states.[31] In 1990 total pharmaceutical exports reached $49 million, most of which went to the Iraqi market ($25 million).[32] This accounted for 5.8 per cent of total Jordanian exports and approximately 60 per cent of pharmaceutical sector revenue. By 1995 total pharmaceutical exports had tripled and totalled just over $142 million – most of which was still to regional markets. Total pharmaceutical exports continued to rise from 1995 and by 2009 export revenue totalled well over $300 million.[33] As a share of sectoral revenue exports now stand at 70 per cent – total revenue in the pharmaceutical sector currently totals more than $400 million – and pharmaceutical exports are now the second-largest exports in value terms after T&C goods, representing approximately 4 per cent of GDP and 12 per cent of total exports.[34]

In comparison to exports, imports of pharmaceutical goods over the past decade have seen a slightly slower pace of growth from approximately $104 million in 1994 to just over

$250 in 2008. This is due to two factors: firstly the Jordanian market for pharmaceuticals remains relatively small and growth in this market is limited by an average population growth rate (2.6 per cent) and the over-saturation of the market with producers. Furthermore, unequal income distribution and relatively modest per capita income growth (equivalent to approximately $300 per year over the past decade) have limited growth in the domestic market. Third, imports had been growing at a slower rate relative to exports (until 2005, when imports began to rise at a higher rate than in previous years) as Jordanian corporations expanded their activities and in particular their exports to traditional markets (which in 2009 still accounted for around 80 per cent of pharmaceutical exports) and expansion into new ones such as Europe and the United States.[35]

In an economy which has traditionally had difficulties providing enough employment opportunities to reduce unemployment figures to a level of perhaps 15 per cent – as opposed to the current (unofficial) 30 per cent – sectors which have seen consistent employment growth are key to the overall health of the economy.[36] Employment in the pharmaceutical sector has witnessed solid growth in the past decade and predictions suggest that this growth is likely to continue.[37] In 2008 the sector employed just under 8,000 workers, with 4,700 employed directly in pharmaceutical manufacturing. This is in comparison with total employment of only 1,800 in 1991 – a 257 per cent increase in a 15-year period.[38] While the growth in employment in the sector is important, the location of employment opportunities and the type of employment are equally important. As discussed above, QIZs and other industrial estates are placed strategically around the kingdom – in part to benefit the local economies and communities. The majority of pharmaceutical manufacturers now operate in these zones and estates. However, unlike T&C manufacturers, most pharmaceutical corporations are located in or around the Amman area. This is partly because of the specific services and facilities needed and to gain access to the relevant labour pools.

According to the Jordanian Association of Manufacturers of Pharmaceuticals and Medical Appliances (JAPM), the main representative body for the pharmaceutical sector, there are currently 17 Jordanian corporations involved in pharmaceutical manufacturing.[39] In 1995 there were only 11 such corporations, with the oldest being Arab Pharmaceutical Manufacturing Co Ltd. (APM), which was established in 1962. The growth in the number of pharmaceutical manufacturers was slow throughout the 1960s, 1970s and 1980s. However, by 1995 a large expansion in the number of manufacturers had taken place, peaking at 18 domestic producers by 2001. Some observers have claimed that this growth in manufacturers shows a dynamic and growing sector.[40] The increase in domestic producers has been partly responsible for an increase in overall sector capital investments, which currently total $400 million with production value for 2008 at over $300 million. In comparison the 1990 figures stood at $192 million and $112 million respectively.[41] However, the increase in private sector actors in the domestic market has also limited domestic market penetration for some of the corporations. The increase in competition for domestic market shares has largely been confined to domestic producers, while European producers maintain their overall position in the market.[42] Furthermore, only three of the Jordanian pharmaceutical manufacturers have been able to compete in international markets in any sustained manner. The three most significant corporations account for 80 per cent of domestic production, 90 per cent of exports and over 75 per cent of market capital.[43] These are Hikma Pharmaceuticals, APM and Dar Al-Dawa and it is to these three corporations that we shall now turn.

Hikma Pharmaceuticals is currently the largest Jordanian manufacturer operating in the pharmaceutical sector. Founded in 1978 in Amman, Hikma has pursued a policy of internationalising its activities and expanding into external markets in order to increase profits.[44] In its first decade of operation Hikma pursued expansion into regional markets, namely Saudi Arabia (where it is the fourth-largest operating pharmaceutical corporation) and Algeria (the second-largest operating pharmaceutical corporation). Following successful operation in these two markets as well as the domestic market, Hikma began to implement a set of policies in 1990 aimed at gaining access to the European and US markets. This policy has been successful to some extent and this is attributable to two factors. The first method used to gain greater access to these key markets was to acquire manufacturing capabilities in them (discussed below). The second method pursued was to target niche markets for certain pharmaceutical products by focusing on research and development (R&D) and gaining approval for products by the relevant regulatory bodies such as the Food and Drug Agency (FDA) in the United States.[45] As a result Hikma has transformed itself from a domestic-focused producer to a regional actor into an MNC with international operations and sales. In 2008 Hikma had sales in 28 states.[46] Significantly, sales have doubled since 1996 and the US market now represents 50 per cent of all Hikma sales while Europe accounts for 7.8 per cent and the MENA region, including the domestic market, accounts for 42.2 per cent of sales revenue.

In order to expand into the US market (the world's largest pharmaceutical market) Hikma purchased West-Ward, a New Jersey, US-based corporation in 1991. By 2006 the Hikma subsidiary had been transformed from a loss-making manufacturer into a profitable operation bringing in $120 million of sales revenues.[47] Through West-Ward, Hikma has gained stable and sustainable access to the US market, and the expansion of R&D activities as well as an increasing number of USFDA-approved products have spurred US sales. In the

European market production facilities in Portugal and Italy have allowed Hikma to penetrate the world's second-largest pharmaceuticals market. An injectable manufacturing facility was built in Portugal in 2002 consisting of four production lines. One line produces cephalosporins, while the other three lines produce liquid injectables for sale in all Hikma markets. A new 7,500 square metre cephalosporin manufacturing facility was opened in Portugal in summer 2007. Also developed and operational in 2007 was a production facility for injectables in Italy. This plant focuses on producing lyophilized products and works in conjunction with a new warehouse and packaging facility.[48]

In the MENA region too, greater access to markets has been pursued by acquisitions and the development of manufacturing facilities. In Saudi Arabia Hikma has a number of manufacturing facilities owned by Jazeera Pharmaceutical Industries (JPI), which is now fully owned by Hikma (final acquisition of the remaining shares of JPI took place in autumn 2006).[49] These facilities produce solid, semi-solid and liquid products but not injectables. In Algeria construction of a production facility for solid, semi-solid and liquid branded generics begun in 2006 supplies the Algerian market.

Of more importance to increased product sales and market access is the attainment of regulatory body approval for Hikma products. Prior to 1999, as mentioned above, Jordanian manufacturers of pharmaceutical goods operated in a relatively lenient IPRs regime. However, following membership of the WTO and compliance with the TRIPs agreement, and implementation of the JUSFTA this regime was significantly altered. In order for Hikma, as well as all other domestic manufacturers, to comply with new legislation and maintain domestic and export sales licences would have to be obtained for in-patent products. Furthermore, in order to gain access to the main international markets not only would licences for in-patent products be needed but the registration and approval of new products developed by Jordanian manufacturers would also be required. As discussed in more detail below, the pharmaceutical industry is largely driven (at least in the medium to long term) by development of new products. To sell products in the US market approval of both the products and manufacturing facilities by the USFDA is first needed.[50] Likewise, in Europe approval of both products and facilities is required from the Medical and Healthcare Products Regulatory Agency (MHRA).[51]

With regard to generic pharmaceutical goods manufactured by Hikma, the main production facilities for these products are located in Jordan and Eaton Town, New Jersey, USA. Both of these facilities have been given USFDA and MHRA approval, allowing goods produced in them access to the US and European markets. The production facilities in Saudi Arabia, Portugal and Italy have also been given approval by the US and EU bodies. The Algerian facility is also being developed to USFDA and MHRA-approved standard and so should gain approval once fully operational.[52] Between 1995 and 2006 Hikma received USFDA approval on 33 products, the vast majority of them approved in the post-2001 regime. A further 21 products are awaiting approval, most of which are CNS, cardiovascular, anti-infective and musculoskeletal products. The cephalosporins, lyophilized and injectable goods produced in the Portuguese and Italian facilities have received MHRA approval and as a result sales in the European market expanded from 1 per cent of total sales in 1995 to 7.8 per cent in 2007.

The growth of Hikma Pharmaceuticals over the past 15 years or so, and in particular following Jordanian membership of the WTO in 1999, has been dynamic. By focusing on gaining access to international markets by locating production facilities through acquisitions and licensed development, products have been given a degree of comparative advantage over other producers. By gaining regulatory body approval for many of its pharmaceutical products and by investing in R&D in order to gain approval on products in development, Hikma has managed to capitalise on competitive advantages and has increased sales in external markets – including the US market, which is now its most important sales market. However, Hikma has also pursued greater market share of the domestic and regional markets quite aggressively and by the end of 2007 Hikma had made a successful bid to purchase APM as a subsidiary. Through this purchase Hikma has been able to gain access to APM's resource base, infrastructure, R&D and licences.

APM was the first Jordanian pharmaceuticals manufacturer to begin operations. It was established in Salt in 1962 and its first production facility began operating in 1966. Its core product lines include intravenous solutions, chemical and nutritional products, a small range of cosmetics and a wide range of medications.[53] APM has grown at a steadily increasing rate: from $16 million in revenue in 1991 to over $89 million in 2008. As a result of the change in management regime of the industry in Jordan, overall sales dropped 12.2 per cent in 1999 and a further 6.4 per cent in 2000.[54] However, in both years net income increased slightly as a result of the move towards the production of higher-value goods and decreased production costs. Since 2001 sales have recovered and posted strong growth. Sustained growth was also supported by the issuance of production rights by external MNCs operating in the pharmaceutical industry (discussed below). With the small size and relatively high level of competition in the domestic market, exports have dominated APM revenue since the 1970s. In 2008 export sales constituted 71 per cent of total revenues while domestic sales (17 per cent) and public tenders (12 per cent) made up the remaining sales revenues.[55]

As mentioned above, the pharmaceutical industry is extremely competitive both within Jordan and in international markets. The only method of sustaining growth as well as competitiveness in the medium to long term is to invest in R&D activities to produce new and quality assured goods. In a sector which has become highly saturated with relatively small corporations, market share and overall capital resources can be reduced. According to Fakhry Hazimeh this has been the case in Jordan since the early 1990s.[56] APM realised relatively early on in the first period of transformation in the Jordanian pharmaceutical sector (the second being the post 1999 change in governing regime) that the combining of resources would be necessary to maintain competitiveness. In light of this APM negotiated a total merger with Advanced Pharmaceuticals, a small corporation established in 1994.[57] According to Issam Hamdi Saket, the Managing Director of APM, the merger was seen to be beneficial as Advanced Pharmaceuticals brought with it a number of new products as well as an MHRA-certified production facility. In return APM offered relatively large capital resources, a large labour pool and highly established regional marketing systems.

The APM strategy since the mid-1990s has been to adapt to the emerging TRIPs-dominated regime governing the international pharmaceutical industry. After 1999 this strategy intensified. According to Saket, production has diversified away from the generic pharmaceutical goods which had dominated production since APM's establishment towards high value-added USFDA- and MHRA-approved products.[58] Other efforts to facilitate the flow of technology and know-how to APM include the arranging of conferences, seminars and trade missions between Jordanian physicians and pharmacists (most working for APM) and experts from other states and corporations.[59] While APM has not made extensive efforts to gain USFDA and MHRA approval for its production facilities and products it has constantly pursued licensing agreements from patent holders.[60] The largest such licensing agreement is held with Takeda Chemical Industries Ltd., a Japanese pharmaceutical MNC for the production of goods such as Takepron and Danzen, which are prescribed for ulcer treatment and antibiotic treatment respectively.

The overall growth and development of APM has not been as successful as that of Hikma Pharmaceuticals. However, the general pattern of performance has been similar. The change in governing regime has presented both opportunities and challenges to Jordanian pharmaceutical manufacturers. Both Hikma and APM have developed strategies to combat the challenges and exploit the benefits of complying with the TRIPs-dominated international environment. The growth pattern is similar for Dar Al-Dawa (DAD), the third leading Jordanian pharmaceuticals corporation, as well as the other smaller actors.

DAD was established in 1975 in Amman as a public shareholding corporation. While smaller in size than Hikma and APM, DAD still boasts capital resources of over $28 million (in 2008).[61] While maintaining a significant presence in the domestic market, DAD is largely an export-oriented corporation, obtaining over 70 per cent of its revenues from the export of goods to international markets. Overall growth has increased steadily since 1991, becoming particularly rapid after 1999. Most of this growth has come from further penetration of regional markets, most notably in Saudi Arabia and the UAE. Other major markets include Iraq, Libya, Russia and Romania.[62]

In 2002 DAD was issued with current Good Manufacturing Practice (cGMP) from the MHRA for its manufacturing facility located in Na'ur, Jordan.[63] All goods produced in this facility therefore qualified for sale in the EU market. Other facilities operated by DAD include one in Algiers, Algeria and one in Tripoli, Libya. Both facilities are geared to serve their respective markets but exports from them to external markets are limited.[64] Approval of facilities and products has not been attained from the USFDA, although extensive efforts have been made since 2002 to gain USFDA-approved status. DAD manufacturing processes and products have come into line with USFDA regulations and applications for USFDA approval have been made for the Na'ur facility. Even without approval by the USFDA, DAD operations have to take place in a relatively strict quality assurance environment in Jordan.

While manufacturing standards are important in all manufacturing industries, quality assurance is usually a matter for corporate policy. However, in Jordan extensive governmental regulations, which have been further strengthened since 1999, have resulted in a relatively strict domestic quality assurance regime.[65] Gaining USFDA approval would allow DAD to expand its international operations and gain access to the US market, joining Hikma as the only Jordanian pharmaceuticals corporation to enjoy such access. As will be discussed below, Jordanian membership in the WTO and the JUSFTA present Jordanian corporations with more opportunities to gain access to the US market and so USFDA approval has been sought by several other corporations, although not yet achieved.

In order to remain competitive in both the domestic market and more importantly in international markets, DAD has also pursued a policy of under-licence production of internationally approved products. There are currently six joint ventures between DAD and its subsidiaries with international partners across the MENA region and in Eastern Europe. These include Dar Al Dawa (Algeria), an Algiers-based marketing and distribution specialist for pharmaceutical goods (DAD now owns 90 per cent of this corporation), and Dar Al Dawa Pharma (Romania), a DAD-owned manufacturing subsidiary.[66] DAD produces under-licence goods for New York-based Pfizer and Switzerland-based Novartis.[67] Joint ventures in the domestic market have also been pursed. DAD owns a 43 per cent share in NutriDar, a corporation based in

Jordan since 1994 which produces baby food for the domestic and external markets. Its export markets are based solely in the MENA region with sales totalling just over $8 million in 2008.[68] A second joint venture is with DADVet (32 per cent share), a corporation specialising in veterinary medicines and equipment and in particular the conducting of field trials of products developed by regional and global actors.[69]

Joining the WTO in 1999 and having to comply with TRIPs agreement regulations transformed the Jordanian pharmaceutical sector. Prior to 1999, government legislation and regulation of the industry had begun to strengthen quality assurance and compliance with some international agreements on IPRs. However, the vast majority of Jordanian corporations producing both generic, off-patent and under-licence products did so without fully complying with both contemporary good manufacturing practices (cGMP) and, in many circumstances, patent-holder permission.[70] After 1999 this would no longer be possible in the case of the latter point and in the case of the former would not allow for sustained growth of the sector. All pharmaceutical goods produced in Jordan which were not under licence or off-patent prior to 1999 immediately became illegal as a result of the Jordanian government's decision to forego the allowed five-year transition period to full TRIPs compliance. It was claimed by many observers, both within and outside the industry, that sustained competitiveness in the domestic and external markets as well as future growth would be seriously undermined by the change in governing regime.[71] In addition, the JUSFTA would strengthen this regime with regard to bilateral trade with the United States. However, according to Fakhry Hazimeh, decision-makers in government and those involved in negotiating WTO membership and the JUSFTA saw opportunities for further expansion in the sector. Furthermore, the possibility of strengthening the comparative advantages already enjoyed by Jordanian corporations vis-à-vis regional and international competitors was anticipated.[72]

The change in regime was seen as a bad thing because TRIPs laws and FTA provisions would have to be enforced, thus hindering domestic production and raising the cost of both manufacturing and products for domestic consumers. It was feared that there would be a loss of revenues resulting from the inability to produce certain goods or the loss of profits due to remuneration of relevant patent-holders. The resulting decline of Jordanian corporations would then lead to a loss of international and domestic market share as they would not be able to compete with European MNCs, which enjoy larger capital resources.[73]

However, these fears have not been entirely realised. Even the smaller corporations have been able to maintain sales and activity in the domestic market. Companies have adjusted to the new governing regime and exploited the new opportunities created by this shift. Conformity with international standards has led to USFDA and MHRA approval of certain products made by Hikma Pharmaceuticals, and some facilities for APM, DAD and a range of smaller corporations – allowing for greater market access.[74] In the case of Hikma, as mentioned above, US sales now constitute a large part of revenues, while European sales have increased rapidly since 2001 for APM and regional exports have risen for DAD. Access to the US and European markets would not have been possible prior to conformity with international standards and laws. In order to combat the challenges presented by TRIPs and FTA provisions as well as gaining USFDA and MHRA approval, the leading Jordanian corporations have pursued a number of strategies. The most effective has been to comply fully with the necessary regulations and improve both manufacturing processes and products.

Joint ventures with domestic pharmaceutical manufacturers have also been pursued. The results have been technology and knowledge transfer, greater external market access greater capital investment, and increased funds for R&D activity.[75] Prior to WTO accession Jordanian manufacturers did comply with some process and product patents and so further compliance has had measured impact. As other regional states join the WTO and conform with TRIPs regulations, Jordanian manufacturers will not be disadvantaged but instead will be in a better position to enjoy advantages stemming from already having adjusted to the dominant international regime. In short, the Jordanian pharmaceutical sector has become an export-driven sector moving towards the following goals: a greater share of the domestic market; a greater share of international markets propelled by both increased shares in current export markets and access to non traditional markets (mainly the US and EU); conformity with international standards to improve quality and thus attractiveness to FDI; some knowledge and technology transfer through joint ventures with external MNCs; and increased R&D activity while increasing production levels of generic and licensed pharmaceutical products.[76]

The Jordanian pharmaceutical sector has become much more attractive to external actors since 1999. Growth has been strong and successful export expansion is likely to continue. The overall investment climate in Jordan was negatively affected by the build-up to and the actual US-led invasion of Iraq in 2002–03. Furthermore, continuing problems in both Palestine and Lebanon have kept some FDI away from the region as a whole. However, the Jordanian market has proven resilient for a number of decades and the investment climate has recovered strongly. As further USFDA approval is sought Jordanian exports to and investments in the US market may increase. This would be a dramatic shift in bilateral trade relations between the two states. Potential for greater US pharmaceutical exports exists and, following the implementation of the JUSFTA, US pharmaceutical corporations have actually increased their share of the Jordanian market (although European and Jordanian actors still dominate).[77] However, what is perhaps of more interest in relation to the assessment of contemporary and future trade between Jordan and the United States in pharmaceutical goods is the potential for cooperation between US and Jordanian corporations.

The US pharmaceutical industry and government policy

United States policy with regard to international IPRs deviates slightly from the overall structure of contemporary US trade policy outlined in Chapter 3. To briefly recap, this study claims that US trade policy has become increasingly bilateral in nature as opposed to focusing on the multilateralism of the post-Second World War and post-Cold War eras. In particular the negotiation of bilateral FTAs, or Preferential Trade Agreements (PTAs) as some observers called them,[78] under the Bush administrations became a policy tool used in order to achieve broader political and economic goals. In short, bilateral FTAs between the United States and other states are not necessarily solely about economic benefit but they are also about US foreign policy goals. However, in the case of US policy on international IPRs, foreign policy plays a minor role compared with domestic and international economic policy.[79] Indeed, the inclusion of stringent provisions relating to IPRs in the Moroccan and Australian FTAs, for example, presented major negotiating problems.[80] In the case of the JUSFTA the provisions relating to IPRs are not as severe as the FTAs the United States has since implemented with other states.

While the bilateral FTAs the United States has negotiated since 2000 have included articles on IPRs, they do not act as the only policy approach that the United States has pursued in order to bolster international respect and enforcement of property rights laws. Rather, the issue was at the forefront of US foreign economic and trade policy from the late 1980s and became an increasingly important issue through the 1990s and the period of multilateralism pursued under the Clinton administrations.[81] During the Uruguay Round of trade nego-tiations, the United States had two primary policy goals. The first was the creation of a more concrete governance body for the international trading regime to replace the GATT system. The second key policy goal was the internationalisation of IPRs and a system of laws and regulations which would create a strict and enforceable regime.[82] As mentioned above, many observers have noted that the TRIPs agreement and its en-forcement through the WTO does not necessarily meet all of the expectations of the US government or those of many actors in the private sector. Bilateral FTAs can therefore be seen as a mechanism through which the United States can strengthen the regime governing international IPRs with FTA partners.[83]

With regard to the provisions of the JUSFTA relating to the T&C sector there is little evidence that the agreement with Jordan was ever expected to have, or has had, a significant impact on the US T&C sector. The Jordanian market is too small to allow for increased US T&C exports and using Jordan as an access point to a larger market in the MENA region and beyond would not be of much benefit as US T&C manufac-turing exports to the MENA region are relatively small and static anyway. There has been no large-scale lowering of the price of T&C goods in the US market as a result of cheaper Jordanian T&C goods being imported on an increased scale since 2001. Likewise there has been no significant increase in US exports in T&C goods or related material to Jordan.[84] Much of the Jordan–US trade has taken this form, with no significant impact on the US economy and a significant im-pact on the Jordanian economy. However, emphasis on IPRs has been more for economic rather than political or strategic reasons.[85]

There are a number of core economic reasons why the United States has focused on IPRs when negotiating and implementing bilateral FTAs. A 2005 research study conducted by the US Congressional Research Service concluded that intellectual property is a cornerstone of both the health and competitiveness of the US economy in the twenty-first century.[86] US manufacturing industries have been in relative decline vis-à-vis other states since the 1980s. This is partly a result of the industrialisation of other states around the world in the past three decades and partly because the nature of the US economy has changed. The US economy is now very much a knowledge-based economy with high value-added products and services accounting for increasingly large amounts of the state's GDP.[87] The US pharmaceutical industry is just one example of this, as is the finance sector – which is discussed in the following chapter. The US pharmaceutical industry and consumer market are the largest in the world. There are over 750 corporations involved in pharmaceutical manufacturing in the United States and total revenue for the pharmaceutical sector in 2008 surpassed $289 billion.[88] Total employment in the same year amounted to over 173,000 employees (compared to 23,000 employees for the United Kingdom and only 18,000 employees in Germany – the second- and third-largest pharmaceutical sectors in terms of employment).[89] These figures depict an industry and market far surpassing any other. This sector, as well as other knowledge-based and high value-added sectors, is therefore extremely important to the US economy. Protecting IPRs such as patents, trademarks and copyrights is seen as key to maintaining the strength and revenues of these sectors.[90]

The JUSFTA, while ensuring that Jordanian manufacturers abide by a strict regulatory regime for IPRs, does little in terms of preserving the competitiveness and revenues of US manufacturers on its own. Likewise, no single bilateral FTA is entirely significant on its own in these terms. However, the spread of the international regime for IPRs through the WTO and the TRIPs agreement, coupled with a rising number of bilateral FTAs is significant. Furthermore, the bilateral FTAs the Bush administrations signed after 2000 all have the potential of expanding into larger multilateral FTAs. The proposed US–MENA FTA is an example of this, with the JUSFTA being followed by the Bahrain–US FTA, the Morocco–US FTA, the Oman–US FTA and proposed FTAs with other regional states such as Egypt.

US corporations operating in the Jordanian pharmaceutical market

Unlike the Jordanian pharmaceutical sector, the US sector is not dominated by a small number of corporations and actors. Instead there are a large number of pharmaceutical manufacturers, many of which have extremely large capital resources and wide-ranging activities in many markets. However, even these large corporations only occupy a small percentage of the US market.[91] It is possible for US-based corporations to have such high levels of revenue with only a limited share of the US market for three core reasons. Firstly, the sheer size of the domestic market means that large profits can be made even with a small percentage share of the market. Second, US pharmaceutical corporations are among the most competitive in the world and dominate many international markets, leading to large revenues from exports. And finally, the large amounts of capital and human resources employed by US corporations in R&D activity (the highest in global terms) allows them to remain competitive and own the rights to new products and processes.[92] It is these latter two issues which are of most relevance to pharmaceutical trade with Jordan.

US pharmaceutical exports to the Jordanian market have expanded relatively rapidly, particularly since 1999. In 1995 total US exports stood at just under $5.08 million; this figure grew to $7.6 million in 1999 and just under $19 million in 2008.[93] This quadrupling of export value in the 12-year period is quite dramatic and translates into US corporations having an increased share of the Jordanian market relative to European firms – Jordanian manufacturers have also slightly increased domestic market share, as highlighted above. US corporations have also begun to expand their activities in the Jordanian market through investment and joint projects with Jordanian counterparts. This has only been possible as a direct result of the Jordanian government's implementation of TRIPs agreement provisions and the JUSFTA provisions relating to IPRs. As the Jordanian pharmaceutical sector's operating practices and regulatory regime come further into line with those of the US sector, US corporations have been able to capitalise on some of the advantages presented by involvement in the Jordanian market.

In short, these advantages are greater access to the MENA market through Jordan, lower operating costs in the development of new products and processes through joint R&D activity, and investment opportunities in the expanding Jordanian pharmaceutical industry. However, thus far only a small number of US corporations have been involved in the Jordanian sector in these ways. In fact, according to Fakhry Hazimeh the expectation in Jordan was that there would be far greater investment and joint projects between Jordanian corporations and US entities following 1999.[94] An examination of the activities of US corporations in Jordan reveals this tendency to engage with the Jordanian market only at a limited level.

Pfizer is one of the largest pharmaceutical MNCs in the world, ranking third in global sales ($32.4 billion per annum).[95] However, although Pfizer accounts for approximately 10 per cent of global sales, sales and activity in the MENA region have remained relatively limited. This is largely due to the fact that this region only accounts for 10 per cent of the global market and is relatively saturated with domestic, European and other US pharmaceutical manufacturers.[96] A second factor hindering or otherwise discouraging greater activity in the MENA market as a whole has been the growth of other markets such as India, which has diverted investtments and sales from the MENA region.[97] Nevertheless, the global pharmaceutical industry has maintained steady growth over the past decade and a half and Pfizer, as one of the leading corporations, has continued to expand its global presence.[98]

As mentioned above, the changes in the governing regime for the pharmaceutical (and other intellectual property related fields) in Jordan since 1999 have created an environment which is more in line with the US industry. This should theoretically facilitate the operation of US pharmaceutical corporations in Jordan, whether that is investment, sales or joint projects such as R&D activity. Pfizer has explored these opportunities – although only to a limited extent.[99] Pfizer is typical of large pharmaceutical MNCs in terms of its profit-making activities. While it is a major producer of pharmaceutical goods, it is largely a research-driven global entity, constantly developing new products and processes. Due to this reliance on R&D for profits Pfizer has been increasingly outsourcing its R&D activities to markets with lower R&D costs but appropriately high standards of operating procedures and IPRs protection.

Since 2000 Pfizer has been expanding its operations in the Jordanian market. This is a trend which has not been seen before in the small Jordanian market due to its previously weak IPRs regime. The number of employees working in the pharmaceutical sector in Jordan on behalf of Pfizer increased between 2000 and 2006.[100] As mentioned above, DAD produces goods which are licensed by Pfizer – this licence was granted in 2001 following the implementation of the TRIPs agreement and Pfizer's decision to start to expand in the Jordanian market. In 2004 Pfizer took the decision to conduct clinical trials in Jordan as part of its R&D process for cardiovascular drugs. In total four clinical trials were conducted over a two-year period in conjunction with the King Hussein Medical Centre and Hospital in Amman. The trials are believed to have involved up to 200 patients. According to Fakhry Hazimeh, Pfizer was attracted by the lower operating costs for the trials in Jordan, along with the highly skilled professionals available to conduct them and the high-quality facilities in Amman. These incentives were coupled with the now strong IPRs governing regime in Jordan.[101]

The majority of large and successful pharmaceutical MNCs are relatively old – due to the length of time it takes to develop new products and processes, pharmaceutical corporations tend to need many years to develop and grow – and Merck & Co. is no exception to this rule. The company was originally established in Germany in the late seventeenth century and a US-based branch of Merck KGaA was set up in New York in 1891. This corporation was confiscated in 1917 during the First World War and became an independent US corporation that same year. By 2006 Merck & Co. had grown to become the largest global pharmaceutical MNC with total sales of $51.8 billion per annum.[102]

In a similar manner to Pfizer's expansion in Jordan, Merck & Co. has increased its number of staff working in Jordan five-fold since 2000. The vast majority of these employees are employed in clinical trial projects conducted in collaboration with Jordanian corporations. In the period 2003–06 Merck and Co. carried out three clinical trials at the King Hussein Medical Centre and Hospital. However, these trials were more limited than those carried out by Pfizer.[103] Perhaps the activities of Merck and Co. in Jordan which are most important are a series of educational meetings and academic programmes held in Amman. These peaked in 2004, when 75 were held.[104] There were two main aims of these events, which included meetings, seminars and lectures. Firstly, events have been focused on IPRs and strengthening the IPRs regime in Jordan through the dissemination of information pertaining to the TRIPs and JUSFTA agreements. Second, events were used to share and develop both products and processes as well as R&D activities being conducted in Jordan by Merck and Co.[105] While the Jordanian pharmaceutical industry has not received as great a benefit as could have been expected as a result of implementing TRIPs and JUS-FTA IPRs provisions, observers such as Keith Maskus note that this form of technology transfer and engagement is in itself a significant investment.[106]

There are in total six US-based pharmaceutical MNCs operating in the Jordanian market through sales and investments. Pfizer and Merck & Co. have the largest investments in Jordan but the remaining four corporations also have a significant presence in the market in the form of sales, investment and clinical trials. Aventis has tripled its workforce in Jordan since 2000. Six local and relatively small clinical trials as well as a relatively large clinical R&D trial were conducted through 2004 and 2005 in conjunction with the King Hussein Medical Centre and Hospital.[107]

Organon was the first US-based pharmaceutical MNC to conduct clinical R&D trials in Jordan. In 2000 Organon initiated a number of trials for its new fertility therapy. However, in recent years Organon has had limited activity in Jordan.[108] Likewise Bristol Myers Squibb has conducted R&D trials in Amman, including a three-year 5,000-patient trial initiated in 2001 to study risk factors affecting cardiovascular health in Jordan.[109] The corporation is also part of the Jordanian Ministry of Health's participation in the HIV/AIDS Accelerated Access Initiative – which is a joint initiative between a number of MNCs and international organisations which includes UNAID, the World Health Organisation (WHO), the WB and UNICEF among others.[110] Continuing this same pattern of activity, Eli Lilly has also conducted a number of clinical trials and further R&D projects were planned for 2009 onwards.[111] However, Eli Lilly has not restricted its activity to this form of investment alone; rather it is currently the only US MNC which has a marketing partnership with a Jordanian counterpart (Hikma Pharmaceuticals) where co-promotion activity takes place in both the US and Jordanian markets for both corporations. These initiatives have been driven by the private sector following the liberalisation of the investment and privatisation laws since 2000 and the firming up of the IPRs protection regime in Jordan.

The US pharmaceutical industry is driven by the development of new products through R&D activity – as well as by financial flows and capital investments. In order for US pharmaceutical corporations to maintain their profit margins and market presence they continue to develop new products. However, R&D activity is very costly in terms of capital resources, time and manpower. In the pursuit of reducing R&D costs and increasing profits, corporations such as Pfizer and Merck and Co. have pursued the outsourcing of some R&D activities to other states and markets where R&D costs are lower but where high standards and operating procedures are met and IPRs protection is also guaranteed.[112] In markets where IPRs are not enforced or respected there is little incentive for pharmaceutical manufacturers to conduct R&D for fear of the likely theft of technology, information, products and processes. However, through the US government vigorously pursuing the implementation of the TRIPs agreement and more stringent bilateral provisions relating to IPRs, more markets are becoming 'business friendly' for pharmaceutical manufacturers.[113] As a result, outsourcing of R&D activity is taking place at an increasing pace and this is likely to continue. This includes outsourcing to the Jordanian pharmaceutical sector. The lack of enforcement of IPRs in neighbouring states such as Syria, Iraq and Egypt has further helped promote the Jordanian market as a regional market for R&D outsourcing.

The very nature of the pharmaceutical industry means

that the outsourcing of production is not often witnessed. In the T&C industry moving manufacturing plants to less developed states usually has the benefit of lowering production costs and thus increasing profits. However, the production of pharmaceutical goods is characterised by relatively low production costs (as opposed to very high R&D costs) and low transport costs no matter where they are produced due to the fact that the goods are small, light and mass produced. Of course, the production facilities are relatively expensive to construct, operate and maintain. This is necessary in order to gain approval by regulatory bodies such as the USFDA in order to sell the goods in the largest markets and so is unavoidable. Also, it is the development of the products and not their actual manufacture which is expensive – again this has little to do with where they are actually manufactured.[114] According to Professor Michael Ryan, the fact that the manufacture of pharmaceutical goods is rarely outsourced is precisely why US corporations have not invested in Jordan in that way.[115] Rather, Ryan suggests that investment in the pharmaceutical sector comes in the form of R&D, product licensing and clinical trials (in the case of the latter usually because payment and compensation costs are extremely low in developing states such as Jordan).[116] It is in these areas that US corporations have begun to invest in the Jordanian pharmaceutical sector.

As mentioned above, US corporations have recently increased their range of activities in Jordan. Sales have grown relatively rapidly but investment has been slightly slower. However, a number of key R&D and clinical trial projects have been conducted or are currently underway. With the continued strengthening of the Jordanian IPRs regime and further marketing by Jordanian corporations the experiences of Pfizer, Merck and Co. and Aventis may lead to more investment and clinical trials. Furthermore, this is likely to take place not just between Jordanian actors and the above mentioned US corporations but also other US-based actors.

This chapter has discussed a second form of trade activity between Jordan and the United States: trade in high value-added, capital-intensive and high-technology manufactured pharmaceutical goods. Studying this form of trade develops the overall analysis in this study as it offers an analysis of a different form of trade in a number of ways. Not only is the type of economic activity very different to the activity in the T&C sector discussed in the previous chapter but it also entails different institutional frameworks, different types of actors and different processes. As explained in Chapter 4, Jordanian state and non-state actors as well as foreign actors operating in Jordan dominated bilateral trade in T&C goods. This is quite fitting due to the nature of the Jordanian economy as a less developed one which has had only measured success industrialising and so specialises in labour intensive, often low value-added manufactures. However, the United States represents the most advanced economy in global terms and has by far the greatest resources dedicated to R&D in high-technology industries.

As discussed above the pharmaceutical industry is driven by R&D and large capital pools. Thus the US economy would naturally be expected to be more dominant in trade in pharmaceutical goods. However, the analysis presented in this chapter demonstrates that trade between Jordan and the United States in pharmaceutical products is much more than would be expected. Trade levels are much higher even in value terms than, say, trade in T&C goods. However, this is not simply because actors based in either market are as competitive as each other. It would be more appropriate to claim that trade between the two markets is in fact *limited* to the same extent. Jordan-based actors are largely uncompetitive in the more advanced international markets such as the US and EU. Furthermore, they have relatively low capital assets and limited access to some of the latest technologies and either have not attempted to or have failed to receive approval from the relevant regulatory bodies in foreign markets. Only Hikma Pharmaceuticals has managed to penetrate the US market to any great extent. Nevertheless, even this corporation's levels of trade with the US market are quite insignificant in overall market terms. For actors based in the United States the Jordanian market is simply not attarctive. Over-saturation of the market supply due to large numbers of quite small Jordanian corporations and larger European MNCs along with the limited population size, limited income and resulting small size of the market, have largely discouraged US-based actors.

Regardless of the low levels of overall trade in pharmaceutical goods between the two states, significant elements of the political economy of trade between them can be discussed. Here there are two main features which are important in understanding both the nature of Jordan–US economic interaction and the role of the international institutions the states have engaged with. In the first instance, trade liberalisation seems to have had little impact on overall levels of trade in pharmaceutical products. The expansion of Hikma Pharmaceuticals into the US market dates back to the early 1990s and so predates the period of liberalisation and increased state-level cooperation. Exports of goods from the US market to the Jordanian market are very limited in value even though they have seen significant increases since bilateral trade liberalisation was embarked upon. However, some US corporations have begun to operate in the Jordanian market since 2001 in the form of joint R&D ventures with Jordanian actors and clinical trials – albeit in a limited capacity. This has only been made possible due to Jordanian involvement in IOs such as the WTO and adherence to various regimes such as the TRIPS agreement and JUSFTA. This form of activity (while not overly significant in scope) has thus emerged as a result of the state-level facilitation of trade through international institutions.

The question regarding which state interests have been pursued and if these are being achieved must be addressed again here. Referring back to the discussions in chapters 3 and 4, it was determined that the Jordanian government has pursued policies of political and economic reform and engaged with international institutions in order to pursue sustained economic growth. With regard to the United States the proposition was put forward that the US government maintains traditional interests in Jordan and the MENA region based largely on security and support for its foreign and economic policies there. The state-level cooperation with Jordan and the resultant facilitation of bilateral trade through trade liberalisation and international institutions is one element in the United States' efforts to deepen state-level cooperation and market integration with Jordan. The analysis of trade in pharmaceutical products does offer some insights into how successful the pursuit of these interests has been. The reorientation of the Jordanian domestic regulatory regime and engagement with global regulatory regimes for pharmaceutical goods, especially protection for IPRs, has begun to lead to an adjustment in the domestic sector and competetiveness of actors involved in it. However, trade liberalisation with the United States, as mentioned above, has had limited impact thus suggesting that economic growth in the sector and thus the broader economy may be slow to materialise. The United States' facilitation of trade in this sector has not significantly deepened the integration of the two markets. There are signs that greater state-level cooperation through joint engagement in the WTO-led regime governing IPRs, for example, could lead to greater cooperation through unifying some state interests.

The issue of the balance between multiple relations between different actors at the domestic and international levels and the gains sought and achieved at these different levels is also illuminated by the analysis presented here. Unlike the rather unipolar gains achieved by the Jordanian state and market due to trade in T&C goods, there seem to be more even gains with regards to trade in pharmaceutical products, although the United States could be seen as gaining more. Trade levels are not very high and Jordanian exports to the US market account for a slightly greater share of the overall trade. Nevertheless, the Jordanian adherence to various international agreements and the JUSFTA and thus international regulatory regimes for pharmaceutical goods means that US actors gain to some extent in economic terms while the US government gains by expanding the network of (largely US-inspired) international institutions governing these products. The impact on broader state-level cooperation and integration in both the economic and political spheres, however, does not seem to be greatly impacted upon by the liberalisation of trade in pharmaceutical products. Some measure of economic integration and political cooperation is evident within this sector but there is little evidence that suggests this cooperation can go beyond sector-specific interests. In order to develop the analysis of the political economy of trade between Jordan and the United States and to answer the core questions it is necessary to examine one final form of trade relations in the following chapter.

6

BILATERAL TRADE IN BANKING AND INSURANCE SERVICES

This third case study chapter examines the framework for and nature of trade in banking and insurance services between Jordan and the United States. The assessment and analysis presented develops the overall examination of the political economy of trade between the two states by looking at a 'third form of trade activity', broadly defined as services. This chapter examines and analyses Jordan–US trade in banking and insurance services as case studies of financial services trade. While the previous two chapters have presented analyses of trade in low value-added and high valued-added goods respectively, the analysis here presents yet another unique picture. Despite the increasing integration of, and rising trade levels between, the two economies, low levels of trade in banking and insurance services persist. The significance of this lack of trade activity lies not in contemporary economic opportunities being missed but in the overall potential for Jordan–US trade relations. Furthermore, this analysis offers an insight into the ways in which the political economy of

Jordan–US trade may hinder rather than promote trade in banking and insurance services.

This chapter also includes a discussion of how cooperation between the United States and Jordan over the past decade has led the latter to engage with a number of regulatory regimes through the General Agreement on Trade in Services (GATS) and the JUSFTA. This discussion examines the nature of inter-state cooperation regarding these institutions and, coupled with the developments in actual market interaction, assesses the impacts upon state-level interaction and cooperation. As with the previous four chapters a multitude of both state and non-state actors are examined and the multiple links between these actors and relevant issues are considered. The impact of trade liberalisation and interaction in the banking and insurance sectors upon the state policy interests outlined in chapters 3 and 4 is also assessed.

Any study of trade in financial services is at the same time both complex and limited. The very nature of financial services presents a number of problems for the quantification and regulation of such activity, even at the domestic level. At the international level this is even more difficult. The result is that studying trade in financial services can be restricted. However, some forms of financial services are easier to study than others and, indeed, there is a great variation in these service sectors which need to be clearly defined. The first section of this chapter thus defines what is meant by 'financial services', what the various forms are and how they differ, and which forms are most important with regard to trade in banking and insurance services between Jordan and the United States. The banking and insurance service sectors are introduced as the sectors analysed here, and the rationale is given for the study of these services and the exclusion of others.

Due to the nature of financial services and their importance to economic activity at all levels, the international framework governing these services directly shapes the domestic framework. The second section of this chapter thus examines the international and domestic regulatory frameworks within which Jordan–US financial services trade takes place. Much the same as with trade in T&C and pharmaceutical goods, trade in financial services is governed by a comprehensive international framework. Through the WTO-negotiated GATS, trade in all forms of services has been liberalised (an ongoing process) and governed since the mid- to late 1990s. As members of the WTO, both Jordan and the United States are thus members of GATS and the international framework for services trade. Furthermore, the JUSFTA includes provisions on trade in services which strengthen and advance the provisions of the GATS agreement.

Due to the limited nature of trade in banking and insurance services between Jordan and the United States it is useful to examine the condition of their domestic financial service sectors. Section four offers a discussion of the Jordanian banking and insurance sectors followed by a discussion of the counterpart sectors in the United States in section five. An in-depth assessment of all financial services trade and the relevant sectors in the domestic markets is not possible in this project. In order to offer as accurate and representative an analysis as possible of trade in financial services between Jordan and the United States two of the most prominent sectors are analysed here. The overall characteristics of the sectors and the activities of the most prominent non-state actors are discussed. The involvement of Jordanian-based financial services actors in the US financial services market is insignificant and so only a brief discussion is included in this section. An analysis of US-based corporations' involvement in the Jordanian banking and insurance market is also presented. As mentioned above, quantifying and monitoring trade in financial services is not completely possible and so the scale of trade in empirical terms is not comprehensively included here. Rather this section offers a discussion based on the actors involved and the type of activities and services provided, as well as the scope of activity as can best be presented. A final section summarises the main points and arguments presented in this chapter. Conclusions are offered on the complexities and limitations of trade in financial services between Jordan and the United States, arguing that the political economy of Jordan–US trade coupled with market specificities limit trade in financial services and banking and insurance services in particular.

Trade in financial services

Financial services are in many ways the most integral element to both economic activity (of all forms, both official and non official) and to economies in general.[1] In fact, all areas of modern economic activity are dependent on access to financial services of one kind or another. Furthermore, the modern global economy could not have developed without the diversified intermediation and risk management services supplied by the global financial system.[2]

It is perhaps most appropriate to refer to the definition of financial services agreed upon during the Uruguay Round of trade negotiations when the liberalisation of trade in financial services was ushered to the fore of international trade discussion. The participants at this round of negotiations listed a great many services, broadly split into two separate categories. The first category is insurance and related services, while the second is banking and other financial services.[3] The former includes the following services: life and non-life insurance, insurance intermediation (broking and agency services) and trade insurance as well as others.[4] The latter includes: 'acceptance of deposits; [...] consumer credit, mortgage credit, factoring and financing of commercial transactions; financial leasing; money broking and settlement; [and] clearing services for financial assets'.[5]

Trade in financial services includes a great many activities, some of which are officially recognised and some not. A range of different types of actors may be involved in financial services – as suppliers or consumers – including corporations, governments, individuals or groups (highlighted by Susan Strange in a number of her works[6] as groups such as the Mafia and other criminal syndicates), NGOs and so on. In relation to international trade in financial services, the most common definition is the occurrence of one actor residing in one state supplying a consumer in a second with a service(s) without the establishment of a branch or subsidiary in the said second state. The actor providing the financial services could be located in the state where it is headquartered or in a third state, and supplies a consumer of the service(s) in a second state.[7] However, for the purposes of this study it is relevant to include also the activities of financial services suppliers based in one state (either the United States or Jordan in this case) *in the second state* as opposed to just *for actors based in the second state.* For example, this entails the study of operations of actors such as the American Life Insurance Corporation (ALICO), a US-based MNC that has offices located in Jordan to supply services to the Jordanian market.

A more comprehensive outline of the modes of supply of international financial services as described by Allan Webster and Philip Hardwick includes four elements. These are as follows: cross-border movements of financial services (as in the OECD definition above); movements of consumers to the importing country (including tourism, work placements and so on); establishment of a commercial presence in a foreign country (as with ALICO's operations in Jordan); and finally temporary movement of persons to a foreign country to provide the service.[8] In this study the approach to trade in financial services incorporates these four modes.

Measuring trade in financial services is, unfortunately, not an easy task and there is still a serious shortfall in available and reliable data on trade flows in financial services.[9] According to Webster and Hardwick, while data is stronger for trade flows between the larger economic centres in the Triad of North America, Europe and South East Asia,[10] data for intra-regional trade in financial services for less developed states including the MENA economies is relatively weak.[11] Furthermore, data pertaining to trade in financial services between MENA economies and international markets is also weak and can be unreliable. However, the data for Jordanian–US trade that has been collected for this study is from reliable sources,[12] and is reinforced with data gathered during field research work in Amman, Washington and Geneva. It must also be noted here that in order to study trade in financial services, banking and insurance operations which equate to financial goods or products are excluded from this chapter. For example, trade in corporate and government bonds is not examined as these are deemed here to be financial products and not services.

Established in 1995, the GATS agreement is the only comprehensive set of multilateral rules and commitments pertaining to state regulation of trade in services.[13] There are two elements to the agreement which governments must abide by: the first is the framework agreement which outlines the rules and disciplines governing trade in services; and the second element is the national schedules.[14] This latter is the mechanism by which national governments list the service sectors which they wish to liberalise and allow foreign access to. Furthermore, these schedules outline the extent to which the chosen sectors will be liberalised.[15] Sally Stewart has suggested that GATS has been less scrutinised than other multilateral trade agreements due to the relatively flexible nature of the schedule element.[16] This is because national governments themselves create their individual schedules according to national positions and are not (at least formally) obliged under GATS to include all service sectors.[17]

The agreement covers service sectors including financial services in this same manner, through the two elements mentioned above. There are, however, two broad service sectors which are excluded: services provided in support of government authority, and air transport. Furthermore, GATS includes all of the four modes of the supply of services outlined above, thus aiming to comprehensively liberalise trade in services for WTO member states. Under the agreement the Jordanian and US governments included financial services in their respective schedules. It is worth briefly assessing these provisions which, while superseded by the JUSFTA in relation to US–Jordan trade, form the basis of the FTA provisions and continue to shape their respective trade in financial services with other states.

The GATS schedule of the United States is relatively more complex than that of Jordan. This is a result of the difference in size and complexity of the financial service sectors and overall economy of the United States in relation to those of Jordan, and the position of the United States in the global economy and the resultant intricacy of trade-related financial service activities.[18] With regard to the insurance and insurance-related sub-sectors the complexity of provisions for market access and national treatment in the four modes of supply (as outlined above) originate with the fact that there are varying provisions for different states. Constant across the majority of states is that government-owned or government-controlled corporations, whether US or foreign, are not allowed to participate in the US insurance sector.[19] National treatment of foreign entities is for the most part equal across all states and equivalent to treatment given to domestic entities. There is one major exception to this rule pertaining to maritime insurance: '[w]hen more than 50 per cent of the value of a maritime vessel whose hull was built under federally guaranteed mortgage funds is insured by a non-US insurer, the insured must demonstrate that the risk was substantially first offered in the US market'.[20]

In relation to all non-insurance-related financial services, including trading of securities, trading in derivative products and participation in the issues of government debt securities, market access and national treatment are liberalised under the four modes of supply. Mechanisms and provisions vary across US states, resulting in an occasionally contradictory governing regime for trade in financial services in the US market. For example, some states, such as Tennessee, Mississippi and Missouri, do not have the mechanisms to register a new branch or subsidiary of a foreign firm if it is not already registered in another US state which does have the mechanisms in place.[21] There are also restrictions on the status of natural persons operating in the US market. US citizenship is required for higher-level employees of insurance firms in many states, while residency status is required for lower level employees wishing to operate in a large number of states. Furthermore, licences for some insurance- and non-insurance-related activities such as consultancy and risk assessment are not issued to non residents of the United States in some states such as Alabama, Hawaii and Georgia.[22]

Overall, the schedule of the United States under GATS allows for the liberalisation of the domestic financial services sector and international trade in financial services. However, there are variations in the liberalisation allowed under the provisions of the schedule between different states. The Jordanian schedule also allows for much liberalisation of the sector and related trade; however, it is much less complex and imposes fewer limits than the US schedule. The provisions result in a largely unbound governing regime in the modes of supply for insurance-related and non-insurance activities, except for several forms of insurance activity where suppliers either have to be based in Jordan or have branches located in Jordan.[23] Furthermore, 100 per cent foreign ownership of firms located in Jordan is allowed. Much like the schedule of the United States, the Jordanian schedule places relatively strict limits on the presence of natural persons. For most financial services the presence of natural persons from abroad, whether employed by a foreign or Jordanian entity, is restrictted to high-level employees or professionals with skills lacking in the Jordanian workforce either in number or quality.[24] Market access under the four modes of supply for non-insurance related activity is limited to registered banks and financial services companies – as is the case in the United States. Only registered entities are permitted to operate in the market in areas such as the taking of deposits or other repayable transactions.[25]

According to Lawrence Summers, '[b]uilding a more effective international financial architecture that can ensure that capital flows are sustainable as well as strong is of profound importance around the world'.[26] It is precisely this perception of the global financial services market that fashioned the elements of the JUSFTA which deal with trade in financial services. The FTA text incorporates all of the provisions of the GATS schedules for Jordan and the United States as well as the framework agreement of rules and regulations. The result is to further strengthen the governing regime between the United States and Jordan for trade in financial services.

The Jordanian banking and insurance sectors

The Jordanian economy has traditionally been service oriented. The wide-ranging processes of economic and political reform discussed in Chapter 2 have included liberalisation of the banking and insurance sectors in much the same way as in non-service sectors such as the T&C and pharmaceutical sectors. However, according to Dihel and Kardoosh the success of reform in financial service sectors has been relatively mixed and is seen as being limited.[27] Nevertheless, the banking and insurance sectors are significant components of the Jordanian economy and since 2000 have seen solid growth. However,

Jordanian banks and insurers remain small in relation to their counterparts in other markets, are generally not competitive in international markets and as a result have failed to exploit the opportunities in the US market for financial services provided by the GATS agreement and JUSFTA provisions.

While reform and liberalisation of the insurance and banking sectors has not been overly robust, growth in activity in these sectors has been quite strong since 2000. The first 'modern' domestic banks were established in the kingdom in the early 1950s, shortly after independence. As the banking sector in Jordan is a relatively young sector, it is worth looking back at the historical data from as early as the 1960s. Through the 1960s the number of banks remained limited and total capital assets were perpetually small, even in comparison to similar markets in states such as Lebanon and Israel. For example, total deposits with licensed banks in 1964 were a mere $68 million while by 1970 this had only risen to $81.4 million.[28] Dew, Wallace and Shoult argue that this lack of growth was due to the small size of the market and its low level of maturity.[29] However, with increasing economic activity, rising income levels and increased integration with regional capital markets through aid and worker remittances from the oil-producing states,[30] the 1970s saw significant growth in the banking sector – with deposits totalling $1.14 billion by 1980.[31]

The economic recession and crises (discussed in Chapter 2) which characterised the 1980s led to stagnation in the banking sector. Following the implementation of the economic reform policies devised in the early 1990s the banking sector once again began to grow in line with the overall economy. The boom-bust cycles in the banking sector now seem to have been broken, or at least limited to minor adjustments. Since the growth of the early 1990s the banking sector has remained relatively strong with growth since 2000 being healthy.[32]

A number of factors have contributed to the growth witnessed since 2000. In the first instance, transformation in the regulation of the sector began to attract foreign investment and foreign exchange. Coupled with rising levels of international trade and overall rising levels of income, the banking sector was able to capitalise on greater capital flows.[33] Third, the increase in and sustained high levels of oil and natural gas prices since 2001, while resulting in higher import costs for the economy as a whole, have led to a rapid increase in investments, savings and remittances from oil- and gas-producing markets.[34] The fourth factor sustaining the current boom in Jordanian banking is the repatriation of petro-dollars from Western markets (mainly US but also European) in the post-9/11 environment, and their investment in MENA markets. The Jordanian market is seen as stable and so has benefited form further investment.

The development of the banking sector is apparent when conducting a brief quantitative study of the capital assets of licensed banks (both domestic and foreign) and the foreign reserves of the Central Bank of Jordan (CBJ) – which is the banking sector's main regulatory body. With regard to the latter, through 2008 the CBJ held foreign currency reserves of just under $8 billion – equivalent to six months' worth of the kingdom's imports of goods and services. This was an increase of $216.4 or 3.5 per cent on the end level for 2006. The CBJ's foreign reserves stood at only $3.56 billion at the end of 2002 and at $2.268 billion in 1997.[35] Furthermore, total deposits at licensed banks totalled over $21.3 billion, an increase of over $646 million, or 3.1 per cent on the end level for 2006.[36] The equivalent figures for 2002 and 1997 were $13.2 billion and $9.1 billion respectively.

Expanding credit facilities are also another key quantitative indicator of the size and robustness of any banking sector. Credit creation and distribution has traditionally been the weakest element of the Jordanian banking sector and was a main characteristic of the sector's lack of maturity until the 1990s. However, this too has seen growth since 2000. By the end of the first quarter 2007, outstanding credit facilities extended by licensed banks totalled $14.598 billion, a 3.1 per cent increase on the end level for 2006, or $645.9 million.[37] The equivalent figures for 2002 and 1997 were $7.238 billion and $5.61 billion respectively.[38] According to Sabri Al-Khassib the banking sector has seen significant growth over the past decade and especially since 2000. This growth has been driven by both Jordanian and international actors operating in the domestic market.[39] However, Jordanian actors have not witnessed much growth in international markets (discussed in more detail below).

The insurance sector has experienced a similar process of establishment and expansion. According to the Jordan Insurance Federation (JIF), the main regulatory body for the insurance sector in Jordan, it was during the late 1940s and early 1950s that the insurance sector began to emerge. The initial impetus came as a result of the expansion of marine transport through the port of Aqaba and the small but growing number of cars owned.[40] Growth in the 1960s and 1970s was extremely slow as there was a limited market for insurance services due to the small population and low levels of income. However, by the 1980s the number of insurance companies had risen dramatically from just three at the end of the previous decade to 33 – ten of which were foreign insurance firms. This rise came as a result of the improved economic environment associated with the oil boom of the 1970s.

Nevertheless, while strong growth had been witnessed in the early 1980s, by the end of the decade the economic recession and subsequent crises which so drastically affected the banking sector also resulted in the rapid decline of the insurance sector. By 1987 the total number of insurance firms had fallen to just 18 and only one of the international firms remained.[41] As a result of new legislation introduced in 1995

(Insurance Law No. 9) repealing previous legislation enacted in 1984 (the Insurance Practice Monitoring Act) – which prevented the entrance of new insurance firms into the market – the number of insurance firms once again began to grow. Included in the 1995 legislation, however, were provisions which to a certain extent acted as restraints on market investment. These provisions included requiring domestic firms to have capital assets of a minimum of $3.5 million and $35 million for direct insurance and re-insurance operation respectively. International firms wishing to enter the market were obliged to have $7 million in capital assets.[42]

The insurance sector has thus developed with some similarities to the banking sector. Firstly, there has been a history of uneven growth accompanied by periods of decline. Secondly, Jordanian insurance firms have had limited success in competing in international markets. Indicative of this latter point is that in 2005 Jordanian insurance firms witnessed a 40.1 per cent decline in insurance premiums written outside of the kingdom on the previous year.[43]

Again, a brief quantitative assessment of the growth of the insurance sector is quite revealing. However, unlike an assessment of the banking sector, it is only fruitful to conduct this analysis from 1997 onwards, because of the extremely limited size of the insurance sector prior to this year. Total assets of insurance firms operating in the Jordanian market totalled over $770 million at the end of 2008. At the end of 2002 this figure stood at only $368.5 million and in 1997 a much smaller $173 million.[44] Furthermore, the insurance sector has seen strong growth in inward investment which by the end of 2008 amounted to over $575 million, up from $237 million in 2002 and $81 in 1997. [45] However, the growth in the sector is slightly misleading. While the sector has witnessed a large increase in activity, investment and total assets especially since 2000, this is in fact only a reflection of the maturation of the insurance sector in the Jordanian economy and not necessarily its profitability. Total retained earnings in the sector are quite low and in 2006 only amounted to $21.1 million – a drop of 78 per cent on the previous year and only a $2.7 million increase on the 2002 figure of $18.4 million.[46]

Of the seven main types of insurance offered in the Jordanian market,[47] motor insurance and medical insurance have traditionally been the strongest. For example, in 2006, motor insurance operations accounted for $170.7 million total premiums and medical insurance $60.5 million. The total premiums for 2006 equalled $365.1 million.[48]

In this environment of increasing activity and growth but low levels of retained earnings, saturation of the market with a large number of small firms represents a key structural weakness. The Jordanian banking sector is much larger than the insurance sector and has witnessed even stronger sustained growth since 2000. However, it too faces the structural problem of being relatively saturated with smaller entities. A discussion of these weaknesses follows a brief description of the domestic regulation of these sectors.

There are two regulatory bodies in the Jordanian banking sector: the CBJ and the Association of Banks in Jordan (ABJ). The former acts as the public management body while the latter acts as the private sector counterpart. The CBJ was established in 1964 following the 1959 Law of the Central Bank of Jordan with the purpose of acting as the exclusive regulatory body of the banking sector.[49] The Law of the CBJ states that the bank's purpose is to maintain monetary stability, ensure the convertibility of the JD and to promote sustained growth in the overall economy.[50] In order to achieve these goals the CBJ's functions have evolved over the past four decades to include the following: the issuing and regulating of bank notes and coins – the CBJ is the sole issuer of the JD; the maintaining and management of the kingdom's reserves of gold and foreign exchange; acting as a banker and fiscal agent to the government of Jordan and to public institutions; acting as a banker to private banks and financial institutions; to maintain the safety of the banking system – to ensure the protection of depositors and shareholders; to act as advisor to the government on fiscal and economic policies; to manage monetary problems and participate in the management of domestic economic problems; and finally to regulate credit.[51] The CBJ's decision-making body is independent of the government; however, the bank's capital is entirely owned by the government and the overall operations of the bank are coupled with those of the Ministry of Finance.

The ABJ on the other hand acts as a professional association for private banks and was established by the private sector in 1978. The General Assembly of the association is constituted of the director generals of the 23 banks operating in the Jordanian market while the association's capital is entirely supplied by the member banks.[52] Through the 1970s, as mentioned above, the banking sector grew relatively rapidly. As a result there was seen to be a need to develop a mechanism for the coordination of policies between the banks as well as to improve the overall efficiency of the sector through shared information. Thus the ABJ was established, with the following roles: to facilitate coordination and cooperation between member banks; to deal with mutual problems faced by private banks and generate solutions; to facilitate the exchange of information and experiences between member banks; to promote the development of banking methods; to standardise banking forms and expressions; to facilitate coordination with the CBJ; to seek to establish cooperative relations between Jordanian banks and international banking associations; and to act as a dispute settlement mechanism for member banks.[53]

Like the banking sector, the insurance sector has two main regulatory bodies, one public and one private: the Insurance Commission (IC) and the JIF. The latter was established in 1956 as the Jordan Association for Insurance Companies but was renamed following a royal decree in 1989. It has been presided over by members of the private sector and operates as an independent body of the private sector. Its purpose has traditionally been to promote the insurance sector and develop the coordination of insurance practices between insurance firms operating in the market.[54] It also seeks to provide market research in order to both improve the efficiency of insurance firms through the sharing of information, and enhance customer awareness.

The IC acts as the primary regulatory body having ultimate regulatory control over the insurance sector – including all forms of insurance operations. It was established in 1999 following the approval of the Insurance Supervision Act No. 33 and acts as an independent regulatory body. The IC is a private sector actor with an independent management structure constituted by a General Council, Director General and Executive Staff.[55] Furthermore, the IC's financial budget is entirely sourced from the private sector with minimal links to the Jordanian government. In a similar manner to the JIF, the IC seeks to regulate the insurance sector to ensure that the rights of insured parties as well as insurance firms are protected; to facilitate the efficient operation of private actors and act as a link between the government of Jordan and insurance firms.[56]

Unlike the banking sector the insurance sector also has a third regulatory body which acts in one specific sub-sector: motor insurance. The Compulsory Unified Insurance Office (CUIO), established in 1987, carries out all work related to vehicular insurance in cooperation with the various government licensing departments at the governorate level.[57] The CUIO also acts as a governing authority over insurance firms operating in the motor insurance sector, allocating market share and compulsory pricing ranges. In this sense the CUIO acts in a more authoritative manner than the JIF and IC.

These three regulatory bodies all act in much the same way as the organisations discussed in Chapter 4, such as JEDCO, JIEC and JIB. They have all been created or have evolved in a regulatory framework created by the government of Jordan in line with its macro-economic policies. Furthermore, they not only act as authorities managing and serving the insurance sector to ensure it operates efficiently for both private insured parties and insurance firms, but they also act as a link between the insurance sector and the government. Through the JIF, the IC and the CUIO the government of Jordan is able to strengthen the sector by promoting growth and stability. Meanwhile, through these three regulatory bodies private actors operating in the insurance sector are able to exploit the opportunities presented by the government for support (both political and economic). The result is a mutually beneficial and relatively close relationship between the public and private spheres in the domestic insurance market.

According to the Association of Banks in Jordan, the banking sector currently comprises 23 banks (excluding the Central Bank of Jordan), including eight which are branches of foreign banks and two which are Islamic banks.[58] The largest of these banks in terms of assets assigned to the Jordanian market are the Arab Bank and the Housing Bank for Trade and Finance, with asset bases of $23.7 billion and $4.5 billion respectively.[59] For a small state with only a limited market due to its relatively small population and low overall GDP, the large number of banks means that the banking sector is quite saturated.[60] While strong growth has been sustained in this sector over the past decade and is likely to continue, the relatively limited size in terms of deposit and credit facilities along with the high number of banks already operating in Jordan limits the attractiveness of the sector for foreign banks. Thus Jordanian banks have remained dominant in the Jordanian market. However, many of these banks have not witnessed any sustained success in international markets.

None has penetrated the US market beyond offering Jordan-based customers access to funds through international financial service providers such as Visa and MasterCard.

Likewise the insurance sector has traditionally been over-supplied by insurance firms. According to the IC there are currently 26 firms operating in the insurance sector.[61] Significantly, 20 of these firms are Jordanian (both public and private), four are joint Jordanian–foreign private firms (not American), one is a Yemeni firm and only one is a US-based firm – ALICO. The largest of these firms in terms of total assets assigned to the Jordanian market are Jordan Insurance with $108 million (or 14 per cent of the market), ALICO with $100 million (or 13 per cent of the market), and Middle East Insurance with $93 million (or 12 per cent of the market).[62] Profits in the Jordanian insurance sector are extremely limited, standing at only approximately $21 million in 2008. When this low profit margin is coupled with the saturated nature of the market, it is evident that for foreign insurance firms, including highly competitive firms such ALICO, expansion into the Jordanian insurance market is not attractive. This point goes some way towards explaining the lack of international actor involvement in this sector. The effect of this structure has been that Jordanian insurance firms have maintained their dominance in the Jordanian market, but at the expense of further development and expansion into international markets. The lack of competition from highly developed and capitalised international firms has contributed to the relative weakness of Jordanian firms. Thus, like Jordanian banks, Jordanian insurance firms have not penetrated the US market.

Nevertheless, it is worth briefly examining the performance and activities of the leading Jordanian banks and insurers operating in the Jordanian market. This short analysis illustrates the lack of capability of these leading Jordanian actors to penetrate the US market and offer financial services there, thus explaining why trade in financial services between the Jordanian and the US markets is non-existent when the services would emanate from Jordan.

The Housing Bank for Trade and Finance was established in 1973 as a public shareholding limited company with the sole purpose of providing finance for housing. By the late 1990s the bank had grown rapidly and had evolved into a comprehensive bank supplying full commercial and investtment banking services to the Jordanian market. It is now the second leading Jordanian bank with total capital of over $355 million.[63] Furthermore, the bank's total asset base stood at $5.78 billion by the end of 2008, a 28 per cent increase on the 2005 figure. (For further financial indicators see Table 6.1.) Importantly, the yearly profit earnings of the bank have rapidly increased in recent years, rising from $41.2 million in 2002 to over $180 million in 2008. However, despite the banks' strong performance in the Jordanian market, expansion into international markets has been very limited. The Housing Bank for Trade and Finance has 96 branches across Jordan (the largest number of branches of any bank operating in Jordan), four in Palestine and one in Bahrain. A further five subsidiary bank branches are located in Algeria (Algiers), Syria (Damascus), Iraq (Baghdad), United Arab Emirates (Abu Dhabi) and Libya (Tripoli).[64] However, as yet there have been no attempts by the bank to penetrate into more advanced banking markets in Europe, North America or South East Asia.

The Arab Bank represents a slightly different story. Established in 1930 in Jerusalem, Palestine, it has grown to be the largest MENA-based bank in terms of total assets, annual revenues and extent of international operations. While the Arab Bank was established in Palestine and not Jordan by Abdul Hameed Shoman, following the 1967 Six Day War and the occupation of the West Bank the company relocated its headquarters to Amman and became a public shareholding company. Since this time it has remained a Jordan-based financial institution.[65] The company now has 400 branches in operation in 29 states (most in the MENA region) across five continents and has managed to penetrate the advanced financial markets in Europe and North America with branches in London, Paris, Frankfurt, Zurich and New York. The Jordanian market represents the Arab Bank's most important market in terms of branch operations with 79 branches spread across the kingdom. The Arab Bank has total assets of over $35.5 billion and a capital base of $5.5 billion.[66]

Within Jordan, the Arab Bank has total assets of $7.76 billion and accounts for 24 per cent of the Jordanian market, occupying the largest single portion.[67] With regard to the Arab Bank's operations in the United States and its role in international trade in banking services between Jordan and the United States, the corporation has much less significance than in the MENA region or even in European markets. Total assets for its operations in the US market amount to only a little over $500,000, accounting for only an insignificant percentage of the overall market in value terms – it must be highlighted again that the Arab Bank only has operations in New York.[68] The Arab Bank is the largest and arguably the most stable financial institution of its kind in the MENA region and will continue to post solid and sustainable growth in the foreseeable future. It is likely to continue to dominate the Jordanian market for banking services and further expand its operations in the region and in European and South East Asian markets. However, the growth of its operations in the US market is less clear and it is most likely that the corporation will not expand its services in the US market by a significant extent in the short to medium term. Furthermore, the Arab Bank's role in international trade in banking services between Jordan and the United States will remain relatively limited, confined mostly to the supply of services to Jordanian citizens visiting the United States for short periods of time.

Table 6.1: **Major financial indicators of the Housing Bank for Trade and Finance 2002–06 in US$ million**[69]

Item / Year	2002	2003	2004	2005	2006
Total Assets	2501.9	2864	3527.3	4510.4	5780.2
Customer's Deposits	1806.8	2154	2708	3345	3996.3
Credit Facilities-Net	846.6	887.3	1241.8	17817	2243
Shareholder's Equity	379.3	413.6	447	557.4	1178
Gross Income	111.5	126.3	146	245	287.5
Profit Before Income Tax	41.2	43.5	66.5	148.5	183.6
Profit After Income Tax	30.9	31.75	42.8	104.6	133.6
Return on Average Assets %	1.26	1.18	1.34	2.6	2.6
Return on Average Equity %	8.34	8.01	9.71	20.42	15.4
Dividends	0.2	0.2	0.28	0.35	0.35
Share price in ASE	3.41	6.11	11.29	28.2	9.24

The Jordan Insurance Co. was established in 1951 by a number of private businessmen as the first major insurance firm in the country. Within seven years of its founding Jordan Insurance expanded regionally and opened up branches in Kuwait, Saudi Arabia and the United Arab Emirates. By the end of 2006 the corporation operated seven regional branches.

Throughout its five-decade existence the company has dominated the insurance sector, offering a comprehensive range of insurance services. Unlike many of the insurance firms in the market, including ALICO, Jordan Insurance Co. supplies all the types of insurance services listed above. However, while the firm's total assets are the largest of any Jordanian-based insurance firm as well as the assets dedicated to the Jordanian market of the non-Jordanian firms, totalling $17.5 million at the end of 2006, its annual profits remain small.[70] In 2008 net profits after tax and fees amounted only to slightly over $2 million. This does however, equate to almost 10 per cent of total profits after tax and fees for the whole insurance sector – with 25 other firms competing for the remaining 90 per cent. With this narrow profit margin it is highly unlikely that Jordan Insurance Co. will be able to expand internationally and offer insurance services in other markets, especially those outside the MENA. In fact, according to Khaldun Abuhassan, the Chairman of Jordan Insurance Co., there are no plans for expansion into new markets for the foreseeable future – and certainly not for operation in the US market.[71]

The activities and financial particulars of the Housing Bank for Trade and Finance, Arab Bank and the Jordan Insurance Company outlined above are indicative of the problems facing Jordan-based banks and insurance firms. The actors discussed here are the largest, most competitive and technologically advanced corporations in their respective sectors, yet they do not operate in the US market or offer financial services to actors based or operating in the US market through the first three modes of delivery for the former or all four modes of delivery for the latter. It is therefore fair to conclude that there is unlikely to be any expansion into the US market by Jordan-based banks or insurance firms in the medium term future, and thus trade in financial services emanating from the Jordanian market to the US will remain extremely limited. The story, however, may be slightly different for trade flows in financial services going in the opposite direction. It is now appropriate to turn to an assessment of the US banking and insurance sectors and the flow of trade in such financial services from US-based actors to the Jordanian market.

The US banking and insurance sectors

As with the previous two chapters covering the T&C and pharmaceutical industries, a full overview of the US banking and insurance sectors is neither possible nor strictly necessary for the purposes of this chapter. An in-depth assessment of the US banking and insurance sectors would yield little in terms of furthering the analysis presented here. Instead, attention is best placed on the US-based actors which are operating in the Jordanian market, in order to determine how the supply of financial services by these actors to the Jordanian market has developed in light of the structural weaknesses of this market and what prospects for future trade in financial services exist.

It is, however, necessary to present an assessment – albeit a relatively brief one – of the Jordanian banking and insurance sectors, in order to put forward the argument and main analysis of this chapter. One must recall that trade in financial services between the United States and Jordan is very small in quantitative terms and largely restricted qualitatively in terms of the four modes of supply. The aim of this study is to determine why this is in fact so. It has already been illustrated that trade in banking and insurance services emanating from the Jordanian market and being supplied to the US market is largely not possible due to the lack of capabilities of Jordan-based actors to provide these services.

A large number of US-based actors, as will be illustrated below, do possess the capabilities to provide financial services to the Jordanian market. However, it is the Jordanian market itself that prevents this supply from being realised by its structural weaknesses — namely in size and saturated market supply. A brief introduction to the US banking and insurance sectors provides an insight as to what structural limitations and opportunities there are for non-US based actors to offer financial services to the US market. National banking in the United States began in Philadelphia in 1781 with the establishment of the Bank of North America, which acted as the sole central bank of the United States, having a monopoly on currency. A decade later this bank was succeeded by the First Bank of the United States. However, this bank ceased operations in 1811 when the US Congress failed to renew its charter. A Second Bank of the United States was created in 1816 with a similar charter to its two predecessors but was also to expire in 1836.[72] The result of this lack of a central banking authority led to state banks emerging independent of any central regulation.

By 1863 this system had become known as the dual banking system as a result of resurgence in congressional regulation of the banking sector with the passing of the National Bank Act, which provided for the chartering of banks on a national scale. This system has endured to the present era, where banks may operate on the state or national level, adhering to state or national regulations respectively.[73] In terms of national regulation, following the 1913 Federal Reserve Act the Federal Reserve System was established bringing all banks operating in the United States under the authority of the federal government. Twelve Federal Reserve Banks exist across the country and are supervised by the Federal Reserve Board.[74] The purpose of this system is to control the overall money supply in the United States, to implement monetary policy and to financially support the banking system.

Under this system the US banking sector has maintained rapid growth to become the world's largest such sector. Total assets of commercial banks operating in the United States totalled over $10 trillion at the end of June 2007 while total deposits stood at just under $6.3 trillion at the end of the same period.[75] The respective figures for the end of the corresponding period in 2006 were $9.2 trillion and $5.8 trillion. Significantly non-US based banks occupy approximately 10 per cent of the market. Foreign-related corporations accounted for slightly over $1 trillion of the US banking sector's total assets at the end of June 2006 and $1 trillion at the end of June 2007. Meanwhile total deposits in these banks stood at $652 billion and $871 billion for the same periods.[76] When compared with the figure for 2000 the growth in the US banking sector is quite extraordinary. At the end of June 2000, for example, total assets of all banks operating in the United States equalled $5.8 trillion while total deposits amounted to $3.6 trillion.[77] The growth of market share for foreign-related banks has remained constant at approximately 10 per cent as total assets and deposits in non-US banks amounted to $690.8 billion and $387.4 billion at the end of June 2000. Nevertheless, while market share has not increased – and in some instances has actually decreased for non-US banks – overall assets and deposits, as well as other indicators, have grown rapidly.

There are currently around 200 foreign banks from 60 different countries operating in the United States.[78] Under the complex system of dual banking mentioned above, foreign banks wishing to operate in the US market enjoy the same national treatment as US-based banks. The International Banking Act of 1978 underpins this 'national treatment' for foreign banks, meaning that subsequent trade agreements such as bilateral FTAs which have provisions for trade in banking services do not offer preferential treatment to actors based in the FTA partner(s). While foreign banks are given the same market access treatment as US banks they are also subject to the same regulatory measures. A range of Congressional Acts since 1990 have been passed, further harmonising regulation of domestic and foreign banks.[79] Access to the US banking sector for non-US banks is therefore quite liberalised. This ease of access is, however, offset by the high level of competition found in this sector and the dominance of medium and large banks with large total assets and capitalisation. As described above, Jordanian banks simply cannot compete and offer financial services in this market.

The insurance sector in the United States shares similar characteristics with the banking sector. In short, the sector is very large in capital terms, is highly liberalised, is saturated with a large number of insurance service providers, and is dominated by medium-sized and large firms with high levels of capital, total assets and profits. By the end of 2006 the US insurance sector had a total market value of $1.2 trillion, making it by far the largest single insurance sector in the world.[80] The corresponding figure for 2001 was $909.6 billion. Average growth in the sector over the five-year period spanning 2002–06 amounted to 5.9 per cent and forecasts suggest that by 2010 the sector will have grown by over 23 per cent since 2005 to total over $1.4 trillion.[81] The US insurance sector accounts for 36.3 per cent of all premiums written within the global insurance market, with the EU being the closest single market with annual premiums representing 35.8 per cent of the global market in 2006.[82] Significantly, over the past decade non-life insurance has increased in importance and market share in the United States and now accounts for around 54 per cent of the insurance market in terms of premiums written.[83]

Regulation of the insurance sector in the United States is unique in comparison to other financial services in that it is the responsibility of state authorities, not federal authorities.[84] However, according to Susan Randall, the content of insurance sector regulation between states does not differ greatly. This is due largely to the efforts of the National Association of Insurance Commissioners (NAIC), a national private sector organisation comprising insurance firms.[85] This organisation was established in 1871[86] to act as a forum for private sector actors along with state insurance commissioners to pursue the organisation of insurance regulation: identified as fair pricing, protecting insurance firm solvency, preventing unfair practices and ensuring insurance availability.[87] Over the past 50 years the role of the NAIC has increased significantly as tension grew between state-level regulation of the insurance sector and the need for broader uniformity as insurance firms first expanded across state lines and then internationally. Furthermore, as insurance firms based outside the United States have increasingly penetrated the US market, more unified regulatory processes have been required.

As mentioned above, national treatment of non-US based insurance firms operating in the United States is provided and there are few limitations to market access. Under the US–GATS schedule and the JUSFTA, Jordanian insurance firms wishing to enter the US market can do so with no limitations as long as they are not owned by or affiliated to the Jordanian government. It must be noted, however, that some states do not have the mechanisms to register foreign insurance firms.[88] As with the banking sector (apart from the New York operations of The Arab Bank), there are no Jordanian insurance firms operating in the United States – although insurance is provided for Jordanian nationals entering the United States as in mode two of the supply modes described above. This is not due to a lack of regulatory facilitation or limitations on market access for Jordanian actors and firms. Rather it is due to a lack of ability on the part of the Jordanian insurance firms to penetrate the US market. The relatively small total assets of these firms, low annual profits and lack of competitiveness result in the opportunities for access to the US market being unexploited. On the other hand, the reciprocal regulatory treatment that US insurance firms and banks receive in the Jordanian market combined with greater total assets, annual profits and overall competitiveness, has led to US-based actors operating in the Jordanian market.

US banks and insurers operating in the Jordanian market
United States banks and insurance firms are amongst the largest in the world in their respective fields and amongst the largest MNCs of any sort. The largest banks such as Citibank – part of the financial services giant Citigroup – operate in dozens of states on all continents. The largest insurers such as ALICO – a member of American International Group – also operate on all continents in dozens of states. However, by 2009 the only US-based bank operating in the Jordanian market was Citibank and the only US insurance firm operating in Jordan was ALICO. As highlighted above, there are a number of reasons for the lack of interest by international firms and banks in entering the Jordanian market, and certain factors which act as deterrents to inward investment. These include, specifically for the banking and insurance sectors, small market size in overall capital terms and population size, over saturation and over-supply of actors already involved in the market and low levels of profit returns. Nevertheless, ALICO and Citibank have been operating in the Jordanian market for a number of years and it is worth analysing the activities of both corporations in Jordan and determining whether there have been any changes in this activity since 2001, as well as assessing the prospects for future activity.

Citibank is the largest bank of its kind in the United States and one of the largest five globally. It was founded in 1812 as the City Bank of New York and is now the consumer and corporate banking division of Citigroup – the second largest corporation of its kind in the world. By 1865 the bank joined the newly formed national banking system in the United States and was renamed the National City Bank of New York. It soon became one of the largest US banks. The rapid expansion continued and by 1897 it became the first US bank to establish operations overseas.[89] In 1974 Citibank Jordan – the Jordanian branch of Citibank – was established as a fully licensed corporate and commercial bank. Since 1974, Citibank has been the only US-based bank to operate in the Jordanian market and is the only non-Jordanian bank operating in Jordan to have senior local management for the Mashreq region – serving as the regional headquarters for Citibank, responsible for operations in Syria and Palestine as well as Jordan.

Despite being one of the largest global banks, Citibank has refrained to a certain extent from investing in Jordan and expanding operations in the kingdom. At the end of 2008 Citibank Jordan ranked seventeenth in the Jordanian market in terms of total assets, which amounted to around $325 million – as compared to a total of $1.1 trillion in global assets for Citibank as a whole at that time. In comparison, the Arab Bank holds approximate total assets in the Jordanian market of $4.6 billion and accounts for almost 30 per cent of the banking market.[90] Furthermore, despite over three decades of operating in the Jordanian market Citibank only has two branches in the kingdom, both of which are located in the affluent western areas of Amman. Little intention to further expand operations has been expressed since 2001. When taking into account the total assets of Citibank in the MENA region, the low intensity of Citibank's operations in Jordan are highlighted further. For example, in Bahrain, Citibank has total assets of over $30 billion.[91]

The further liberalisation of trade in financial services between Jordan and the United States, and greater access to the Jordanian financial services market for US-based corporations, has had little impact on the activities of Citibank. In terms of market share, the US bank has consistently accounted for only 1.5 per cent of the overall market in terms of total assets, total deposits and credit facilities. However, since 2001 a number of new financial services have been launched in the Jordanian market. These include the following: the introduction of the first fully automated system for custody safekeeping and settlements, electronic banking for banks for currency management – both domestic and foreign – exchange forward contract systems for foreign exchange, electronic banking for cash and trade for banks in Palestine and the creation of debt swap mechanisms for the Jordanian government.[92] It must be noted, however, that the development of services offered by Citibank Jordan is consistent with the competitive processes at work in any banking market and is not due to any substantial increase in investment or trade potential within the Jordanian market or between the US and Jordanian markets. According to Ghada Bahous, the Head of Operations for Citibank Jordan, there are currently no indications that Citibank will seek to further exploit opportunities in the Jordanian market.

ALICO was established in 1921 in Shanghai, China by C.V. Starr and was originally named the Asian Life Insurance Company. Within ten years of its founding ALICO was providing a range of commercial and personal insurance services across South East Asia. However, following the start of the Second World War, insurance operations in the region largely ceased. In need of new markets to operate in, ALICO established operations in Europe, Central and South America, Africa, the Caribbean and the MENA regions. By 1951 ALICO's name had been changed to American Life Insurance Company and by 2008 it was supplying over 50 markets across five continents with life, accident and health insurance services. It is worth highlighting that ALICO, while a US-based corporation headquartered in Wilmington in the United States and hence subject to US regulation, provides insurance services exclusively outside the US market.[93] International diversification has therefore been the key to the sustained growth of the corporation.

Jordan was one of the first states in the MENA region to receive insurance services from ALICO, which established operations in the kingdom in 1958 and was one of the first insurance firms in Jordan. Over the first three decades of operations in Jordan, ALICO maintained a market share of 20 per cent in life, health and accident insurance services (the firm has never supplied marine, transport, fire, theft or property damage insurance). However, in the past two decades this market share has dwindled to slightly over 6.6 per cent in 2008, down from 11.7 per cent in 2000.[94] This means ALICO has slipped from having the single largest market share for any insurance provider in Jordan to being the fifth largest. The decrease in overall share and paid up capital is indicative of decreasing market operations. In terms of paid up capital ALICO had only $2.8 million invested in the Jordanian market (ALICO has over $40 billion in global assets), as compared with the three leading insurance firms, the Jordan Insurance Company, Arab Orient and the Arab German Insurance Company, all of which had paid up capitals of over $7 million by 2006.[95] These figures may be slightly misleading in some ways. For example, while ALICO does not possess the largest capital assets among insurance firms in Jordan, it does have the largest total of gross premiums in value terms – $13 million – and one of the smallest per cent tage shares of market claims – at 4.1 per cent. Coupled with the market share as mentioned above, this means ALICO is the most profitable insurance firm in Jordan, with profits reaching just under $1 million.[96]

Regardless of the level of profitability of ALICO in comparison to the other firms operating in Jordan, activity does not appear to have altered significantly since 2001. Since the signing of the FTA ALICO has lost market share, and there has not been a significant increase in the supply of insurance services to the Jordanian market. Significantly, ALICO has not diversified the services which it does offer to the Jordanian market since 2001. It seems that the market access already enjoyed by ALICO prior to the JUSFTA and Jordanian accession to the WTO and GATS was such that the further liberalisation in trade in financial services between Jordan and international markets means that any opportunities in Jordan were already being exploited. It can thus be predicted that ALICO will maintain a similar level of market share in the Jordanian insurance sector over the medium term and will not witness significantly increased levels of gross premiums.

There is a relatively complex international system of institutions which regulate and manage trade in financial services, centred on the GATS agreement and the WTO. The creation of the JUSFTA further strengthened both the management of and liberalisation of trade in banking and insurance services between Jordan and the United States. These are two markets with very different characteristics, with the US market being the largest single market in the world and the Jordanian market a very small one. The nature of financial services and their intertwined relationship with markets overall mean that these services and the overall market which they service are interdependent. Thus the banking and insurance services and these service markets in the United States are very different from those found in the Jordanian market. This large disparity in market characteristics manifests itself in a number of ways as highlighted in this chapter.

In the case of Jordan the banking and insurance sectors are relatively small in comparison to other markets in the region and farther afield. While the market has seen strong relative growth in the past decade, and especially since the Jordanian government engaged further with international institutions in the pursuit of trade liberalisation, it still remains small in overall capital terms. Furthermore, much the same as with the pharmaceutical sector, the banking sector is quite saturated with domestic banks – although not with international banks. The capital-intensive nature of this sector as opposed to, say, the T&C sector, means that a market with limited size cannot carry a large number of suppliers. The insurance sector suffers from the same market restrictions. A small overall population in Jordan, limited income and a relatively immature insurance sector mean that insurance services in Jordan are relatively unprofitable. These market characteristics serve as a limitation or restriction on greater external supply of banking and insurance services. In short, the banking and insurance service markets in Jordan are not attractive to foreign actors. At the same time, Jordanian actors are generally small and limitations on the development of economies of scale restrict their ability to be competitive internationally. Thus Jordanian corporations have failed to penetrate or supply more advanced markets in much the same manner as Jordanian pharmaceutical corporations in their respective sector.

The Arab Bank Corporation has managed to evolve into a large international banking corporation and does operate and supply services to European markets but has very limited involvement in the US market – almost insignificant in terms of the size of that market. No other Jordanian banking actor operates in the US market. At the same time, no Jordanian insurance corporation is involved in Jordan–US trade or supply to the US market. The implications of trade liberalisation and engagement with international institutions such as the GATS-dominated international regime for services has done little since 1999 to increase Jordanian supply of banking and insurance services to the US market.

The US market is quite different, representing the largest banking and insurance sectors in the world. Many of the largest banking and insurance service corporations are also based or operate in the US market. These actors are far more competitive than their Jordanian counterparts. However, US corporations have very little activity in the Jordanian market and trade between the two markets – while extremely difficult to measure in empirical terms, as discussed above – can be regarded as very limited. Thus, while in low value-added goods such as T&C, trade liberalisation has had a significant impact on market interaction and integration, and in high value-added goods sectors such as pharmaceutical products, trade liberalisation has had some impact on market interaction and integration, with financial services this has not been the case. It is the conclusion of this chapter that market characteristics as opposed to state-level facilitation are the determining factors of trade between Jordan and the United States in financial services.

It is difficult to develop the discussion about relative and absolute gains at varying levels with regards to financial services. There seem to be very limited gains in economic terms to both state and non-state actors as a result of state-level cooperation and subsequent trade liberalisation. In a sense the United States has sought to expand the network of international institutions governing financial services. By helping to include Jordan in these institutions this network is expanded, but only on a very limited level. This point is discussed further in the concluding chapter to this book. For the Jordanian government there seems to be no significant negative impact on the banking and insurance service sectors as a result of trade liberalisation with the United States or broader international system as a result of engagement in international institutions. The sectors in fact seem to have grown more rapidly in the post-cooperation era and Jordanian actors have not been faced with significant competition from external actors. At the same time, however, gains have also been limited. Market interaction with the United States has been negligible and market integration non-existent beyond the inherent levels – remember that there is in fact a global financial system within which national markets exist.

Jordan–US state-level cooperation and integration do not

seem to have been altered significantly when trade in banking and insurance services is considered. The main significance here is the initial cooperation between the two governments in the late 1990s and early twenty-first century in pursuing the creation of the JUSFTA and the US-assisted engagement of Jordan in international institutions which govern trade in financial services. It was stated in the introduction to this book and has been evident throughout that assumptions are made on the basis of liberal economic thought and liberal institutionalist theory. These assumptions hold that trade liberalisation through international institutions leads to greater economic interaction, which in turn leads to economic integration. This market integration will result in greater state cooperation and integration. However, the limited increase in market interaction in the banking and insurance sectors do not provide any evidence that greater state-level cooperation or integration is occurring between the United States and Jordan. This discussion, along with those in the previous chapters, will be taken further in the following concluding chapter.

CONCLUSIONS

There are, broadly speaking, two types of conclusions of this study. The first type is what could be called 'hard' conclusions, and the second type is 'soft' conclusions which are less strongly argued but are nonetheless significant. This chapter will discuss these in order starting with the 'hard' conclusions, followed by the 'soft' conclusions.

This study uses a critical liberal institutionalist approach to assess and analyse the political economy of trade relations between the United States and Jordan in the framework of a heterodox IPE and a re-conceptualisation of MENA and US foreign policy studies. The hypothesis tested is grounded in liberal political and economic theory and holds that trade liberalisation between the two states has led to, and will continue to lead to, greater economic growth and integration between the markets and subsequently an increase in inter-state cooperation. Throughout this research project four key research questions have been discussed. The first question asked if bilateral trade liberalisation through the creation of and engagement with international institutions has in fact led to greater levels of bilateral trade between Jordan and the United

States. The second core question was whether greater levels of bilateral trade have led to greater levels of market integration. A third question was whether or not greater political cooperation between the two states has followed. The final research question considered in this study has sought to ask what the interests of Jordan and the United States as state actors have been, why they engaged with international institutions in order to facilitate trade and if their goals have been met through doing this.

Throughout this study the roles played by the US and Jordanian governments in facilitating bilateral trade have been discussed. These analyses are based on literature studies as well as field research in Jordan, the United States and Geneva, Switzerland, which included a number of individual interviews with members of government, IGOs and the private sector. The conclusion of these analyses is that both governments have constructed a bilateral framework within which trade can take place in a wholly liberalised manner through the JUS-FTA. Both state actors have engaged in multilateral and bilateral IOs and trade regimes in order to pursue respective national interests which are defined by changing domestic and international environments. Nevertheless, the discussions in chapters 3 and 4 identify different interests and relatively overlapping policy decisions taken in pursuit of these interests. In bilateral relations the differing national interests and foreign and economic policies taken in the past decade or so have converged to a great extent. The result has been the mutual engagement with international institutions and creation of a trade-facilitating bilateral regime.

In the case of Jordan, domestic and international demands and constraints which emerged in the late 1980s resulted in macroeconomic structural adjustment throughout the 1990s and broader political and economic reform at the domestic level. By 1999 and the ascension to the throne of King Abdullah II, political reform in the kingdom had halted but economic reform continued apace. The subsequent post-1999 governments in Jordan have maintained and accelerated processes of economic reform in pursuit of the newly primary interests of economic growth and stability. Traditional national interests which revolved around security and regime survival were replaced by economic concerns and domestic governance. It seems that the identification by the Jordanian government of economic interests as the primary interests of the state in the early twenty-first century have resulted in a number of policies. Many of the major domestic and foreign policies taken by Jordan since the mid-1990s and discussed in Chapter 2 have revolved around reform at home and integration at the international level, and involve cooperation through international institutions.

Accession to the WTO in 1999, the JEUAA, various MENA initiatives such as the GAFTA and MAFTA, and bilateral FTAs such as the JUSFTA all represent significant elements of Jordanian involvement in international institutions related to trade. Taken together these policy directions signify an overall move towards facilitating international trade as a means to increase economic growth and stability and by extension attend to various security concerns – largely pertaining to regime survival. The JUSFTA in particular is a key element of Jordanian facilitation of trade due to the importance and size of the United States as both state and market. However, the relationship with the United States with regard to trade and economic interaction that has developed since 1997 should not be seen as independent from the policies taken in the broader facilitation of trade with international economy. In short, Jordanian trade policy towards the United States and engagement with the United States in international institutions is aimed primarily at increasing economic growth through trade liberalisation and not necessarily at increasing state-level cooperation and interdependence with the United States.

In the case of the United States, the analysis in Chapter 3 introduced a reinterpretation of US interests with regard to the MENA region and Jordan in particular. Some of these interests were of an economic nature, much the same as the main Jordanian interests, and some were political or security oriented. For the United States, a stable and friendly MENA region is not only a key policy goal in itself but is also pivotal in order for the United States to pursue its other traditional policy goals in the region. These include secure and sustainable access to the region's natural resources which are indispensable to the US and global economies and to maintaining the United States' position in international relations. The second main traditional interest has been access to the region's markets for goods and services both in terms of markets to export to and import from. A final traditional policy interest in the region is the encouragement of cooperation with states in the region in a relationship characterised by US leadership or hegemony. The reinterpretation of traditional interests in the MENA region presented in this study has led to one main conclusion. This conclusion is that the United States is pursuing economic cooperation and market integration with states in the region and the encouragement of economic growth there as the primary method through which the United States wishes to achieve its main interests. Thus US engagement with Jordan in international institutions in order to liberalise bilateral trade has been pursued to promote bilateral market integration in order to increase state-level cooperation.

The analyses of state interests and resultant facilitation of trade demonstrate little by way of answering the first three core research questions. However, chapters 3 and 4 define what state-led trade liberalisation is, thus enabling the study to progress towards analysing the actual trade that takes place and which actors are involved in this trade.

Three chapters have been dedicated to analysing the nature and characteristics of, as well as the change in, bilateral trade in three economic sectors. The sectors chosen permit the study of trade in three very different sectors, allowing as representative a study as is possible. The first sector studied was trade in textiles and clothing, a low value-added, labour intensive manufacturing sector. The analysis of this sector in Chapter 4 concludes that bilateral trade in T&C goods is dominated by Jordanian exports to the US market, has grown rapidly since the implementation of the JUSFTA and displays signs of limited asymmetric market integration. Furthermore, the growth of this sector in the Jordanian economy has had significant effects on overall economic growth. The sector developed largely after 1997 and the creation of the QIZs as a new element in the bilateral trade regime between the United States and Jordan, and has since grown largely due to exports to the US market following the implementation of the JUS-FTA in 2001. A complex relationship between public and private sector actors has served to promote the sector both within the Jordanian economy and in terms of market access abroad.

A comparison between Jordanian exports of T&C goods to the EU market and exports to the US market reveals a stark contrast. Even with the JEUAA in place and adherence to the post-MFA governance of trade in T&C goods, Jordanian exports to the EU are very limited. At the same time exponential growth to average levels of over $1 billion is seen in exports to the US market. Furthermore, comparison between the success of Jordanian exports to the US market with more well established and larger T&C export sectors in the MENA region also is dramatic. Compared to Tunisia, Morocco and Egypt, Jordan exports far more to the US even though its T&C sector is much smaller and younger than its regional counterparts. The indications are that the increase in trade in T&C along with the overall growth of the sector in Jordan have led to, and are likely to maintain, a greater level of importance of the sector in Jordan and bilateral market integration for the medium-term future.

The second economic sector studied in this study was pharmaceutical manufacturing, a high value-added, capital-intensive manufacturing sector which differs from the T&C sector. This analysis concluded that bilateral trade in this sector is far more limited than in the previous sector studied and is characterised by more equal trade levels. Here private actors based in the United States operate in the Jordanian market on a small scale, as does one Jordanian-based actor in the US market. However, of importance here is that this market interaction and integration has largely developed in the few years since the implementation of the JUSFTA. This sector is different in many ways from the T&C industry and both the institutional framework governing trade in pharmaceutical products and the actors involved in the sector vary greatly from those of the T&C sector. While there may only be small levels of trade in actual products there has been some measure of market integration through the activity of US-based actors in the Jordanian market. This activity is centred on collaborative projects related to research and development of new products. Without Jordanian cooperation in the international institutions governing pharmaceutical production and trade this activity would not be possible.

Nevertheless, the overall conclusion of the analysis of this sector is that trade liberalisation has had only a small impact on economic growth in Jordan and no real impact on economic growth in the United States. Furthermore, the indications are that there are significant market characteristics which will prevent market integration and actor cooperation in the pharmaceutical sectors in Jordan and the United States in the future. Concrete gains from trade liberalisation in pharmaceutical products are limited for both states. For the United States the inclusion of Jordan in regulatory institutions further expands this network – which is a key US interest with regard to issues such as IPRs and so on. Jordan also has achieved some gains through this process. These include the restructuring of Jordanian pharmaceutical producers and their adherence to cGMPs, which will make them more competitive in both the domestic and international markets in the long run. Overall though, the gains are limited and bilateral trade in pharmaceutical products has not added to greater bilateral economic and political integration, and is unlikely to do so in the short to medium term.

In order to complete the study of trade relations as thoroughly as possible the third sector studied was financial services in the form of banking and insurance services, which are capital-intensive service sectors. These sectors again differ greatly in characteristics to the sectors studied in chapters 4 and 5. The analysis in Chapter 6 produced an interesting set of conclusions, the first being that historically there has been very little bilateral trade in financial services between the two markets and this has not significantly changed in the liberalised trade era. Furthermore, the lack of market integration is a result of two factors. Firstly, the small size and saturated nature of the Jordanian financial services market does not present profitable opportunities for US-based private sector actors and thus does not attract activity, even in the context of liberalised trade. Secondly, Jordanian-based actors are ill-equipped to compete in the US financial services market. Again, this is the case even with the added benefit of unfettered access granted as a result of the JUSFTA.

The final conclusion drawn here is that there is unlikely to be a significant change in bilateral trade in banking and insurance services and in fact possibly other high value-added services in the short to medium term. Therefore, once again, trade liberalisation between the United States and Jordan has not led to greater economic growth, increased market integration or political and economic cooperation at the state level. Furthermore, neither state actor has significantly gained from trade liberalisation in these forms of service trade nor achieved their main interests of economic growth and inter-state cooperation.

The overall conclusions drawn from this study provide answers to the four core research questions and test the hypothesis presented in the introduction. With regard to the supposition that bilateral trade liberalisation leads to greater bilateral trade, this study shows that this is not necessarily the case for every economic sector. State facilitation of bilateral trade through trade liberalisation and engagement with international institutions simply establishes a framework within which trade can take place. However, Jordan and the United States as state actors are not involved to any great extent in the trade which actually takes place. Rather it is non-state actors, sometimes public sector or government-affiliated actors, but mostly private sector actors, which are actually involved in trade between the markets. Thus it is these non-state actors and the market characteristics which determine levels of bilateral trade. The framework within which bilateral trade takes place is merely complementary. The difference in the levels and nature of trade in the three sectors studied here demonstrate this to great effect.

Because the answer to the first research question is rather complicated and at any rate is not a simple 'yes', the answer to the second question is also complicated. The second research question asked whether or not increased trade levels have led to increased economic growth and market integration. The evidence in this study does not suggest that a definite answer can be given either way. The study of trade in T&C goods suggests that increased integration has been witnessed, albeit in a slightly asymmetric manner with the Jordanian market being more dependent on the US market for exports. However, the small levels of trade in pharmaceutical goods and banking and insurance services as assessed in chapters 5 and 6 do not suggest that these sectors are becoming more integrated across the markets. The overall answer to this question must therefore be that increased trade can lead to increased market integration under some circumstances, but only in some sectors. As stated in the introduction, however, there is much scope for the further study of bilateral trade between Jordan and the United States in different economic sectors and as the framework for trade established through international institutions further solidifies.

In conclusion to the third research question regarding the impacts of market integration on state-level cooperation, the discussions in chapters 4 through 6 must again be drawn upon. Overall, the limited levels of increase in trade levels and subsequent limited levels of market interaction and integration do not suggest that there is greater state-level integration or cooperation. Certainly increased trade in T&C goods has led to increased bilateral economic interests on the part of Jordanian actors. However, the asymmetric nature of this integration reflects a form of relationship closer to dependence than interdependence. Furthermore, the low levels of market integration in pharmaceutical products, banking and insurance services suggest that there has been little increase in shared interests with regard to these sectors and little by way of growth in interdependence. In short, the markets have remained relatively independent of each other and so state-level interests have not converged to a great extent, thus limiting the need for cooperation. On the other hand, Jordanian involvement in IOs such as the WTO and WIPO along with the United States, as well as adherence to various regimes governing IPRs and services such as TRIPs and GATS, does constitute a significant form of cooperation with the United States at the state level. Furthermore, the cooperation between Jordan and the United States with regard to formulating the TRIPs-Plus provisions within the JUSFTA is also significant. Again, here the significant difference between TRIPs and TRIPs-Plus provisions must be noted. However, this cooperation is sector-specific and confined to unique issues and so does not represent a major paradigmatic shift towards greater inter-state cooperation on non-related issues.

The fourth question addressed by this study considered what the main national interests for the United States and Jordan have been over the past decade or so in relation to their bilateral relations and if these are being met as a result of the policies taken to liberalise trade between them. As earlier discussed, both states have engaged with bilateral trade liberalisation through international institutions in pursuit of various national interests. In the case of Jordan these interests revolve around economic growth and stability. For the United States these interests revolve around greater cooperation and integration with the MENA region as a whole using Jordan as an initial step in a much broader project. For both states no simple conclusion can be drawn about whether or not these interests have been met.

Jordanian exports to the US market have increased since bilateral trade liberalisation began and overall economic growth in Jordan has been impacted. Furthermore, the successful reorientation of the bilateral trade relationship with the United States has further solidified Jordanian efforts to liberalise trade and integrate economically at the international level. The United States certainly has become a more important economic market for the Jordanian market and thus state, and as such has been able to increase its integration with Jordan. It is possible to venture the conclusion, although it cannot be argued from a position of absolute authority that the increasing importance of the United States to Jordan should result in greater cooperation. However, asymmetric market integration and issue-specific cooperation in IOs and trade regimes do not necessarily equate to greater inter-state cooperation on other issues. Perhaps this fourth research question was too bold and ambitious and cannot be answered through this study on its own, but instead requires further study of market interactions and bilateral state relations.

The conclusions of this study demonstrate that trade liberalisation between Jordan and the United States through engagement with international institutions has not led to significantly greater levels of trade, economic growth and market integration. Instead some increases in bilateral trade, economic growth and market integration have occurred in some sectors but not others. Market characteristics and the activity of non-state actors are the keys to determining levels of trade, economic growth and market integration and unfortunately, as demonstrated in this study, these at present seem to restrict greater market interaction and integration between Jordan and the United States in some sectors. Furthermore, even if these conditions are met there is only limited proof that suggests that inter-state cooperation and stable relations between Jordan and the United States will necessarily follow, even if trade liberalisation does encourage greater economic growth and market integration.

NOTES

Introduction

1 Cohen, B.J., 2008, *International Political Economy: An Intellectual History*, Princeton: Princeton University Press.

2 Halliday, F., 2005, *The Middle East in International Relations: Power, Politics and Ideology*, Cambridge: Cambridge University Press.

3 Murphy, C., Tooze., R (eds), 1991, *The New International Political conomy*, Boulder: Lynne Rienner Publishers, p. 4.

4 Gills, B., 'Forum: Perspectives on New Political Economy: Reorienting the New (International) Political Economy', *New Political Economy*, 6(2), 2001, pp. 234–236.

5 Abu-Hammour, M., 2005, *Jordan's Economic Reforms*, Abu Dhabi: S.n.; 'Singh, R., 'Liberalisation or Democratisation?: The Limits of Political Reform and Civil Society in Jordan', in Joffé, G. (ed), 2002, *Jordan in Transition: 1990–2000*, London: MacMillan Press, pp. 66–90.

6 Ward, A., 'US Policy to the Middle East: Utopianism and Realism', *IISS Strategic Comments*, 1(1), Jan. 2003, p. 2.

7 Rosen, H., 'Free Trade Agreements as Foreign Policy Tools: The US–Israel and US–Jordan FTAs', in Schott, J.J. (ed), 2004, *Free Trade Agreements: US Strategies and Priorities*, Washington: Institute for International Economics.

8 See for example: Little, D., 2002, *American Orientalism: The United States and the Middle East Since 1945*, London: I.B.Tauris & Co. Ltd.

9 Simons, G., 2003, *Future Iraq: US Policy in Reshaping the Middle East*, London: Saqi Books.

Chapter 1

1   Burch, K., Denemark, R., 1997, *Constituting International Political Economy*, Boulder: Lynne Rienner.

2   'Editorial, Forum for Heterodox International Political Economy', *Review of International Political Economy*, 1(1), 1994, p. 2.

3   Murphy, C., Nelson, D., 'International Political Economy: a Tale of Two Heterodoxies', *British Journal of Politics and International Relations*, 3(3), Oct. 2001, p. 393.

4   Dickens, A., 'The Evolution of International Political Economy', *International Affairs*, 82(3), 2006, p. 480.

5   Blyth, M., Spruyt, H., 'Our Past as Prologue: Introduction to the Tenth Anniversary Issue of Review of International Political Economy', *Review of International Political Economy*, 10(4), 2003.

6   Katzenstein, P.J., Keohane, R., Krasner, S., 'International Organisation and the Study of World Politics', *International Organization*, 52(4), 1 October 1998, pp. 645–685.

7   Tooze, R., 1982, *World Political Economy*, New York: Continuum International Publishing Group, p. 2.

8   Strange, S., 1988, *States and Markets: An Introduction to International Political Economy*, London: Pinter Publishers, p. 18.

9   Ibid.

10 Gilpin, R., 1987, *The Political Economy of International Relations*, Princeton: Princeton University Press, p. 11.

11 Gills, B., 'Forum: Perspectives on New Political Economy; Reorienting the New (International) Political Economy', *New Political Economy*, 6(2), 2001, pp. 234–236.

12 Tooze, R., 'The Unwritten Preface: International Political Economy and Epistemology', *Millennium: Journal of International Studies*, 17(2), 1988, pp. 285–294.

13 Murphy, C., Tooze, R. (eds), 1991, *The New International Political Economy*, Boulder: Lynne Rienner Publishers, p. 4.

14 Stubbs, R., Underhill, G., 2000, *Political Economy and the Changing Global Order*, 2nd edition, Oxford: Oxford University Press, p. 21.

15 Ibid.

16 Krasner, S., 'International Political Economy: Abiding Discord', *Review of International Political Economy*, 1(1), 1994, pp. 13–19.

17 Krasner, S., 1996, 'The Accomplishments of IPE', in Smith, S., Booth, K., Zalewski, M. (eds), *International Theory: Positivism and Beyond*, Cambridge: Cambridge University Press.

18   Denmark, R., O'Brien, R., 'Contesting the Canon: International Political Economy at UK and US Universities', *Review of International Political Economy*, 4(1), 1997, pp. 214–238.

19   Taylor, I., 'Globalisation Studies and the Developing World: Making International Political Economy Truly Global', *Third World Quarterly*, 26(7), 2005.

20   While international trade has been the most cited issue area, others have also been the focus of much attention in IPE. These include: interdependence, development and economic regimes.

21   Hay, C., Marsh, D., 'Introduction: Towards a New (International) Political Economy', *New Political Economy*, 4(1), 1999, p. 6.

22   Murphy, C., Tooze, R., *The New International Political Economy*, p. 11.

23   See Krasner, S., 1996, for a discussion on the level of effectiveness of IPE research.

24   Katzenstein, P.J., Keohane, R., and Krasner, S., 'International Organisation and the Study of World Politics', pp. 645–685.

25   Cox, R., 'Social Forces, States and World Orders: Beyond International Relations Theory', *Millennium: Journal of International Studies*, 10(2), 1981, p. 123.

26   Gramsci, A., 1971, *Selections From the Prison Notebooks*, New York: International Publishers.

27   Ibid.

28   Groom, A., Light, M. (eds), 1994, *Contemporary International Relations: a Guide to Theory*, London: Pinter Publishers.

29   Cox, R., 'Ideologies and the New International Economic Order: Reflections on Some Recent Literature', *International Organization*, 33(2), 1979, p. 269. For a thorough analysis of knowledge production in the broader social sciences see Gibbons, M. *et al.*, 1994, *The New Production of Knowledge / the Dynamics of Science and Research in Contemporary Societies*, London: Sage.

30   Murphy, C., Tooze, R., *The New International Political Economy*, p. 13.

31   Cox, R., 'Social Forces, States and World Orders: Beyond International Relations Theory', p. 127.

32   Higgott, R., 'Toward a Non-Hegemonic IPE: An Antipodean Perspective', in Murphy, C., Tooze, R., *The New International Political Economy*, p. 98.

33   Cox, R., 'Social Forces, States and World Orders: Beyond International Relations Theory'; Strange, S., *States and Markets: An Introduction to International Political Economy*; Murphy, C., Tooze, R., *The New International Political Economy*.

34   Haas, E.B., 1997, *Nationalism, Liberalism and Progress: The Rise and Decline of Nationalism*, Ithaca: Cornell University Press.

35   Amin, A., Palan, R., 'Towards a Non-Rationalist International Political Economy', *Review of International Political Economy*, 8(4), 2001, pp. 561–564.

36   Cox, R., 'Ideologies and the New International Economic Order: Reflections on Some Recent Literature', p. 269.

37   Jessop, B., Sum, N.L., 'Pre-Disciplinary and Post-Disciplinary Perspectives', *New Political Economy*, 6(1), 2001, p. 90.

38   Murphy, C., Tooze, R., *The New International Political Economy*, p. 14.

39   'Editorial, Forum for Heterodox International Political Economy', *Review of International Political Economy*, 1(1), 1994, p. 10.

40   Strange, S., 'Political Economy and International Relations', in Booth, K., Smith S., 1995, *International Relations Theory Today*, Cambridge: Polity.

41   Gilpin, R., *The Political Economy of International Relations*.

42   Ibid, p. 3.

43   Spero, J., 1990, *The Politics of International Economic Relations*, 7th edition, London: Routledge.

44   Gilpin, R., 1987 *The Political Economy of International Relations*, p. 3.

45   Ibid, p. 25.

46   Reference taken from: Helbroner, R., 1985, *The Nature and Logic of Capitalism*, New York: W.W. Norton, p. 107.

47   Amoore *et al.*, 2000, 'Paths to a Historicized International Political Economy', *Review of International Political Economy*, 7(1), Spring 2000, pp. 54–56.

48   Murphy, C., and Tooze, R., *The New International Political Economy*, p. 18.

49   Keat, R., Urry, J., 1975, *Social Theory as Science*, London: Routledge.

50   Halfpenny, P., 1982, *Positivism and Sociology*, London: Allen & Unwin.

51   Lloyd, C., 1993, *The Structures of History*, Oxford: Blackwell.

52   Quine, W., 1961, *From a Logical Point of View*, New York: Harper & Row.

53   Thompson, E.P., 1978, *The Poverty of Theory*, London: Merlin Press, p. 211.

54   Ayer, A.J., 1940, *The Foundations of Empirical Knowledge*, London: Macmillan.

55   Kuhn, T.S., 1970, *The Structure of Scientific Revolution*, 2nd edition, Chicago: Chicago University Press.

56   Feyeraband, P., 1975, *Against Method: Outline of an Anarchistic Theory of Knowledge*, London: Verso.

57   Deardorff, A., Stern, R., 'What You Should Know About Globalization and the World Trade Organization', *Review of International Economics*, 10(3), 2002, pp. 417–423.

58   Dobson, J., 'The Battle in Seattle: Reconciling Two World Views on Corporate Culture', *Business Ethics Quarterly*, 11(3), 2001, pp. 403–413.

59   Mayo, M., 2004, *Global Citizens: Social Movements and the Challenge of Globalization*, London: Zed Books.

60   Macrory, P., Appleton, A., Plummer, M., 2005, *The World Trade Organization: Legal, Political and Economic Analysis*, New York: Springer.

61   Murphy, C., Tooze, R., *The New International Political Economy*, p. 19.

62   Amin, A., Palan, R., 'Towards a Non-Rationalist International Political Economy', pp. 561–564.

63   Sjolander, C., Cox, W., 1994, *Beyond Positivism: Critical Reflections on International Relations*, Boulder: Lynne Rienner.

64   Krasner, S., 'Structural Causes and Regime Consequences: Regimes as Intervening Variables', *International Organization*, 36(2), 1982, pp. 185–206.

65   Ibid, p. 195.

66   Murphy, C., Tooze, R., *The New International Political Economy*, p. 20.

67   Lewis, B., 2002, *What Went Wrong: Western Impact and Middle Eastern Responses*, London: Phoenix.

68   Marx, K., 1890, *Das Kapital*, Washington: Regnery Publishing Inc.

69   See Milner, H., 1997, *Interests, Institutions and Information: Domestic Politics and International Relations*, Princeton: Princeton University Press.

70   Farrands, C., Worth, O., 'Critical Theory in Global Political Economy: Critique? Knowledge? Emancipation', *Capital and Class*, 85, 2005, pp. 49–51.

71   Krasner, S. (ed), 1983, *International Regimes*, Cornell: Cornell University Press.

72   Underhill, G., 'State, Market and Global Political Economy: Genealogy of an (Inter-?) Discipline', *International Affairs*, 76(4), 2000, pp. 805–824.

73   Murphy, C., Tooze, R., *The New International Political Economy*, p. 22.

74   Lapid, Y., 'The Third Debate: On the Prospects of International Theory in a Post-Positivist Era', *International Studies Quarterly*, 33(3), 1989, p. 240.

75   Cairncross, F., 1975, *The Second Great Crash: How the Oil Crises Could Destroy the World's Economy*, London: Meuthen.

76   Rybczynski, T., 1976, *The Economics of the Oil Crisis*, London: Macmillan.

77   Gilpin, R., *The Political Economy of International Relations*, p. 25.

78   Murphy, C., Tooze, R., *The New International Political Economy*, p. 23.

79   Whitworth, S., 'Theory as Exclusion: Gender and International Political Economy', in Stubbs, R., Underhill, G., *Political Economy and the Changing Global Order*, pp. 116–120.

80   Stubbs, R., Underhill, G., 2000 *Political Economy and the Changing Global Order*, p. 6.

81   Rosamund, B., 'Babylon and On: Globalization and International Political Economy', *Review of International Political Economy*, 10(4), 2003, pp. 661–665.

82   Hay, C., Watson, M., 'Globalisation: Sceptical Notes on the 1999 Reith Lectures', *Political Quarterly*, 70(4), 1999, pp. 218–225.

83   Watson, M., 25 Feb.–1 March 2003, *Constructing and Contesting Orthodoxies: General Equilibrium Economics and the Political Discourse of Globalisation*, 44th Annual Convention of The International Studies Association, Portland, USA.

84   Taylor, I., 'Globalisation Studies and the Developing World: Making International Political Economy Truly Global', p. 1031.

85   Lovett *et al.*, 2005, *US Trade Policy: History, Theory and the WTO*, 2nd edition, New York: ME Sharpe.

86   Lawrence, R., 2006, *A US–Middle East Trade Agreement: A Circle of Opportunity*, Washington: Institute for International Economics.

87   Rosen, H., 'Free Trade Agreements as US Foreign Policy Tools: The US–Israel and US–Jordan FTAs', in Schott, J.J. (ed), 2003, *Free Trade Agreements: US Strategies and Priorities*, Washington: Institute for International Economics.

88   Malkawi, B., 2005, *Jordan and the World Trading System: A Case Study for Arab Countries*, Washington: American University, Washington College of Law.

89   Johnston, D., 'Constructing the Periphery in Modern Global Politics', in Murphy, C., Tooze, R. *The New International Political Economy*.

90   Vale, P., 'Engaging the World's Marginalised and Promoting Global Change: Challenges for the United Nations at Fifty', *The Harvard International Law Journal*, 36(2), 1995, pp. 96–100.

91   Hettne, B., 1995, *Development Theory and the Three Worlds: Towards an International Political Economy*, Harlow: Longman.

92   Dasgupta, B., 1998, *Structural Adjustment, Global Trade and the New Political Economy of Development*, London: Zed Books.

93   Frieden, J., Lake, D., 1995, *International Political Economy: Perspectives on Global Power and Wealth*, p. 1.

94   Note that the often lively debate regarding the relationship between IPE and IR is not engaged with at great length in this study. This is intentionally done so as not to distract the reader from the already

numerous and complex aims this piece of work is undertaking. However, this issue will be briefly addressed here. The majority of IPE scholars, works and degree programmes date back only to the 1960s and early 1970s, long after the emergence of IR as a discipline in 1919. This basic examination may lead the student of IPE to the conclusion that the discipline is a sub-field of IR as opposed to an independent discipline. However, accepting this view without attempting to assess the history of IPE further is misleading. Adam Smith, for example, was *doing* (I)PE in the 1770s, as was David Ricardo in the 1890s. It can be argued that studying IPE was simply *forgotten* until the late 1960s and early 1970s when events such as the oil crises and the end of the fixed exchange rate prompted the rediscovery of the discipline.

95   Murphy, C., Tooze, R. *The New International Political Economy*, p. 25.

96   Strange, G., 'Globalisation, Regionalism and Labour Interests in the New International Political Economy', *New Political Economy*, 7(3), 2002.

97   Watson, A., 'Seen But Not Heard: The Role of the Child in International Political Economy', *New Political Economy*, 9(1), 2004.

98   Haggard, S., Maxfield, S., 'The Political Economy of Financial Internationalization in the Developing World', *International Organization*, 50(1), 1996.

99   See Demir, O., Mustafa, A., Toprak, M., 'Anatolian Tigers or Islamic Capital: Prospects and Challenges', *Middle Eastern Studies*, 4(6), 2004.

100   Gills, B., 'Forum: Perspectives on New Political Economy: Re-orienting the New (International) Political Economy'.

101   See Michalet, C.A., 'From International Trade to World Economy', in Makler, H., Martinelli, A., Smelser, N., 1982, *The New International Economy*, London: Sage Ltd.

102   Destler, I.M., 2005, *American Trade Politics*, 4th edition, Washington: Institute for International Economics.

103   Ambrose, E., 1997, *Rise to Globalism: American Foreign Policy Since 1938*, 8th revised edition, London: Penguin Books.

104   Bergsten, F., 1988, *America in the World Economy: A Strategy for the 1990s*, Washington: Institute for International Economics.

105   Zinn, H., 2003, *A People's History of the United States*, 3rd edition, London: Pearson Ltd.

106   Todd, E., 2003, *After the Empire: The Breakdown of the American Order*, Birmingham: Constable.

107 Griswold, D.T., 'Trading Tyranny for Freedom: How Open Markets Till the Soil for Democracy', *Trade Policy Analysis*, 26, 6 Jan. 2004, p. 2.

108 Strange, S., 1991, 'An Eclectic Approach', in Murphy, C., Tooze, R. *The New International Political Economy*, pp. 33–49.

109 Homer-Dixon, T., 1999, *Environment, Scarcity, and Violence*, Princeton: Princeton University Press.

110 Talalay, M., Tooze, R., Farrands, C., 1997, *Technology, Culture and Competitiveness: Change and the World Political Economy*, London: Routledge.

111 Gills, B., 'Forum: Perspectives on New Political Economy: Re-orienting the New (International) Political Economy', p. 238.

112 Murphy, C., Tooze, R. *The New International Political Economy*, p. 28. Note '(orthodox)' added.

113 Tussie, D., 1994, 'Trading in Fear: US Hegemony and the Open World Economy in Perspective', in Murphy, C., Tooze, R., *The New International Political Economy*, pp. 79–97.

114 Worth, O., Kuhling, C., 'Counter-Hegemony, Anti-Globalisation and Culture in International Political Economy', *Capital and Class*, 84, 2004, pp. 31–42.

115 Amoore *et al.*, 2000, 'Paths to a Historicized International Political Economy', p. 55.

116 Murphy, C., Tooze, R. *The New International Political Economy*, p. 28.

117 Nelson, D., 1994, Trade Policy Games, in Murphy, C., Tooze, R., *The New International Political Economy*, p. 129.

118 This constitutes one of the central issues of the post-positivist philosophy of science.

119 Murphy, C., Tooze, R. *The New International Political Economy*, p. 29.

120 Gause, F.G., 1999, *Systemic Approaches to Middle East International Relations*, International Studies Association Annual Convention, published by Blackwells.

121 Halliday, F., *The Middle East in International Relations: Power, Politics and Ideology*.

122 Brown, L.C., 1992, *International Politics and the Middle East: Old Rules, Dangerous Game*, Princeton: Princeton University Press.

123 Said, E., 2005, *Power, Politics and Culture: Interviews with Edward Said*, London: Bloomsbury Publishing.

124 Ali, T., 2003, *Bush in Babylon: The Recolonisation of Iraq*, London: Verso.

125 Mansfield, P., 2003, *A History of the Middle East*, 2nd edition, London: Penguin.

126 Ibid.

127 Braudel, F., 1993, *A History of Civilisations*, London: Penguin Books, pp. 69–93.

128 Ohmae, K., 2005, *The Next Global Stage: The Challenges and Opportunities in Our Borderless World*, New Jersey: Pearson Education Inc.

129 Teti, A., Heristchi, C., 'The Middle East After the Politics of Certainty', *The Journal of Mediterranean Studies*, 14(1), 2004, pp. 1–15.

130 Ismael, T. (ed), 1990, *Middle East Studies International Perspectives on the State of the Art*, London: Greenwood Press, pp. 12–15.

131 Sadiki, L., 2004, *The Search for Arab Democracy*, London: C. Hurst & Co. Publishers Ltd.

132 Said, E., 1978, *Orientalism*, London: Clays Ltd St Ives plc.

133 Wittkopf, E., Kegley, C.W. Jr, Schott, J., 2005, *American Foreign Policy: Pattern and Process*, 7th edition, London: Wadsworth.

134 Rothgeb, J. Jr, 2001, *US Trade Policy: Balancing Economic Dreams and Political Realities*, Washington: CQ Press.

135 Hahn, P., 2005, *Crisis and Crossfire: The United States and the Middle East Since 1945*, Cambridge: Potomac Books Inc.

136 For the United States there have traditionally been three key foreign policy goals with regard to the MENA region. The first policy goal has been maintaining access to the region's markets. The second key goal has been securing accessible and reliable supplies of oil and gas. Finally, the United States has sought cooperation from the region's states – whether coerced or voluntary.

137 Little, D., *American Orientalism: The United States and the Middle East Since 1945*.

138 Laqueur, W., 2000, *The New Terrorism: Fanaticism and the Arms of Mass Destruction*, Oxford: Oxford University Press.

139 Oren, M., 2007, *Power, Faith and Fantasy: America in the Middle East: 1776 to the Present*, London: W. W. Norton and Co. Ltd.

140 Feinberg, R., 2003, *The Political Economy of United States' Free Trade Arrangements*, Washington: Peterson Institute for International Economics.

141 Hanahoe, T., 2003, *America Rules: US Foreign Policy, Globalization and Corporate USA*, Dingle, Co. Kerry: Brandod Ltd.

142 Simons, G., 2003, *Future Iraq: US Policy in Reshaping the Middle East*, London: Saqi Books.

143 Hall, P., Taylor, R., 'Political Science and the Three New Institutionalisms', *Political Studies*, 44(4), 1996, p. 937.

144 March, J., Olsen, J., 'The New Institutionalism: Organizational Factors in Political Life', *American Political Science Review*, 78, 1984, pp. 734–749.

145 Lowndes, V., 'Institutionalism', in Marsh, D., Stoker, G., *Theory and Methods in Political Science*, pp. 90–91.

146 Ibid, p. 90.

147 Martin, L.L., Simmons, B.A., 'Theories and Empirical Studies of International Institutions', *International Organization*, 52(4), 1998, p. 729.

148 Ibid, p. 731.

149 Ibid.

150 Goodrich, L.M., 'From League of Nations to United Nations', *International Organization*, 1(3), 1947; Fox, W., 'The United Nations in the Era of Total Diplomacy', *International Organization*, 5, 1951, pp. 265–273. For the optimistic view, see Bloomfield, L., 1960, *The United Nations and US Foreign Policy*, Boston: Little & Brown.

151 See Knorr, K., 'The Bretton Woods Institutions in Transition', *International Organization*, 2, 1948, pp. 19–38; and Kindleberger, C.P., 'Bretton Woods Reappraised', *International Organization*, 5, 1951, pp. 32–47.

152 Golfer, W., 'GATT After Six Years: An Appraisal', *International Organization*, 8, 1954, pp. 1–18.

153 Johnson, H.C., Niemeyer, G., 'Collective Security: The Validity of an Ideal', *International Organization*, 8, 1954, pp. 19–35.

154 Ibid, p. 27.

155 Niemeyer, G., 'The Balance Sheet of the League Experiment', *International Organization*, 6, 1952, p. 58.

156 Cohen, B.V., 'The Impact of the United Nations on United States Foreign Policy', *International Organization*, 5, 1951, pp. 274–281. For a parallel analysis of institutional effects on Soviet behaviour, see Rudzinski, A.W., 'The Influence of the United Nations on Soviet Policy' *International Organization*, 4, 1951, pp. 282–299.

157 Martin, L.L., Simmons, B.A., 'Theories and Empirical Studies of International Institutions', p. 731.

158 See Matecki, B.E., 'Establishment of the International Finance Corporation: A Case Study', *International Organization*, 10, 1956, pp. 261–275.

159 Keohane, R., 2002, *Power and Governance in a Partially Globalised World*, Suffolk: Bury St Edmunds Press, p. 28.

160 Goodin, R., Klingemann, H. (eds), 1996, *A New Handbook of Political Science*, Oxford: Oxford University Press.

161 Downs, A., 'Social Values and Democracy', in Monroe, K. (ed), 1991, *The Economic Approach to Democracy*, New York: Harper Collins.

162 Wallerstein, I., 1984, *The Politics of the World-Economy: The States, the Movements and the Civilizations*, Cambridge: Cambridge University Press.

163 Alker, H., Russett, B., 1965, *World Politics in the General Assembly*, New Haven: Yale University Press, p. 12.

164 Cox, R., Jacobson, H., 1973, *The Anatomy of Influence: Decision Making in International Organization*, New Haven: Yale University Press.

165 Ibid, p. 214.

166 Haas, E.B., 1958, *The Uniting of Europe: Political, Social, and Economic Forces, 1950–1957*, Stanford: Stanford University Press.

167 Ibid, p. 10.

168 Martin, L.L., Simmons, B.A., 'Theories and Empirical Studies of International Institutions', p. 736.

169 For a brief but authoritative summary of the events leading up to the oil embargo and its immediate impacts see Shlaim, A., 2000, *The Iron Wall: Israel and the Arab World*, London: St. Ives plc.

170 See Ruggie, J., 'Collective Goods and Future International Collaboration', *American Political Science Review*, 66, 1972, pp. 874–893.

171 For an example of this scepticism see Strange, S., 1988, *States and Markets: An Introduction to International Political Economy*.

172 Keohane, R., *Power and Governance in a Partially Globalised World*, p. 29.

173 See, for example, Hopkins, R., Puchala, D., 'Perspectives on the International Relations of Food', *International Organization*, 32(2), 1978, pp. 581–616.

174 Krasner, S., 'Theory of World Politics: Structural Realism and Beyond', in Finifter, A. (ed), 1983, *Political Science: The State of the Discipline*, Washington: American Political Science Association.

175 Ruggie, J., 'Collective Goods and Future International Collaboration'.

176 Grieco, J., 'Anarchy and the Limits of Cooperation: A Realist Critique of the Newest Liberal Institutionalism', *International Organization*, 42(2), 1988, pp. 485–507; and Mearsheimer, J., 'The False Promise of International Institutions', *International Security*, 19, 1994, p. 549.

177 See Keohane, R., 1984, *After Hegemony: Cooperation and Discord in the World Political Economy*, Surrey: Princeton University Press.

178 Martin, L.L., Simmons, B.A., 'Theories and Empirical Studies of International Institutions', p. 738.

179 Rhodes, R.A.W., 1997, *Understanding Governance*, Buckingham: Open University Press.

180 See Pierson, P., 'The Path to European Integration: A Historical Institutionalist Analysis', *Comparative Political Studies*, 29(2), 1996, pp. 122–163.

181 March, J., Olsen, J., 'The New Institutionalism: Organizational Factors in Political Life', p. 747.

182 Ibid, p. 738.

183 Jessop, B., 18–19 December 2000, *Institutional (Re)turns and the Strategic-Relational Approach*, paper presented at the Institutional Theory in Political Science Conference, Ross Priory, Loch Lomond.

184 Peters, G., 1999, *Institutional Theory in Political Science: The New Institutionalism*, London: Pinter.

185 Lowndes, V., 'Varieties of New Institutionalisms: A Critical Appraisal', *Public Administration*, 74(2), 1996, pp. 194–195.

186 Knight, J., 1992, *Institutions and Social Conflict*, Cambridge: Cambridge University Press, p. 17.

187 Weingast, A., 1996, 'Political Institutions: Rational Choice Perspectives', in Goodin, R., Klingemann, H. (eds), *A New Handbook of Political Science*, Oxford: Oxford University Press.

188 For an example of this type of research project see Rittberger, V., 1993, *Regime Theory and International Relations*, Oxford: Clarendon Press.

189 Cohn, T., 2003, *Global Political Economy: Theory and Practice*, 2nd edition, London: Addison Wesley Longman, p. 100.

190 Robert Keohane identifies three types of international institutions: IOs, international regimes and conventions. See Keohane, R., 'Neoliberal Institutionalism: A Perspective on World Politics', in Keohane, R., 1989, *International Institutions and State Power: Essays in International Relations Theory*, pp. 3–4.

191 Haas, E.B., 'Words Can Hurt You: or Who Said What to Whom About Regimes', in Krasner, S. (ed), 1983, *International Regimes*, Cornell: Cornell University Press, p. 27.

192 Keohane, R., 1984, *After Hegemony: Cooperation and Discord in the World Political Economy*, p. 44.

193 It is here held that cooperation between actors in the international system and in particular states is desirable. Liberals advocate international cooperation as the most desirable form of international interaction in order to establish and promote a 'free', prosperous and peaceful world order in which, as John Locke (1632–1704) stated, people's 'lives, liberties and estates' can be preserved. See Locke, J., 1964, *Two Treatises of Government*, Cambridge: Cambridge University Press, p. 368.

194 Keohane, R., 1984, *After Hegemony: Cooperation and Discord in the World Political Economy*, p. 49.

195 Ibid.

196 For an authoritative and informative assessment of how economic interdependence renders violent confrontation obsolete see Angell, N., 1911, *The Great Illusion: a Study of the Relation of Military Power to National Advantage*, London: Read Books.

197 Krugman, P., Obstfeld, M., 2000, *International Economics: Theory and Policy*, 5th edition, Reading, Harlow: Addison-Wesley, p. 3.

198 Griswold, D.T., 'Trading Tyranny for Freedom: How Open markets Till the Soil for Democracy', *Trade Policy Analysis*, 6 Jan. 2004, p. 2.

199 Ibid, p. 6.

200 Lindsey, B., 'The Trade Front: Combating Terrorism with Open Markets', *Trade Policy Analysis*, 5 Aug. 2003, p. 2.

201 Held, D., 1995, *Democracy and the Global Order: From the Modern State to Cosmopolitan Governance*, Cambridge: Polity Press.

202 March, J.G., Olsen, J.P., 1995, *Democratic Governance*, New York: Free Press.

203 Downs, A., 1957, *An Economic Theory of Democracy*, New York: Harper and Row.

204 Mill, J.S., 1991, *On Liberty and Other Essays*, Oxford: Oxford University Press.

205 Axelrod, R.M., 1984, *The Evolution of Cooperation*, New York: Basic Books.

Chapter 2

1 Mansfield, P., 1992, *The Arabs*, London: Clays Ltd., p. 418.

2 Sasley, B.E., 'Changes and Continuity in Jordanian Foreign Policy', *Middle East Review of International Affairs*, 6(1), March 2002, p. 37.

3 Ryan, C., 2002, *Jordan in Transition: From Hussein to Abdullah*, London: Lynne Rienner Publishers Inc, p. 110.

4 Feiler, G., 2000, *The Middle East in the New Millennium: Economic Development and Business Law*, The Hague: Kluwer Law International, pp. 117–124.

5 Dew, P., Wallace, J., Shoult, A., 2004, *Doing Business with Jordan*, London: GMB Publishing Ltd, p. 15.

6 Hamarneh, M., 1994, *The Jordanian Economy: Problems and Prospects*, Amman: Centre for Strategic Studies.

7 Maciejewski, E., Mansur, A., *Jordan: Strategy for Adjustment and Growth*, IMF Occasional Paper No. 136, 20 May 1996.

8 For an overview of political liberalisation in 1989, see Brand, L.A., 'Liberalization and Changing Political Coalitions: The Bases of

Jordan's 1990–1991 Gulf Conflict Policy', *Jerusalem Journal of International Relations*, 13(4), 1991.

9   Milton-Edwards, B., Hinchcliffe, P., 2001, *Jordan: A Hashemite Legacy*, London: Sage.

10 Swaidan, Z., Nica, M., 'The 1991 Gulf War and Jordan's Economy', *Middle East Review of International Affairs*, 6(2), June 2002, p. 3.

11 Halliday, F., 'The Gulf War and its Aftermath: First Reflections', *International Affairs*, 67(2), April 1991, p. 233.

12 Wilson, R., 'The Regional Economic Impact of the Gulf War', *Middle Eastern Studies*, 1991, p. 185.

13 Swaidan, Z., Nica, M., 'The 1991 Gulf War and Jordan's Economy', p. 5.

14 Ibid.

15 Singh, R., 2002, 'Liberalisation or Democratisation: The Limits of Political Reform and Civil Society in Jordan', in Joffé, G., *Jordan in Transition 1990–2000*, pp. 66–90.

16 Brand, A., 'The Effects of the Peace Process on Political Liberalisation in Jordan', *Journal of Palestine Studies*, 28(2), Winter 1999.

17 Singh, R., 'Liberalisation or Democratisation: The Limits of Political Reform and Civil Society in Jordan'.

18 Anon, 8 October 2003, *The Challenge of Political Reform: Jordanian Democratisation and Regional Instability*, Amman/Brussels: International Crisis Group, p. 5.

19 Robins, P., 2004, *A History of Jordan*, Cambridge: Cambridge University Press, p. 193.

20 Saikal, A., Schnable, A., 2003, *Democratization in the Middle East: Experiences, Struggles and Challenges*, New York: United Nations Press, p. 130.

21 Ryan, C., 2005, 'Reform Retreats Amid Jordan's Political Storms', *The Middle East Report*, 10 June 2005.

22 Anon, ICG Report, 8 October 2003.

23 Robins, P., *A History of Jordan*.

24 Ibid.

25 This law required organisers of public events to not only inform the government prior to the event but also to acquire a permit three days in advance and assume liability for any damage to property.

26 Seen as extremely harsh, this law denies those convicted of misdemeanours the ability to appeal.

27 While it had been the case that all municipal council members (outside of the Greater Amman Municipality) had been elected for four-year terms, this law bestowed on the government the right to

appear the Head and approximately half of the members of all municipal councils.

28   Marto, M., ICG Interview, Amman, 13 May 2003.

29   Bouillon, M., 'Walking the Tightrope: Jordanian Foreign Policy from the Gulf Crisis to the Peace Process and Beyond', in Joffé, G., *Jordan in Transition 1990–2000*, pp. 1–23.

30   Anon, ICG, 8 October 2003, p. 5.

31   Ibid.

32   Al-Fayez, F., ICG Interview, Amman, 13 May 2003.

33   For a full introduction to this campaign aimed at strengthening national identity, civil society and democratisation see the Jordan First project section on the Hashemite Kingdom of Jordan, Foreign Ministry website: http://www.mfa.gov.jo/pages.php?menu_id=437

34   Robins, P., *A History of Jordan*.

35   Burns, J.F., 'Jordan's King, in Gamble, Lends Hand to the US', *The New York Times*, 9 March 2003.

36   George, A., 2005, *Jordan: Living in the Crossfire*, London: Zed Books Ltd, p. 53.

37   Ryan, C., 'Reform Retreats Amid Jordan's Political Storms'.

38   Anon, ICG, 8 October 2003, p. 9.

39   George, A., *Jordan: Living in the Crossfire*.

40   Anon, ICG, 8 October 2003, p. 9.

41   Muasher, M., ICG Interview, Amman, 16 June 2003.

42   Ibid.

43   Ibid.

44   George, A., *Jordan: Living in the Crossfire*.

45   Obeidat, A., ICG Interview, Amman, 16 June 2003.

46   Shaban, R.A., Abu-Ghaida, D., Al-Naimat, A.S., 2001, *Poverty Alleviation in Jordan in the 1990s: Lessons for the Future*, Washington: World Bank, p. 4.

47   World Bank 1995, *Country Report – Jordan*, Washington: World Bank.

48   Silva-Jauregui, C. (ed), 2002, *Jordan Development Policy Review: A Reforming State in a Volatile Region*, Washington: World Bank, p. 5.

49   Hourani, A., Khoury, P., Wilson, C., (eds) 2004, *The Modern Middle East*, 2nd edition, London, I.B.Tauris, p. 52.

50   For reasons and details see Kanovsky, E., 'Jordan's Economy: From Prosperity to Crisis', in Ayalon, A., Shaked, H. (eds), 1990, *Middle East Contemporary Survey Volume XII*, Boulder: Westview Press, pp. 333–369.

51 Lucas, R., 2005, *Institutions and the Politics of Survival in Jordan: Domestic Responses to External Challenges*, New York: State University of New York Press, p. 96.

52 World Bank, 1996, *Structural Adjustment in Jordan*, Washington: World Bank.

53 Ibid.

54 Silva-Jauregui, C. *Jordan Development Policy Review: A Reforming State in a Volatile Region*, p. 9.

55 Ibid.

56 Abu-Hammour, M., 2005, *Jordan's Economic Reforms*.

57 World Bank, *Structural Adjustment in Jordan*.

58 Ibid.

59 Moore, P., 2004, *Doing Business in the Middle East: Politics and Economic Crisis in Jordan and Kuwait*, Cambridge: Cambridge University Press, p. 150.

60 CBJ, 1994, *Fiscal Year Report 1994*, Amman: Central Bank of Jordan.

61 Kanovsky, E., 'Jordan's Economy: From Prosperity to Crisis'.

62 World Bank, *Structural Adjustment in Jordan*.

63 Shaban, R.A., Abu-Ghaida, D., Al-Naimat, A.S., *Poverty Alleviation in Jordan in the 1990s: Lessons for the Future*.

64 Al-Khassib, S., Head of the Research and International Agreements Unit, Amman Chamber of Commerce, interview held in Amman, 24 December 2006.

65 World Bank, *Structural Adjustment in Jordan*.

66 Shaban, R.A., Abu-Ghaida, D., Al-Naimat, A.S., *Poverty Alleviation in Jordan in the 1990s: Lessons for the Future*.

67 World Bank, *Structural Adjustment in Jordan*.

68 Joffé, G., *Jordan in Transition 1990–2000*.

69 Anon, 'Foreign Grants up by End of April', *Jordan Times*, 27 June 2008.

70 Jordan Investment Trust, 2005, *Jordan: Growth Despite Difficulties*, Amman: Jordan Investment Trust, p. 14.

71 Robins, P., *A History of Jordan*.

72 El-Said, H., 'Waiting for Privatisation in the Arab World: The Case of Jordan', in El-Said, H., Becker, K., 2001, *Management and International Business Issues in* Jordan, Binghamton: International Business Press, p. 145.

73 Ibid.

74 Abu-Hammour, M., 2006, *Letter from the Chairman*, The Executive Privatization Committee, Amman, Jordan.

75   Al-Khouri, R., Pasch, P., 2002, *Privatisation in Jordan*, Amman: Friedrich Ebert Stiftfung Consultancy.

76   Zu'bi, T., Chief Communications Officer of the Executive Privatisation Committee, interview held in Amman, 21 December 2006.

77   Kandah, A.S., 2004, *Uses of Privatisation Proceeds*, Amman: Centre for Strategic Studies, p. 11.

78   Zu'bi, T., 21 December 2006.

79   Kandah, A.S., *Uses of Privatisation Proceeds*, p. 11.

80   EPC, 2006, *Types of Privatization*, Amman: The Executive Privatisation Committee.

81   World Bank, *World Bank Press Report*, 2006, Washington: World Bank.

82   EPC, 2001, *Privatisation Newsletter*, Amman: The Executive Privatisation Committee.

83   EPC, 2009, *Report on Completed Transactions*, Amman: The Executive Privatisation Committee.

84   Zu'bi, T., 21 December 2006.

85   Page, J., 2002, *Structural Reforms in the Middle East and North Africa*, Washington: World Bank, p. 72.

86   *The Privatization Law 25/2000*, Amman: The Executive Privatization Committee.

87   EPC, *Report on Privatisation Proceeds*, 2006, Amman: The Executive Privatization Committee.

88   Ibid.

89   Ministry of Finance, *Government Finance Bulletin*, Amman: Ministry of Finance, Vol. 3, No. 12, Jan. 2002.

90   Zu'bi, T., 21 December 2006.

91   Anon, 'Jordan's Privatisation Programme is one of the Most Successful in the Region: World Bank', *Jordan Times*, Economy Section, 4 March 2002.

92   EPC, 2000, *Report from the Executive Privatisation Committee*, Amman: Executive Privatisation Committee.

93   Ibid.

94   Kandah, A.S., *Uses of Privatisation Proceeds*, p. 12.

95   Feraboli, O., 2003, *A Dynamic Analysis of Jordan's Trade Liberalisation*, Hamburg: Universität Hamburg - Institut für Wachstum und Konjunktur.

96   Zarouk, J., 'The Greater Arab Free Trade Area', in Hoekman, B., Zarrouk, J., 2003, *Catching Up With the Competition: Trade Opportunities and Challenges for Arab Countries*, Ann Arbor: The University of Michigan Press.

97   Dennis, A., February 2006, *The Impact of Regional Trade Agreements and Trade Facilitation in the Middle East and North Africa Region*, Washington: World Bank, p. 4.

98   Carkoglu, A., Eder, M., Kirisci, K., 1998, *The Political Economy of Regional Cooperation in the Middle East*, London: Clays Ltd, p. 16.

99   Hosoe, N., 'A General Equilibrium Analysis of Jordan's Trade Liberalization', *Journal of Policy Modelling*, 23(6), Aug. 2001.

100 Winters, A.L., April 1996, *Regionalism Versus Multilateralism*, paper presented at the CEPR Conference on Regional Integration, La Coruna, Spain.

101 Sachs, J., Warner, A., 1995, *Economic Reform and the Process of Global Integration, Brookings Papers on Economic Activity*, Washington: The Brookings Institute, p. 1.

102 Vamvakidis, A., 1998, *Regional Trade Agreements Versus Broad Liberalisation: Which Path Leads to Faster Growth? Time-Series Evidence*, Washington: IMF Working Paper 40.

103 Al-Khouri, R., 'Trade Policies in Jordan', in Hoekman, B., Kheir-El-Din, H. (eds), 2000, *Trade Policy Developments in the Middle East and North Africa*, Washington: The World Bank, p. 149.

104 WTO, *Report of the Working Party on the Accession of Jordan*, World Trade Organisation, 3 Dec. 1999, p. 1.

105 Ibid, p. 39.

106 Ibid, p. 46.

107 Anon, 2003, *Annual Report*, Amman: The European Commission in Jordan, p. 19.

108 Patten, C., 2006, *The EU–Jordan Association Agreement: Opportunities and Challenges*, Amman: The European Commission in Jordan.

109 EC, *Summary of the Provisions of the Jordan–EU Association Agreement*, The European Commission in Jordan.

110 Ibid.

111 Dessus, S., Devlin, J., Safadi, R. (eds), 2001, *Towards Arab and Euro-Med Regional Integration*, Paris: OECD.

112 Devlin, J., Page, J., 'Testing the Waters: Arab Integration, Competitiveness and the Euro-Med Agreements', in Dessus, S., Devlin, J., Safadi, R. (eds), *Towards Arab and Euro-Med Regional Integration*.

113 Patten, C., *The EU–Jordan Association Agreement: Opportunities and Challenges*.

114 Haddad, M., 2001, *Export Competitiveness: Where Does the Middle East and North Africa Region Stand?* Cairo: Economic Research Forum.

115   Konan, D., 'Alternative Paths to Prosperity: Economic Integration Among Arab Countries', in Galal, A., Hoekman, B. (eds), 2003, *Arab Economic Integration*, Washington: The Brookings Institute.

116   Signed by the following Arab states: Jordan, Bahrain, UAE, Tunisia, Saudi Arabia, Syria, Iraq, Oman, Qatar, Kuwait, Lebanon, Libya, Egypt, Morocco, Tunisia, Algeria, Mauritania.

117   Zarouk, J., 'The Greater Arab Free Trade Area'.

118   League of Arab States, 1997, *Executive Programme of the Agreement on Facilitating Trade and Developing Intra-Arab Trade for Establishing the Greater Arab Free Trade Area (GAFTA)*, Secretariat of the Arab League, Directorate of Economic Affairs, Cairo, Egypt.

119   Hoekman, B., Zarrouk, J., 2003, *Catching Up With the Competition: Trade Opportunities and Challenges for Arab Countries*, Ann Arbor: The University of Michigan Press, p. 290.

120   Anon, 2007, Foreign Trade Statistics of Jordan 1993–2006, Cairo: Arab Monetary Fund.

121   Al-Atrash, H., Yousef, T., 2000, *Intra-Arab Trade: is it too Little*, Washington: IMF.

122   Peridy, N., 'Toward a Pan-Arab Free Trade Area: Assessing Trade Potential Effects of the Aghadir Agreement', *Developing Economies*, 43(3), Sept. 2005, pp. 329–345.

123   Arab Monetary Fund Statistics Division, 2009.

124   Hamoudeh, M., 2005, *The Aghadir Process*, Amman: Ministry of Industry and Trade.

125   Dennis, A., *The Impact of Regional Trade Agreements and Trade Facilitation in the Middle East and North Africa Region*, p. 4.

126   Konan, D., 'Alternative Paths to Prosperity: Economic Integration Among Arab Countries'.

127   Hoekman, B., Zarrouk, J., 2003, *Catching Up With the Competition: Trade Opportunities and Challenges for Arab Countries*, p. 286.

128   Al-Shamali, Y., Deputy Director of the Foreign Trade Policy Department of the Ministry of Industry and Trade, interview held in Amman, 24 December 2006.

129   Ibid.

130   For a breakdown of US economic and military aid to Jordan see the Embassy of the Hashemite Kingdom of Jordan, Washington: DC. http://www.jordanembassyus.org/new/aboutjordan/uj1.shtml

131   Ibid.

132   US–Jordan Free Trade Agreement, *Schedule of Specific Commitments*.

133   Leverett, F., 2005, *The Road Ahead: Middle East Policy in the Bush Administration's Second Term*, Washington: The Brookings Institute, p. 5.

134 Rosen, H., 'Free Trade Agreements as Foreign Policy Tools: The US–Israel and US–Jordan FTAs', in Schott, J.J. *Free Trade Agreements: US Strategies and Priorities*, pp. 51–53.

135 USTR, 2005, *The US–Jordan FTA Fact Sheet*, Washington: Office of the United States Trade Representative.

136 Jardaneh, D., 2003, *US–Jordan Free Trade Agreement: Reaching the Finish Line*, Amman: Atlas Investment Group.

137 Ibid.

138 Ministry of Industry and Trade, *Implementation of the JUSFTA: Review 2006*, Amman: Ministry of Industry and Trade.

139 US Census Bureau Foreign Trade Statistics, 2007.

140 Ibid.

141 Jardaneh, D., *US–Jordan Free Trade Agreement: Reaching the Finish Line*.

142 Ibid.

143 Ibid.

144 Ibid.

Chapter 3

1 Little, D., 2002, *American Orientalism: The United States and the Middle East Since 1945*, London: I.B.Tauris & Co. Ltd.

2 Oren, M., 2007, *Power, Faith and Fantasy: America in the Middle East: 1776 to the Present*, London: W. W. Norton & Co. Ltd.

3 Khalidi, R., 2004, *Resurrecting Empire: Western Footprints and America's Perilous Path in the Middle East*, London: I.B.Tauris & Co. Ltd.

4 Ambrose, S., Brinkley, D., 1997, *Rise to Globalism: American Foreign Policy Since 1938*, 8th edition, London: Penguin Books, pp. 254–281.

5 Madfai, M.R., 1993, *Jordan, The United States and the Middle East Peace Process 1974–1991*, Cambridge: Cambridge University Press.

6 Ibid.

7 Little, D., *American Orientalism: The United States and the Middle East Since 1945*.

8 See Allison, R.J., 2000, *The Crescent Obscured: The United States and the Muslim World, 1776–1815*, Chicago: University of Chicago Press.

9 Ibid.

10 Mansfield, P., 1992, *The Arabs*, Clays Ltd, St Ives plc, pp. 113–114.

11 Thus the origin of the opening line of the Marine Hymn: 'From the halls of Montezuma to the shores of Tripoli'.

12 Allison, R.J., *The Crescent Obscured: The United States and the Muslim World, 1776–1815*.

13   Oren, M., *Power, Faith and Fantasy: America in the Middle East: 1776 to the Present*, pp. 297–300.

14   See Lewis, B., 2002, *What Went Wrong: Western Impact and Middle Eastern Responses*, London: Phoenix.

15   Deudney, D., Meiser, J., 'American Exceptionalism', in Cox, M., Stokes, D., 2008, *US Foreign Policy*, Oxford: Oxford University Press, p. 36.

16   Adams, Q., 1821, *Seeking Monsters to Destroy*, s.i.: s.n.

17   Hook, S., Spanier, J., 2007, *American Foreign Policy Since World War Two*, Washington: CQ Press, pp. 80–99.

18   Nye, J. Jr, 2004, *Soft Power: The Means to Success in World Politics*, New York: Perseus Books Group.

19   Hall, H.P., 'Editorial', *Middle East Journal*, 1(1), Jan. 1947, pp. 1–2.

20   Oren, M., *Power, Faith and Fantasy: America in the Middle East: 1776 to the Present*.

21   Easton, S.C., 1968, *World History Since 1945*, Unknown Publisher.

22   Kuniholm, B., 1994, *The Origins of the Cold War in the Near East: Great Power Conflict and Diplomacy in Iran, Turkey and Greece*, Princeton: Princeton University Press.

23   Kennan, G., 'Containment Then and Now', *Foreign Affairs*, 65, 1986, pp. 886–890.

24   Ambrose, S., Brinkley, D., *Rise to Globalism: American Foreign Policy Since 1938*, p. 106.

25   Flemming, D.F., 1961, *The Cold War and Its Origins: 1917–1960*, New York: Doubleday Publishers.

26   Gaddis, J.L., 1998, *We Now Know: Rethinking Cold War History*, Oxford: Oxford University Press.

27   Kennan, G., 'Containment Then and Now', p. 888.

28   Ibid.

29   Flemming, D.F., *The Cold War and Its Origins: 1917–1960*.

30   Ambrose, S., Brinkley, D., *Rise to Globalism: American Foreign Policy Since 1938*, pp. 254–255.

31   Yergin, D., 1991, *The Epic Quest for Oil: Money and Power*, London: Simon and Schuster.

32   Shlaim, A., 2000, *The Iron Wall: Israel and the Arab World*, London: Penguin Books, p. 127.

33   Dinerstein, H.S., 1968, *Fifty Years of Soviet Foreign Policy*, Washington: Johns Hopkins University.

34   Shlaim, A., 2000, *The Iron Wall: Israel and the Arab World*, p. 153.

35   Ambrose, S., Brinkley, D., *Rise to Globalism: American Foreign Policy Since 1938*, pp. 153–154.

36   Mansfield, P., *The Arabs*, p. 262.
37   Little, D., *American Orientalism: The United States and the Middle East Since 1945*, pp. 168–171.
38   Ambrose, S., Brinkley, D., *Rise to Globalism: American Foreign Policy Since 1938*, p. 158.
39   Walker, M., 1995, *The Cold War: A History*, Birmingham: Holt Paperbacks.
40   Parmet, H., 1972, *Eisenhower and the American Crusades*, New Jersey: Transaction Publishers.
41   Eisenhower, D.D., *Special Message to the Congress on the Situation in the Middle East*, 5 Jan. 1957, pp. 6–16.
42   Nathan, J., Oliver, J., 1978, *United States Foreign Policy and World Order*, London: Longman.
43   LaFeber, W., 2006, *America, Russia and The Cold War*, 7th edition, Sydney: McGraw Hill.
44   Dinerstein, H.S., *Fifty Years of Soviet Foreign Policy*.
45   Ambrose, S., Brinkley, D., *Rise to Globalism: American Foreign Policy Since 1938*, p. 159.
46   Sprague, R. *et al.*, *Deterrence and Survival in the Nuclear Age*, 7 November 1957, Washington: Security Resources Panel of the Science Advisory Committee, Executive Office of the President.
47   Ambrose, S., 2007, *Eisenhower: The President*, Washington: American Political Biography Press.
48   Brzezinski, Z., 1985, *Power and Principle: Memoirs of the National Security Advisor, 1977–1981*, New York: Farrar, Strauss and Giroux.
49   Smith, G., 1986, *Morality and Reason: American Diplomacy in the Carter Years*, New York: Farrar, Strauss and Giroux.
50   Quandt, W.B., 1986, *Camp David: Peacemaking and Politics*, Washington: The Brookings Institute.
51   Carter, J., 1983, *Keeping Faith: Memoirs of a President*, Fayetteville: University of Arkansas Press.
52   Brzezisnki, Z., *Power and Principle: Memoirs of the National Security Advisor*.
53   Shlaim, A., *The Iron Wall: Israel and the Arab World*.
54   Quandt, W.B., *Camp David: Peacemaking and Politics*.
55   Dayan, M., 1981, *Breakthrough: A Personal Account of the Egypt–Israel Peace Negotiations*, London: Weidenfeld and Nicholson.
56   Kipper, J., Saunders, H., (eds), 1991, *The Middle East in Global Perspective*, Oxford; Boulder: Westview.
57   Kedourie, E., 1992, *Politics in the Middle East*, Oxford: Oxford University Press.

58   Ambrose, S., Brinkley, D., *Rise to Globalism: American Foreign Policy Since 1938*, p. 293.

59   Stempel, J., 1981, *Inside the Iranian Revolution*, Indianapolis: Indiana University Press.

60   Ambrose, S., Brinkley, D., *Rise to Globalism: American Foreign Policy Since 1938*, p. 382.

61   Bresheeth, H., Yuval-Vais, N. (eds), 1991, *The Gulf War and the New World Order*, London: Zed Books.

62   Ibid.

63   Parsons, A., 1995, *From Cold War to Hot Peace: UN Interventions, 1947–1995*, London: Penguin Books.

64   Michaels, J. E., 1997, *The President's Call: Executive Leadership From FDR to George Bush*, Pittsburgh: University of Pittsburgh Press.

65   Almond, M., 1994, *Europe's Backyard War: the War in the Balkans*, 2nd edition, London: Mandarin Press.

66   Bromley, S., 1998, 'Oil and the Middle East: The End of US Hegemony', *Middle East Report* 208, pp. 1–22.

67   Ambrose, S., Brinkley, D., *Rise to Globalism: American Foreign Policy Since 1938*, p. 398.

68   Dumbrell, J., 1997, *American Foreign Policy: Carter to Clinton*, Basingstoke: MacMillan Press.

69   Renshon, S.A., 1995, *The Clinton Presidency: Campaigning, Governing, and the Psychology of Leadership*, Oxford: Westview.

70   Ambrose, S., Brinkley, D., *Rise to Globalism: American Foreign Policy Since 1938*, p. 398.

71   Berman, W.C., 2001, *From the Centre to the Edge: the Politics and Policies of the Clinton Presidency*, Lanham: Rowman and Littlefield Publishers.

72   Ambrose, S., Brinkley, D., *Rise to Globalism: American Foreign Policy Since 1938*, p. 406.

73   Berman, W.C., *From the Centre to the Edge: the Politics and Policies of the Clinton Presidency*.

74   Roper, J., 2000, *The American Presidents: Heroic Leadership from Kennedy to Clinton*, Edinburgh: Edinburgh University Press.

75   Ibid.

76   The full document is available online at the following URL: http://www.fas.org/spp/military/docops/national/1996stra.htm

77   Ibid.

78   Usher, G., 1995, *Palestine in Crisis: the Struggle for Peace and Political Independence After Oslo*, London: Pluto Press.

79   Brinkley, D., 'Democratic Enlargement: The Clinton Doctrine', *Foreign Policy*, Spring 1997.

80 See Woodward, B., 2003, *Bush at War*, London: Pocket Books.
81 Ibid.
82 *The Economist*, 9 June 2001.
83 Ward, A., 'US Policy to the Middle East: Utopianism and Realism', *IISS Strategic Comments*, 1(1), Jan. 2003, p. 2.
84 Rice, C., 'Promoting the National Interest', *Foreign Affairs*, 79(1), Jan.– Feb. 2000, pp. 48–62.
85 Stein, K., 'The Bush Doctrine and Selective Engagement in the Middle East', *Middle East Review of International Affairs*, 6(2), June 2002.
86 Ibid, p. 4.
87 Ward, A., 'US Policy to the Middle East: Utopianism and Realism', p. 2.
88 Yaqub, S., 'US Assessments of Arab Threats Since 1945', *Middle East Policy*, 9(4), Dec. 2002.
89 Ibid, p. 97.
90 Rothgeb, J.M. Jr, 2001, *US Trade Policy: Balancing Economic Dreams With Political Realities*, Washington: CQ Press, p. ix.
91 Ibid, p. x.
92 Destler, I., 2005, *American Trade Politics*, 4th edition, Washington: Institute for International Economics, p. 178.
93 Cohen, S., Paul, J., Blecker, R., 1996, *Fundamentals of US Foreign trade Policy*, Boulder: Westview Press, p. 56.
94 Kress, C., Regional Director for the Middle East and North Africa, US Trade and Development Agency, interview held in Washington, DC on 24 March 2008.
95 Bergsten, F., 2005, *The United States and the World Economy: Foreign Economic Policy for the Next Decade*, Washington: Institute for International Economics.
96 Malloy, M., 2001, *United States Economic Sanctions: Theory and Practice*, London: Kluwer Law International.
97 Schott, J., Senior Fellow at the Peterson Institute for International Economics, interview held in Washington, DC on 23 March 2008.
98 Lovett *et al.*, 2005, *US Trade Policy: History, Theory and the WTO*, p. 84.
99 Volcker, P., Gyothen, T., 1992, *Changing Fortunes: The World's Money and the Threat to American Leadership*, New York: Times Books, p. 189.
100 Hufbauer, C., Goodrich, B., 'Lessons From NAFTA', in Schott, J. (ed), Free Trade Agreements: US Strategies and Priorities, Washington: Institute for International Economics.
101 Schott, J., 23 March 2008.

102   USTR, 2008, *Bilateral FTAs*, Washington: Office of the United States Trade Representative.

103   USTR a, 2006, *The US–SACU FTA*, Washington: Office of the United States Trade Representative.

104   USTR b, 2006, *The US–Andean Community Agreement*, Washington: Office of the United States Trade Representative.

105   Schott, J., 23 March 2008.

106   Yergin, D., *The Epic Quest for Oil: Money and Power*.

107   Lawrence, R., *A US–Middle East Trade Agreement: A Circle of Opportunity*.

108   USTR, 2007, *The US–Middle East Free Trade Area Initiative*, Washington: Office of the United States Trade Representative.

109   Gresser, E., *Draining the Swamp. A Middle East Trade Policy to Win the Peace*, Washington: Progressive Policy Institute, January 2002, p. 1.

110   Richards, A., 'Long Term Sources of Instability in the Middle East', in Russell, J., (ed), 2006, *Critical Issues Facing the Middle East: Security, Politics and Economics*, Basingstoke: Palgrave Macmillan, pp. 13–37.

111   Lewis, B., 2004, *From Babel to Dragomans: Interpreting the Middle East*, London: Orion Books Ltd.

112   Gresser, E., *Draining the Swamp. A Middle East Trade Policy to Win the Peace*, p. 3.

113   Lindsey, B., 'The Trade Front: Combating Terrorism With Open Markets', *Trade Policy Analysis*, 24, 5 Aug. 2003.

114   Griswold, D.T., 'Trading Tyranny for Freedom: How Open Markets Till the Soil for Democracy', *Trade Policy Analysis*, 26, 6 Jan. 2004.

115   Lindsey, B., 'The Trade Front: Combating Terrorism With Open Markets', p. 5.

116   Ibid.

117   Gresser, E., *Draining the Swamp. A Middle East Trade Policy to Win the Peace*, p. 3.

118   Yeats, A., Ng, F., 'Beyond the Year 2000: Implications of the Middle East's Recent Trade Performance', in Hoekman, B., Zarrouk, J., *Catching Up With the Competition: Trade Opportunities and Challenges for Arab Countries*.

119   Bush, G.W., *Freedom in Iraq and the Middle East*, remarks at the 20th Anniversary of the National Endowment for Democracy at the US Chamber of Commerce, 6 Nov. 2003.

120   Ibid.

Chapter 4

1   Kardoosh, M., 2006, *The Institutional Dimension of the Success of Jordanian QIZs*, Amman: Jordan Centre for Public Policy Research and Dialogue.

2   Kanovsky, E., 'The Middle East Economies: The Impact of Domestic and International Politics', *The Middle East Review of International Affairs*, 1(2), 7 July 1997.

3   Schott, J.J., 2005, *Assessing US FTA Policy*, Washington: Institute for International Economics.

4   Al-Shamali, Y., 2004, Deputy Director of The Department of Foreign Trade Policy, Ministry of Industry and Trade, interview held in Amman, Jordan on 26 December 2006.

5   Ibid.

6   Pigato, M. *et al.*, 2006, *Morocco, Tunisia, Egypt and Jordan After the End of the Multi-Fibre Agreement: Impact, Challenges and Prospects*, Washington: World Bank, p. 1.

7   Ibid.

8   Wilson, R., 1995, *Economic Development in The Middle East*, Oxon: Routledge, p. 42.

9   Ibid, p. 15.

10   Al-Shamali, Y., Amman, 26 December 2006.

11   Pigato, M. *et al.*, 2006, *Morocco, Tunisia, Egypt and Jordan After the End of the Multi-Fibre Agreement: Impact, Challenges and Prospects*, p. 1.

12   World Bank, 2006, *Jordan Quarterly Update: Third Quarter 2006*, Washington: World Bank, p. 10.

13   United Nations Comtrade Data, 2009.

14   Ibid.

15   Eurostat Data, 2006.

16   Ibid.

17   Ibid.

18   Abu-Rahmeh, H.F., CEO of The Jordan Exporters Association, interview held in Amman, Jordan on 27 December 2006.

19   The European Commission, 2006, *Jordan: National Indicative Programme 2005–2006*, Brussels: The European Commission.

20   Abu-Rahmeh, H.F., Amman, 27 December 2006.

21   The United States Census Bureau, Foreign Trade Statistics Division, 2007.

22   Ibid.

23   Ibid.

24   Pigato, M. *et al.*, *Morocco, Tunisia, Egypt and Jordan After the End of the Multi-Fibre Agreement: Impact, Challenges and Prospects*. Note: South Asia 4 are: Bangladesh, India, Pakistan and Sri Lanka, CAFTA-DR: Costa

Rica, Salvador, Guatemala, Honduras and Nicaragua, plus the Dominican Republic and Caribbean Basin Initiative (CBI) countries, Greater China: China, Hong Kong and Macao.

25   Abu-Rahmeh, H.F., Amman, 27 December 2006.

26   Volpe, A., Weil, D., 2004, *The Apparel and Textile Industries After 2005: Prospects and Choices*, Cambridge, MA: Harvard Centre for Textile and Apparel Research.

27   Gibson, D., 'Playing Second Fiddle in China', *WA Business News*, 13 October 2005.

28   Lovett *et al.*, *US Trade Policy: History, Theory and the WTO*.

29   Pigato, M. *et al.*, *Morocco, Tunisia, Egypt and Jordan After the End of the Multi-Fibre Agreement: Impact, Challenges and Prospects*, p. 15.

30   Article 7, *Treaty of Peace Between Israel and Jordan*, 1994.

31   Kardoosh, M., 2006.

32   Ibid.

33   Al-Shamali, Y., Amman, 26 December 2006.

34   Atmeh, M., Deputy CEO of the Jordan Industrial Estates Corporation, interview held in Amman, Jordan on 28 December 2006.

35   Ibid.

36   Ibid.

37   Cassing, J., Salameh, A.M., 2006, *Jordan–United States Free Trade Agreement Economic Impact Study: Searching for Effects of the FTA on Exports, Imports and Trade Related Investments*, Amman: USAID Jordan.

38   Atmeh, M., Amman, 28 December 2006.

39   Ibid.

40   Knowles, W., 2005, *Jordan: A Study in Political Economy*.

41   These include the Jordan Industrial Estates Corporation and the Jordan Free Zones Corporation.

42   Such as: the Jordan Investment Board and Jordan Enterprise Development Corporation.

43   JIB, 2006, *Invest in Jordan: The Textiles and Garments Sector*, JIB Report, p. 3.

44   Ali, M., Director of The Foreign Trade Policy Department of The Ministry of Industry and Trade, interview held in Amman, Jordan, 24 December 2006.

45   Atmeh, M., Amman, 28 December 2006.

46   Pigato, M. *et al.*, *Morocco, Tunisia, Egypt and Jordan After the End of the Multi-Fibre Agreement: Impact, Challenges and Prospects*, p. 15.

47   Knowles, W., 2005, *Jordan: A Study in Political Economy*.

48   Abu-Hammour, M., 2005, *Jordan's Economic Reforms*.

49 Silva-Jauregui, C. (ed), 2002, *Jordan Development Policy Review: A Reforming State in a Volatile Region*, Washington: World Bank.
50 Al-Khassib, S., Director of Research at The Amman Chamber of Commerce, interview held in Amman, Jordan on 24 December 2006.
51 Ibid.
52 Ibid.
53 Al-Badri, K., Managing Director of JEDCO, interview held in Amman, Jordan on 19 December 2006.
54 Ibid.
55 Al-Badri, K., Managing Director of JEDCO, interview held in Amman, Jordan on 24 December 2006.
56 Ibid.
57 Al-Badri, K., 24 December 2006.
58 Ibid.
59 Al-Badri, K., 19 December 2006.
60 These are: Ma'an Industrial Estate, Al-Hussein Industrial Estate, Al-Hassan Industrial Estate, Abdullah II Industrial Estate and Amman Industrial Estate.
61 These are to be located in Muagar, Zarqa, Tafila and Madaba. Construction was scheduled to be completed by mid-2010.
62 JIEC, 2006, *Annual Report 2006*, Amman: Jordan Industrial Estates Corporation.
63 Atmeh, M., 28 December 2006.
64 Ibid.
65 Article 6 of the *Investment Promotion Law* 1995.
66 Atmeh, M., 28 December 2006.
67 Ibid.
68 Ibid.
69 Page, S., 1994, *How Developing Countries Trade: The Institutional Constraints*, London: Routledge.
70 Kardoosh, M.A., Al-Khouri, R., 2004, *Qualifying Industrial Zones and Sustainable Development in Jordan*, Amman: Jordan Centre for Pubic Policy and Research.
71 JIB, 2006, *Mission Statement*, Amman: Jordan Investment Board.
72 Farraj, E., Chief Advisor to Maan Nsour, CEO of Jordan Investment Board, interview held in Amman, Jordan, on 24 December 2006.
73 Ibid.
74 Ibid.
75 Ibid.
76 Ibid.
77 Ibid.

78   Ibid.

79   Ibid.

80   Tate, P., 'Jordan Witnesses Investment Boom', *The Jordan Times*, 4 October 2006.

81   World Bank, 2006, *Quarterly Report: Jordan – Third Quarter Report*, Washington: World Bank.

82   Ibid.

83   JIB, 2006, *Invest in Jordan: The Textiles and Garments Sector*, Amman: Jordan Investment Board, p. 3.

84   Dew, P., Wallace, J., Shoult, A., 2004, *Doing Business with Jordan*, London: GMB Publishing Ltd, p. 15.

85   Farraj, E., December 24 2006.

86   Ibid.

87   AFL-CIO, 2006, *Request by the American Federation of Labour and Congress of Industrial Organisations (AFL-CIO) and the National Textile Association (NTA) to the United States to Invoke Consultation Under the United States-Jordan Free Trade Agreement to Address Jordan's Violations of the Agreement's Labour Rights Provisions*, Washington: AFL-CIO, p. 16.

88   Ministry of Labour, 2006, *Report on the Status of Migrant Workers in the Qualifying Industrial Zones and Industrial Estates*, Amman: Ministry of Labour, pp. 5–16.

89   Ministry of Labour, May 2007, *Labour Report*, p. 18.

90   Ibid.

91   Ibid.

92   Harrison, P., 'Jordan Rocked by Abuse Claims', 5 May 2006, Emerging Textiles.com: Textile and Clothing Trade Information.

93   AFL-CIO, *Request by the American Federation of Labour*.

94   Article 6, *Agreement Between the United States of America and the Hashemite Kingdom of Jordan on the Establishment of a Free Trade Area*, 2000.

95   See *Draft Law on Political Associations*, 2005.

96   AFL-CIO, *Request by the American Federation of Labour*, p. 6.

97   Ibid.

98   *Draft Law on Political Associations*, 2005.

99   Ibid, Article 135 (1).

100   Anon, 'Jordan Regrets US Union Action', 30 Sept. 2006, Al-Jazeera News.

101   Sparshott, J., 'Jordan Shutting Abusive Factories', 17 June 2006, *The Washington Times*.

102   Ali, M., 24 December 2006.

103 USITC, 2004, *US–Bahrain Free Trade Agreement: Potential Economy Wide and Sectoral Effects*, Washington: United States International Trade Commission, p. 33.

104 US Census Bureau, Foreign Trade Statistics, 2007.

105 Pigato, M. *et al.*, *Morocco, Tunisia, Egypt and Jordan After the End of the Multi-Fibre Agreement: Impact, Challenges and Prospects*, p. 33.

106 Including with the following states: Australia, Bahrain, Chile, Colombia, Malaysia, Morocco, Oman, Panama, Peru, Singapore.

107 Pigato, M. *et al.*, *Morocco, Tunisia, Egypt and Jordan After the End of the Multi-Fibre Agreement: Impact, Challenges and Prospects*, p. 5.

108 Atmeh, M., 28 December 2006.

109 Lawrence, R., 2006, *A US–Middle East Trade Agreement: A Circle of Opportunity.*

110 Ali, M., 22 December 2006.

111 Ibid.

112 Ali, M., 22 December 2006.

Chapter 5

1 Thomas, J.R., 21 Dec. 2005, *Intellectual Property and Free Trade Agreements: Innovation Policy Issues*, Washington: Congressional Research Service Report, p. 5.

2 See Abbott, F., Cottier, T., 1999, *The International Intellectual Property System: Commentary and Materials*, London: Kluwer Law International.

3 WTO, Sept. 2006, *TRIPs and Pharmaceuticals Factsheet*, Geneva: World Trade Organisation, p. 2.

4 Ibid. Note: it is often the case that with developing economies the product process is recognised as being protected by international property law but not the actual product itself.

5 WTO, 15 April 1994, *Understanding on Rules and Procedures Governing the Settlement of Disputes, WTO Agreement, Annex 2, Legal Instruments – Results of the Uruguay Round*, Vol. 31, No. 33, I.L.M. 1226.

6 Berne Convention for the Protection of Literary and Artistic Works, 9 Sept. 1886, 828 UNTS. 221. Paris Convention for the Protection of Industrial Property, 20 March 1883, 13 UST. 1.

7 TRIPS Agreement Article 12.

8 Ibid, Article 28.

9 Ibid, Article 27(2).

10 Thomas, J.R., *Intellectual Property and Free Trade Agreements: Innovation Policy Issues.*

11 Watal, J., 2001, *Intellectual Property Rights in the WTO and Developing Countries*, New Delhi: OUP.

12   Arafat, A., 2001, *Pharmaceuticals Sector Report*, Amman: Export & Finance Bank, p. 5.

13   Ibid.

14   *TRIPS Agreement* Article 31.

15   Ibid.

16   Maskus, K., 2000, *Intellectual Property Rights in the Global Economy*, Washington: Institute for International Economics, p. 25.

17   Arafat, A., *Pharmaceuticals Sector Report*, p. 5.

18   WTO, 13 August 2001, *Review of Legislation: Jordan*, Washington: Council for Trade-Related Aspects of Intellectual Property Rights, p. 3.

19   Arup, C., 2000, *The New World Trade Organisation,* Cambridge: Cambridge University Press.

20   Braithwaite, J., Drahos, P., 2000, *Global Business Regulation*, Cambridge: Cambridge University Press.

21   Thomas, J.R., *Intellectual Property and Free Trade Agreements: Innovation Policy Issues.*

22   Hazimeh, F., Lead Counsellor for the Jordanian Mission at the WTO, interview held at the WTO in Geneva, Switzerland on 25 April 2007. Mr Hazimeh has been the lead counsellor since 1999 and has been directly involved in the Jordanian accession negotiations to the WTO, the JUSFTA and a number of other bilateral agreements.

23   Adopted by the Assembly of the Paris Union for the Protection of Industrial Property and the World Intellectual Property Organisation in 1999.

24   *Agreement Between the United States of America and the Hashemite Kingdom of Jordan on the Establishment of a Free Trade Area*, Article 4 points 1 through 5.

25   Ibid, pp. 6–7.

26   See El-Said, H., El-Said, M., 2007, 'TRIPs-Plus Implications for Access to Medicines in Developing Countries: Lessons from the Jordan–United States Free Trade Agreement', *The Journal of World Intellectual Property*, 10(6), Nov. 2007, pp. 438–475.

27   Ibid, p. 8.

28   El-Said, H. El-Said, M., 2005, 'TRIPS in Bilateral Agreements: The Jordan–US FTA', *Manchester Journal of International Economic Law*, 2(1), 2005, pp. 59-80.

29   Atmeh, M., Deputy CEO of the Jordan Industrial Estates Corporation, interview held in Amman, Jordan on 28 December 2006.

30   Manneh, J., 2004, *Pharmaceuticals Sector Report*, Amman: Export and Finance Bank.

31 Ryan, M., Shanebrook, J., 2004, *Establishing Globally Competitive Pharmaceutical and Biomedical Technology Industries in Jordan: Assessment of Business Strategies and The Enabling Environment*, Washington: International Intellectual Property Institute Publications.
32 Ministry of Industry and Trade: Trade and Investment Information Database, 2009.
33 Ibid.
34 Ibid.
35 Atmeh, M., 28 December 2006.
36 Knowles, W., 2005, *Jordan: A Study in Political Economy*, London: I.B.Tauris & Co. Ltd, p. 98.
37 Manneh, J., *Pharmaceuticals Sector Report*.
38 JIB, 2005, *The Pharmaceutical Sector*, Amman: Jordan Investment Board, pp. 2–3.
39 Jordan Association of Pharmaceutical Manufacturers: These are as follows: Amman Pharmaceutical Industries Co. (API); Arab Centre for Pharmaceuticals and Chemicals ACPC); The Arab Pharmaceutical Manufacturing Co. Ltd. (APM); Dar Al Dawa Development & Investment Co. (DAD); Hayat Pharmaceutical Industries Co. Ltd.; Hikma Pharmaceuticals; The Jordanian Pharmaceutical Manufacturing Medical Equipment Co. Ltd. (JPM); Jordan River Pharmaceutical Industries L.LC. (Jorivier); Jordan Sweden Medical and Sterilization Co. (JOSWE); Al-Kindi Pharmaceutical Industries; Middle East Pharmaceutical and Chemical Industries and Medical Appliances Co. (Mid Pharma); Pharma International Co. (PIC); Philadelphia Pharmaceuticals; Ram Industries Co. Ltd.; The United Pharmaceutical Manufacturing Co. Ltd. (UPM); IPRC; Triumpharma.
40 JIB, *The Pharmaceutical Sector*.
41 Ministry of Industry and Trade, Trade and Investment Information Database, 2009.
42 Ryan, M., Shanebrook, J., *Establishing Globally Competitive Pharmaceutical and Biomedical Technology Industries in Jordan: Assessment of Business Strategies and The Enabling Environment*.
43 Jordan Association of Pharmaceutical Manufacturers, 2007.
44 Ali, M., Director of Foreign Trade Policy, Ministry of Industry and Trade, interview held in Amman, Jordan on 22 December 2006.
45 Hikma Pharmaceuticals, 2006, *Annual Report*, Amman: Hikma Pharmaceuticals, p. 5.
46 Ibid: these are: United States; United Kingdom; Portugal; Spain; Italy; Germany; The Czech Republic; Slovakia; Ukraine; Finland; Kazakhstan; Uzbekistan; Morocco; Algeria; Tunisia; Libya; Egypt; Sudan;

Chad; South Africa; Syria; Iraq; Saudi Arabia; Yemen; Oman; Lebanon; UAE; Jordan.

47 Ibid, p. 5.

48 Ibid.

49 Ibid.

50 United States Food and Drug Agency, 2007.

51 Medical and Healthcare Products Regulatory Agency, 2007.

52 Hikma Pharmaceuticals, 2006, *Annual Report*.

53 APM, 2007, *Annual Report*, Amman: Arab Pharmaceutical Manufacturing Co. Ltd.

54 Manneh, J., *Pharmaceuticals Sector Report*.

55 Anon, 2008, Arab Pharmaceutical Manufacturing Co. Ltd. export markets include: Saudi Arabia, Kuwait, Qatar, Bahrain, United Arab Emirates, Oman, Yemen, Iraq, Syria, Lebanon, Sudan, Libya, Tunisia, Algeria, Morocco, Nigeria, Ethiopia, Malaysia, Romania, Bulgaria, and Trinidad and Tobago.

56 Hazimeh, F., 25 April 2007.

57 APM, 2007.

58 Saket, H., 2006.

59 Ibid.

60 Ibid.

61 Dar Al Dawa, 2008, *Annual Report*, Amman: Dar Al Dawa..

62 Export markets are as follows: Bahrain, Qatar, Oman, Albania, Iraq, Saudi Arabia, Somalia, UAE, Libya, Yemen, Nigeria, Tunisia, Malta, Algeria, Malaysia, Lebanon, Romania, Sudan, Lesotho, Ethiopia, Russia, Kuwait and Hong Kong.

63 Ryan, M., Shanebrook, J., 2004, *Establishing Globally Competitive Pharmaceutical and Biomedical Technology Industries in Jordan: Assessment of Business Strategies and The Enabling Environment*, p. 15.

64 Manneh, J., *Pharmaceuticals Sector Report*, p. 13.

65 Ryan, M., Shanebrook, J., 2004, *Establishing Globally Competitive Pharmaceutical and Biomedical Technology Industries in Jordan: Assessment of Business Strategies and The Enabling Environment*, p. 15.

66 Dar Al Dawa, 2006.

67 Afram, G., Lloyd, J., Sayegh, L., 2004, *Investment Promotion Sectoral Strategy 2005–2007: Pharmaceuticals*, Amman: United States Agency for International Aid Jordan.

68 NutirDar, 2008, *Annual Report*, Amman: NutirDar.

69 DADVet, 2006, *Annual Report*, Amman: DADVet, p. 9.

70 Anon, *Special 301 Report*, 2000, p. 20.

71 Arafat, A., *Pharmaceuticals Sector Report*, p. 3.

72 Hazimeh, F., 25 April 2007.

73 Arafat, A., *Pharmaceuticals Sector Report*, p. 3.

74 Ryan, M., Shanebrook, J., 2004, *Establishing Globally Competitive Pharmaceutical and Biomedical Technology Industries in Jordan: Assessment of Business Strategies and The Enabling Environment.*

75 Manneh, J., *Pharmaceuticals Sector Report.*

76 Ibid, p. 27.

77 Ministry of Industry and Trade, Trade and Investment Information Database, 2007.

78 Schott, J.J., (ed), 2004, *Free Trade Agreements: US Strategies and Priorities*, Washington: Institute for International Economics, p. 3.

79 Bergsten, C.F., 2005, *The United States and the World Economy: Foreign Policy for the Next Decade*, Washington: Institute for International Economics, pp. 417–419.

80 Thomas J.R., *Intellectual Property and Free Trade Agreements: Innovation Policy Issues*, p. 7.

81 Bergsten, C.F., *The United States and the World Economy: Foreign Policy for the Next Decade*, pp. 19–24.

82 Lovett *et al.*, *US Trade Policy: History, Theory and the WTO.*

83 Ibid.

84 See The United States Census Bureau, Foreign Trade Statistics Division, data on T&C exports.

85 Lovett *et al.*, *US Trade Policy: History, Theory and the WTO.*

86 Thomas J.R., *Intellectual Property and Free Trade Agreements: Innovation Policy Issues*, p. 7.

87 Kress, C., Regional Director Middle East and North Africa, US Trade and Development Agency, interview held in Washington DC, United States, on 24 March 2008.

88 PhRMA, 2008, *Industry Profile: Pharmaceuticals*, Washington: Pharmaceutical Research and Manufacturers of America.

89 Van Beuzekom, B., Arundel, A., 2006, *OECD Biotechnology Statistics*, Paris: OECD, p. 21.

90 Maskus, K., *Intellectual Property Rights in the Global Economy.*

91 Grabowski, H.G., 'An Analysis of US Competitiveness in Pharmaceuticals', *Managerial and Decision Economics*, Spring 1989, pp. 27–33.

92 Ibid.

93 Ministry of Industry and Trade: Trade and Investment Information Database, 2009.

94 Hazimeh, F., 25 April 2007.

95 Afram, G., Lloyd, J. Sayegh, L., *Investment Promotion Sectoral Strategy 2005–2007: Pharmaceuticals*, p. 16.

96   Ibid.
97   See Pfizer, 2006, *Annual Report 2005–2006*, New York: Pfizer.
98   Krebs, R., Greener, M., *A Healthy Business – A Guide to the Global Pharmaceutical Industry*, London: Urch Publishing Ltd.
99   Afram, G., Lloyd, J., Sayegh, L., *Investment Promotion Sectoral Strategy 2005–2007: Pharmaceuticals*, p. 51.
100   Ibid.
101   Hazimeh, F., 25 April 2007.
102   Afram, G., Lloyd, J., Sayegh, L., *Investment Promotion Sectoral Strategy 2005–2007: Pharmaceuticals*, p. 16.
103   Farraj, E., Chief Advisor to Maan Nsour, CEO of the Jordan Investment Board, interview held in Amman, Jordan on December 24 2006.
104   Afram, G., Lloyd, J., Sayegh, L., *Investment Promotion Sectoral Strategy 2005–2007: Pharmaceuticals*, p. 44.
105   Abu Rahmeh, H., Director of the Jordan Exporters Association, interview held in Amman, Jordan on 27 December 2006.
106   Maskus, K., *Intellectual Property Rights in the Global Economy*.
107   Ryan, M., Shanebrook, J., 2004, *Establishing Globally Competitive Pharmaceutical and Biomedical Technology Industries in Jordan: Assessment of Business Strategies and The Enabling Environment*, p. 10.
108   See Organon, 2000, *Annual Report*, New York: Organon.
109   Ryan, M., Shanebrook, J., 2004, *Establishing Globally Competitive Pharmaceutical and Biomedical Technology Industries in Jordan: Assessment of Business Strategies and The Enabling Environment*, p. 10.
110   Hazimeh, F., 25 April 2007.
111   Farraj, E., 24 December 2006.
112   Maskus, K., *Intellectual Property Rights in the Global Economy*, pp. 53–57.
113   Schott, J.J. (ed), 2004, *Free Trade Agreements: US Strategies and Priorities*, Washington: Institute for International Economics, p. 252.
114   Ryan, M., Shanebrook, J., 2004, 2004, *Establishing Globally Competitive Pharmaceutical and Biomedical Technology Industries in Jordan: Assessment of Business Strategies and The Enabling Environment*, Geneva: International Intellectual Property Institute Publications, p. 18
115   Ibid.
116   Ibid.

Chapter 6
1 Kono *et al.*, 2007, 'Opening Markets in Financial Services and the Role of GATS', in *WTO Special Studies*, 2007, p. 1.
2 Ibid.

3 WTO, 1997, Financial Services, in *World Trade Organisation Press Brief.*

4 These are re-insurance and retrocession, services auxiliary to insurance.

5 WTO, 1997.

6 Including: Strange, S., 1986, *Casino Capitalism*, Manchester: Manchester University Press; Strange, S., 1988, *States and Markets: An Introduction to International Political Economy*; Strange, S., 1998, *Mad Money*, Manchester: Manchester University Press.

7 OECD, 1999, 'Cross Border Trade in Financial Services: Economics and Regulation', in *Insurance and Private Pensions Compendium for Emerging Economies*, Paris: OECD Secretariat, p. 3.

8 Webster, A., Hardwick, P., 'International Trade in Financial Services', *The Service Industries Journal*, 25(6), Sept. 2005, p. 724.

9 Ibid, p. 721.

10 For example, The OECD International Trade in Services Statistics Database offers a relatively good range of data for OECD members.

11 See Armdt, H.W., 1986, *Measuring Trade in Financial Services*, Canberra: Australian National University Research School of Pacific and Asian Studies.

12 Data is available from the Jordanian Ministry of Industry and Trade's Trade and Investment Information Database and the United States Census Bureau's Foreign Trade Statistics Database as well as the United Nations data source UNCOM.

13 Das, D.K., 'Trade in Financial Services and the Role of GATS', *Journal of World Trade*, 32(6), Dec. 1998, p. 79.

14 WTO, 2001, *GATS: Fact and Fiction*, Geneva: World Trade Organisation, p. 6.

15 Ibid.

16 Stewart, S., 1993, *The Impact of GATS in the Financial Services*, Manchester: Prentice Hall Ltd.

17 El Hachimi, S., Head of External Relations Division of the WTO, interview held in Geneva, Switzerland on 24 April 2007.

18 Bergsten, C.F., 'A New Foreign Economic Policy for the United States', in Bergsten, C.F. (ed), 2005, *The United States and the World Economy: Foreign Economic Policy for the Next Decade*, Washington: Institute for International Economics, pp. 3–7.

19 Communication from the United States of America, United States Schedule of Specific Commitments Under the General Agreement on Trade in Services, World Trade Organisation, 27/02/2003, S/DCS/W/USA, pp. 51–61.

20 Ibid, p. 51.

21 United States GATS Schedule, 27/02/2003, p. 52.

22   Ibid, p. 64.
23   Communication from the Hashemite Kingdom of Jordan, Schedule of Specific Commitments Under the General Agreement on Trade in Services, World Trade Organisation, 15/12/2000, GATS/SC/128, pp. 23–29.
24   Ibid.
25   Ibid.
26   Summers, L.H., 'Building an International Financial Architecture for the 21st Century', *Cato Journal*, 18(3), Winter 1999, p. 322.
27   Dihel, N., Kardoosh, M.A., 2006, *What Constrains Services Trade in Jordan: Weak Infrastructure, Regulatory Barriers or Both*, Amman: Jordan Centre for Public Policy Research and Dialogue, p. 7.
28   Ministry of Industry and Trade: Trade and Investment Information Database, 2007.
29   Dew, P., Wallace, J., Shoult, A., 2004, *Doing Business with Jordan*, London: GMB Publishing Ltd, p. 15.
30   Bouillon, M., 2002, 'Walking the Tightrope: Jordanian Foreign Policy from the Gulf Crisis to the Peace Process and Beyond', in Joffé, G., *Jordan in Transition 1990–2000*, p. 8.
31   Ministry of Industry and Trade: Trade and Investment Information Database, 2007.
32   El Hachimi, S., 24 April 2007.
33   Dihel, N., Kardoosh, M.A., *What Constrains Services Trade in Jordan: Weak Infrastructure, Regulatory Barriers or Both?*, p. 12.
34   Ibid.
35   CBJ, May 2009, *Research Department Monthly Report*, Amman: Central Bank of Jordan.
36   Ibid.
37   CBJ, May 2007, p. 5.
38   CBJ, 2006, *Yearly Statistical Series: Money and Banking*, Amman: Central Bank of Jordan.
39   Al-Khassib, S., Head of Research, Amman Chamber of Commerce, interview held in Amman, Jordan on 24 December 2006.
40   JIF, 2006, *Historical Background of the Jordanian Insurance Sector*, Amman: Jordan Insurance Federation.
41   Dihel, N., Kardoosh, M.A., *What Constrains Services Trade in Jordan: Weak Infrastructure, Regulatory Barriers or Both?*, p. 14.
42   *Jordan Insurance Law No. 9*.
43   Dihel, N., Kardoosh, M.A., *What Constrains Services Trade in Jordan: Weak Infrastructure, Regulatory Barriers or Both?*, p. 14.

44 JIF, 2006, *Annual Report 2006*, Amman: Jordan Insurance Federation, pp. 3–5.

45 Ibid.

46 Ibid.

47 These are: Marine Insurance, Fire Insurance, Motor Insurance, Credit Insurance, General Accident Insurance, Life Assurance and Medical Insurance.

48 JIF, *Annual Report 2006*, p. 4.

49 CBJ, 2007, *History of the Central Bank of Jordan*, Amman: Central Bank of Jordan.

50 *The Law of the Central Bank of Jordan*, 1959.

51 CBJ, 2007, *History of the Central Bank of Jordan*.

52 ABJ, 2007, *Annual Mission Statement*, Amman: Association of Banks in Jordan.

53 Ibid.

54 JIF, 2006, *Historical Background of the Jordanian Insurance Sector*, Amman: Jordan Insurance Federation.

55 IC, 2006, *Annual Report*, Amman: The Insurance Commission.

56 Ibid.

57 CUIO, 2000, *Mission Statement*, Amman: The Compulsory Unified Insurance Office.

58 The domestic non-Islamic banks are as follows: Bank of Jordan, Jordan Investment & Finance Bank, Arab Jordan Investment Bank, The Housing Bank, Jordan National Bank, Jordan Commercial Bank, Capital Bank of Jordan, Arab Bank, Jordan Kuwait Bank, Arab Jordan Investment Bank, Arab Banking Corp. (Jordan), Societe General Bank. Jordan, Cairo Amman Bank, and Union Bank for Savings & Investment; the foreign banks are as follows: Rafidain Bank, HSBC, Standard Chartered, Citibank, Egyptian Arab Land Bank, Audi Bank S.A.I, National Bank of Kuwait, Bloom Bank; and the two domestic Islamic banks are as follows: Jordan Islamic Bank, International Islamic Arab Bank.

59 ABJ, 2006, *Annual Report*, Amman: Association of Banks in Jordan.

60 Dew, P., Wallace, J., Shoult, A., 2004, *Doing Business with Jordan*, London: GMB Publishing Ltd, pp. 299–309.

61 IC, 2006, *Annual Report*, p. 6. These are as follows: Jordan Insurance; Middle East Insurance; National Ahlia Insurance; United Insurance; Arabian Seas Insurance; General Arabia Insurance; Jerusalem Insurance; Al-Nisr Al-Arabi Insurance; Jordan French Insurance; Arab Union International Insurance; Delta Insurance; Oasis Insurance; Al Yarmouk Insurance; Holy Land Insurance; Arab Lief and Accidents

Insurance; Philadelphia Insurance; American Life Insurance (ALICO); Jordan International Insurance; Arab German Insurance; Euro Arab Insurance Group; Islamic Insurance; Arab Assurers; Al Barakah Takaful Company Ltd; Arab Jordanian Insurance Group; Arab Orient Insurance; Gerasa Insurance.

62   Ibid, p. 35.
63   HBTF, 2006, *Annual Report*, Amman: The Housing Bank for Trade and Finance.
64   Ibid.
65   Arab Bank, 2007, *Historical Overview*, Amman: Arab Bank, pp. 4–5.
66   Arab Bank, 2007, *Semi-Annual Report*, Amman: Arab Bank, p. 3.
67   Arab Bank, 2006, *Annual Report*, Amman: Arab Bank, pp. 33–34.
68   Ibid.
69   Ibid.
70   JIC, 2006, *Annual Report*, Amman: Jordan Insurance Company Ltd., p. 12.
71   Abuhassan, K., 2007, *Mission Statement*, Amman: Jordan Insurance Co.
72   Rothbard, M.N., 1983, *History of Money and Banking in the United States: The Colonial Era to World War Two*, Auburn, Ludwig von Mises Institute, pp. 62–73.
73   Ibid.
74   Ibid.
75   Federal Reserve Statistical Release, 20 July 2007, *Assets and Liabilities of Commercial Banks in the United States*.
76   Ibid.
77   Ibid, 21 July 2001.
78   Anon a, 2006, *Regulatory Guide for Foreign Banks in the United States*, Washington: PriceWaterhouseCoopers.
79   These include: The Foreign Bank Supervision Enhancement Act of 1991; The Riegle–Neal Interstate Banking and Branching Efficiency Act of 1994; The Economic Growth and Paperwork Reduction Act of 1996; The Gramm–Leach–Bliley Act of 1999; The USA Patriot Act of 2001; and The Sarbanes–Oxley Act of 2002.
80   Anon b, 2006, *Insurance in the United States: Industry Profile*, Washington: Datamonitor, p. 3.
81   Ibid, p. 7.
82   The Asia–Pacific region accounts for 24.2 per cent of the global market and the rest of the world has a 3.7 per cent share.
83   Anon b, *Insurance in the United States: Industry Profile*, p. 3.

84 Randall, S., 'Insurance Regulation in the United States: Regulatory Federalism and the National Association of Insurance Commissioners', *Florida State University Law Review*, 26, 1999, p. 629.

85 Ibid.

86 The NAIC was established after the 1868 Supreme Court decision establishing state supremacy over insurance following the Paul v. Virginia court case.

87 Randall, S., 'Insurance Regulation in the United States: Regulatory Federalism and the National Association of Insurance Commissioners', p. 629.

88 US–GATS Schedule of Commitments: These states are as follows: Maryland, Minnesota, Mississippi, and Tennessee.

89 Citibank, 2005, *Historical Background*, New York: Citibank.

90 ABJ, 2007, *Statistical Report: Banks Rating Upon Their Assets*, Amman: Association of Banks in Jordan.

91 Citibank Bahrain, 2006, *Annual Report*, Manama: Citibank Bahrain.

92 Citibank Jordan, 2006, *Annual Report*, Amman: Citibank Jordan.

93 ALICO, 2004, *Historical Background*, Wilmington: ALICO.

94 EFB, 2007, *Report on the Insurance Sector*, Amman: Export and Finance Bank, p. 11.

95 IC, 2008, *Annual Report*, Amman: The Insurance Commission.

96 Ibid.

BIBLIOGRAPHY

Book sources:

Abbott, F., Cottier, T., 1999, *The International Intellectual Property System: Commentary and Materials*, London: Kluwer Law International.

Abu-Hammour, M., 2005, *Jordan's Economic Reforms*, Abu Dhabi: s.n.

Afram, G., Lloyd, J., Sayegh, L., 2004, *Investment Promotion Sectoral Strategy 2005–2007: Pharmaceuticals*, Amman: USAID Jordan Publications.

Ali, T., 2003, *Bush in Babylon: The Recolonisation of Iraq*, London: Verso.

Alker, H., Russett, B., 1965, *World Politics in the General Assembly*, New Haven: Yale University Press.

Al-Khouri, R., 2000, 'Trade Policies in Jordan', in Hoekman, B., Kheir-El-Din, H. (eds), *Trade Policy Developments in the Middle East and North Africa*, Washington: The World Bank.

Al-Khouri, R., Pasch, P., 2002, *Privatisation in Jordan*, s.l.: Friedrich Ebert Stiftung Consultancy.

Allan, G., 1991, 'Qualitative Research', in Allan, G., Skinner, C. (eds), *Handbook for Research Students*, London: Falmer Press.

Allison, R.J., 2000, *The Crescent Obscured: The United States and the Muslim World, 1776–1815*, Chicago: University of Chicago Press.

Almond, M., 1994, *Europe's Backyard War: the War in the Balkans*, 2nd edn, London: Mandarin.

Ambrose, E., 1997, *Rise to Globalism: American Foreign Policy Since 1938*, 8th edn, London: Penguin Books Ltd.

Angell, N., 1911, *The Great Illusion: a Study of the Relation of Military Power to*

National Advantage, London: Read Books.

Arup, C., 2000, *The New World Trade Organisation*, Cambridge: Cambridge University Press.

Axelrod, R.M., 1984, *The Evolution of Cooperation*, New York: Basic Books.

Ayer, A.J., 1940, *The Foundations of Empirical Knowledge*, London: Macmillan.

Baldwin, D.A., 1993, *Neorealism and Neoliberalism: The Contemporary Debate*, New York: Columbia University Press.

Bechofer, F., Paterson, L., 2000, *Principles of Research Design in the Social Sciences*, London: Routledge.

Benton, T., Craib, I., 2001, *Philosophy of Social Science: The Philosophical Foundations of Social Thought*, London: Palgrave MacMillan.

Bergsten, C.F., 1988, *America in the World Economy: A Strategy for the 1990s*, Washington: Peterson Institute for International Economics.

Bergsten, C.F. *et al.*, 2005, *The United States and the World Economy: Foreign Policy for the Next Decade*, Washington: Institute for International Economics.

Berman, W.C., 2001, *From the Centre to the Edge: the Politics and Policies of the Clinton Presidency*, Lanham: Rowman & Littlefield Publishers,

Bevir, M., Rhodes, R., 2002, 'Interpretive Theory', in Marsh, D., Stoker, G. (eds), *Theory and Methods in Political Science*, 2nd edn, Basingstoke: Palgrave MacMillan.

Bloomfield, L., 1960, *The United Nations and US Foreign Policy*, Boston: Little, Brown.

Bouillon, M., 2002, 'Walking the Tightrope: Jordanian Foreign Policy from the Gulf Crisis to the Peace Process and Beyond', in Joffé, G. (ed), *Jordan in Transition 1990–2000*, London: Hurst and Company.

Braithwaite, J., Drahos, P., 2000, *Global Business Regulation*, Cambridge: Cambridge University Press.

Brand, H.W., 1993, *The Devil We Knew: Americans and the Cold War*, Oxford: Oxford University Press.

Braudel, F., 1993, *A History of Civilisations*, London: Penguin Books, pp. 69–93.

Bregman, A., El-Tahri, J., 1998, *The Fifty Years War: Israel and the Arab World*, London: Penguin Books.

Bresheeth, H., Yuval-Vais, N. (eds), 1991, *The Gulf War and the New World Order*, London: Zed Books.

Brown, L.C., 1992, *International Politics and the Middle East: Old Rules, Dangerous Game*, Princeton: Princeton University Press.

Bryman, A., 1988, *Quantity and Quality in Social Research*, London: Routledge.

Brzezinski, Z., 1985, *Power and Principle: Memoirs of the National Security Advisor, 1977–1981*, New York: Farrar, Strauss and Giroux.

Bulmer, M., 1984, 'Facts, Concepts, Theories and Problems', in Bulmer, M. (ed), *Sociological Research Methods: An Introduction*, 2nd edn, London: MacMillan.

Burch, K., Denemark, R., 1997, *Constituting International Political Economy*, Boulder: Lynne Rienner.

Cairncross, F., 1975, *The Second Great Crash: How the Oil Crises Could Destroy the World's Economy*, London: Meuthen.

Cardinal, D., Hayward, J., Jones, G., 2004, *Epistemology: The Theory of Knowledge*, London: Holder Murray.

Carkoglu, A., Eder, M., Kirisci, K., 1998, *The Political Economy of Regional Cooperation in the Middle East*, London: Clays Ltd.

Carter, J., 1983, *Keeping Faith: Memoirs of a President*, Fayetteville: University of Arkansas Press.

Cohen, W., 1993, *America in the Age of Soviet Power*, Cambridge: Cambridge University Press.

Cohen, B. J., 2008, *International Political Economy: An Intellectual History*, Princeton: Princeton University Press.

Cohn, T., 2003, *Global Political Economy: Theory and Practice*, 2nd edn, London: Addison Wesley Longman.

Cox, R., Jacobson, H., 1973, *The Anatomy of Influence: Decision Making in International Organization*, New Haven, CT: Yale University Press.

Cox, M., Stokes, D., 2008, *US Foreign Policy*, Oxford: Oxford University Press

Creswell, J., 1994, Research *Design: Qualitative and Quantitative Approaches*, London: Sage.

—— 2002, *Research Design: Qualitative, Quantitative and Mixed Methods Approaches*, London: Sage.

Dasgupta, B., 1998, *Structural Adjustment, Global Trade and the New Political Economy of Development*, London: Zed Books.

Dayan, M., 1981, *Breakthrough: A Personal Account of the Egypt–Israel Peace Negotiations*, London: Weidenfeld and Nicolson.

Denzin, N., 1970, *Sociological Methods: A Sourcebook*, Chicago: Aldine.

Denzin, N., Lincoln, Y., 2003, *Strategies of Qualitative Inquiry*, London: Sage.

DePaul, M., 2001, *Resurrecting Old-Fashioned Foundationalism*, Birmingham: Rowman & Littlefield Publishers.

Dessus, S., Devlin, J., Safadi, R. (eds), 2001, *Towards Arab and Euro-Med Regional Integration*, Paris: OECD.

Destler, I.M., 2005, *American Trade Politics*, 4th edn, Washington: Institute for International Economics.

Devine, F., Heath, S., 1999, *Sociological Research Methods in Context*, London: Palgrave MacMillan.

Devine, F., 2002, in Marsh, D., Stoker, G. (eds), *Theory and Methods in Political Science*, Basingstoke: MacMillan.

Devlin, J. and Page, J., 2001, 'Testing the Waters: Arab Integration, Competitiveness and the Euro-Med Agreements', in Dessus, S., Devlin, J., Safadi, R. (eds).

Dew, P., Wallace, J., Shoult, A., 2004, *Doing Business with Jordan*, London: GMB Publishing Ltd.

Dihel, N., Kardoosh, M.A., 2006, *What Constrains Services Trade in Jordan: Weak Infrastructure, Regulatory Barriers or Both?*, Amman: Jordan Centre for Public Policy Research and Dialogue.

Dinerstein, H.S., 1968, *Fifty Years of Soviet Foreign Policy*, Washington: Johns Hopkins University.

Downs, A., 1957, *An Economic Theory of Democracy*, New York: Harper and Row.

——1991, 'Social Values and Democracy', in Monroe, K. (ed), *The Economic Approach to Democracy*, New York: Harper Collins.

Dumbrell, J., 1997, *American Foreign Policy: Carter to Clinton*, Basingstoke: Macmillan.

Easton, S.C., 1968, *World History Since 1945*, s.i.: s.n.

Ehteshami, A., Nonneman, G. with Tripp, C., 1991, *War and Peace in the Gulf: Domestic Politics and Regional Relations into the 1990s*, Exeter: Ithaca.

El-Said, H., Becker, K., 2001, *Management and International Business Issues in Jordan*, Binghamton: International Business Press.

Feiler, G., 2000, *The Middle East in the New Millennium: Economic Development and Business Law*, The Hague: Kluwer Law International.

Feinberg, R., 2003, *The Political Economy of United States' Free Trade Arrangements*, Washington: Institute for International Economics.

Feraboli, O., 2003, *A Dynamic Analysis of Jordan's Trade Liberalisation*, Universität Hamburg: Institut für Wachstum und Konjunktur.

Feyeraband, P., 1975, *Against Method: Outline of An Anarchistic Theory of Knowledge,* London: Verso.

Fielding, N., 1993, 'Qualitative Interviewing', in Gilbert, N. (ed), *Researching Social Life*, London: Sage.

Finch, J., 1984, 'It's Great to Have Someone to Talk to: The Ethics and Politics of Researching Women', in Bell, C., Roberts, H. (eds), *Social Researching: Politics, Problems and Practice*, London: Routledge and Kegan Paul.

—— 1986, *Research and Policy*, London: Sage.

Finifter, A. (ed), 1983, *Political Science: The State of the Discipline*, Washington: American Political Science Association.

Flemming, D.F., 1961, *The Cold War and Its Origins: 1917–1960*, New York: Doubleday Publishers.

Frieden, J., Lake, D., 1995, *International Political Economy: Perspectives on Global Power and Wealth*, London: Routledge.

Gaddis, J.L., 1998, *We Now Know: Rethinking Cold War History*, Oxford: Oxford University Press.

George, A., 2005, *Jordan: Living in the Crossfire*, London: Zed Books Ltd.

Gibbons, M. *et al.*, 1994, *The New Production of Knowledge / the Dynamics of Science and Research in Contemporary Societies*, London: Sage.

Giddens, A. (ed), 1974, *Positivism and Sociology*, London: Ashgate.

Gilpin, R., 1987, *The Political Economy of International Relations*, Princeton: Princeton University Press.

Goodin, R., Klingemann, H. (eds), 1996, *A New Handbook of Political Science*, Oxford: Oxford University Press.

Gramsci, A., 1971, *Selections from the Prison Notebooks*, New York: International Publishers.

Groom, A., Light, M. (eds), 1994, *Contemporary International Relations: a Guide to Theory*, London: Pinter Publishers.

Guzzini, S., *Realism in International Relations and International Political Economy*, London: Routledge.

Haas, E.B., 1958, *The Uniting of Europe: Political, Social, and Economic Forces, 1950–1957*, Stanford: Stanford University Press.

— 1997, *Nationalism, Liberalism and Progress: The Rise and Decline of Nationalism*, Ithaca: Cornell University Press.

— 1983, 'Words Can Hurt You: or Who Said What to Whom About Regimes', in Krasner, S. (ed), *International Regimes,* Cornell: Cornell University Press.

Haddad, M., 2001, *Export Competitiveness: Where Does the Middle East and North Africa Region Stand?* Cairo: Economic Research Forum.

Hahn, P., 2005, *Crisis and Crossfire: The United States and the Middle East Since 1945*, Cambridge: Potomac Books Inc.

Halfpenny, P., 1982, *Positivism and Sociology*, London: Allen & Unwin.

Halliday, F., 2005, *The Middle East in International Relations: Power, Politics and Ideology*, Cambridge: Cambridge University Press.

Hamarneh, M., 1994, *The Jordanian Economy: Problems and Prospects*, Amman: Centre for Strategic Studies.

Hammersley, M., 1995, *The Politics of Social Research*, London: Sage.

Hamoudeh, M., 2005, *The Aghadir Process*, Amman: Ministry of Industry and Trade.

Hanahoe, T., 2003, *America Rules: US Foreign Policy, Globalization and Corporate USA*, Dingle, Co. Kerry: Brandod Ltd.

Helbroner, R., 1985, *The Nature and Logic of Capitalism*, New York: W.W. Norton.

Held, D., 1995, *Democracy and the Global Order: From the Modern State to*

Cosmopolitan Governance, Cambridge: Polity Press.

Hettne, B., 1995, *Development Theory and the Three Worlds: Towards an International Political Economy*, Harlow: Longman.

Higgott, R., 1991, 'Toward a Non-Hegemonic IPE: An Antipodean Perspective', in Murphy, C., Tooze, R. (eds), *The New International Political Economy*, Boulder: Lynne Rienner.

Hobbes, T., 1996, *Leviathan*, Cambridge: Cambridge University Press.

Hoekman, B., Zarrouk, J., 2003, *Catching Up With the Competition: Trade Opportunities and Challenges for Arab Countries*, Lansing: The University of Michigan Press.

Hogan, M., 1987, *The Marshall Plan*, Cambridge: Cambridge University Press.

Hollis, M., Smith, S., 1991, *Explaining and Understanding International Relations*, Cambridge: Clarendon Press.

Hollis, M., 1994, *The Philosophy of Social Science: An Introduction*, Cambridge: Cambridge University Press.

Homer-Dixon, T., 1999, *Environment, Scarcity, and Violence*, Princeton: Princeton University Press.

Hourani, A., Khoury, P., Wilson, C. (eds) 2004, *The Modern Middle East*, 2nd edn, London: I.B.Tauris.

Howarth, D., 1995, 'Discourse Theory', in Marsh, D., Stoker, G. (eds), *Theory and Methods in Political Science*, Basingstoke: MacMillan.

Ismael, T. (ed), 1990, *Middle East Studies: International Perspectives on the State of the Art*, London: Greenwood Press.

Joffé, G. (ed), 2002, *Jordan in Transition 1990-2000*, London: Hurst and Company.

Johnston, D., 1991, 'Constructing the Periphery in Modern Global Politics', in Murphy, C., Tooze, R. (eds).

Jones, J.M., 1965, *The Fifteen Weeks*, London: Harcourt.

Kandah, A.S., 2004, *Uses of Privatisation Proceeds*, Amman: Centre for Strategic Studies.

Kanovsky, E., 1990, 'Jordan's Economy: From Prosperity to Crisis', in Ayalon, A., Shaked, H. (eds), *Middle East Contemporary Survey Volume XII*, Boulder: Westview Press.

Kardoosh, M.A., Al-Khouri, R., 2004, *Qualifying Industrial Zones and Sustainable Development in Jordan*, Amman: Jordan Centre for Public Policy and Research.

Kardoosh, M., 2006, *The Institutional Dimension of the Success of Jordanian QIZs*, Amman: Jordan Centre for Public Policy Research and Dialogue.

Keat, R., Urry, J., 1975, *Social Theory as Science*, London: Routledge.

Kedourie, E., 1992, *Politics in the Middle East*, Oxford: Oxford University Press.

Keohane, R., Nye, J., 1977, *Power and Interdependence: World Politics in Transition*, Boston: Little, Brown and Company.

Keohane, R., 1984, *After Hegemony: Cooperation and Discord in the World Political Economy*, Surrey: Princeton University Press.

—— 1989, *International Institutions and State Power: Essays in International Relations Theory*, Boulder: Westview Press.

—— 2002, *Power and Governance in a Partially Globalised World*, Suffolk: Bury St Edmunds Press.

Khalidi, R., 2004, *Resurrecting Empire: Western Footprints and America's Perilous Path in the Middle East*, London: I.B.Tauris.

Kipper, J., Saunders, H., (eds), 1991, *The Middle East in Global Perspective*, Oxford/ Boulder: Westview.

Kirk, J., Miller, M., 1986, *Reliability and Validity in Qualitative Research*, London: Sage.

Knight, J., 1992, *Institutions and Social Conflict*, Cambridge: Cambridge University Press.

Knowles, W., 2005, *Jordan: A Study in Political Economy*, London: I.B.Tauris.

Konan, D., 2003, 'Alternative Paths to Prosperity: Economic Integration among Arab Countries', in Galal, A., Hoekman, B., (eds), *Arab Economic Integration*, Washington: Brookings Institution Press.

Krasner, S. (ed), 1983, *International Regimes*, Cornell: Cornell University Press.

Krasner, S., 1996, 'The Accomplishments of IPE', in Smith, S., Booth, K., Zalewski, A. (eds), *International Theory: Positivism and Beyond*, Cambridge: Cambridge University Press.

Krebs, R., Greener, M., 2001, *A Healthy Business: A Guide to the Global Pharmaceutical Industry*, London: URCH Publishing Ltd.

Krugman, P.R., Obstfeld, M., 2000, *International Economics: Theory and Policy*, 5th edn, Reading: Addison-Wesley.

Kuhn, T S., 1970, *The Structure of Scientific Revolution*, 2nd edn, Chicago: Chicago University Press.

Kuniholm, B., 1994, *The Origins of the Cold War in the Near East: Great Power Conflict and Diplomacy in Iran, Turkey and Greece*, Princeton: Princeton University Press.

LaFeber, W., 2006, *America, Russia and The Cold War*, 7th edn, Sydney; McGraw Hill.

Laqueur, W., 2000, *The New Terrorism: Fanaticism and the Arms of Mass Destruction*, Oxford: Oxford University Press.

Lawrence, R., 2006, *A US–Middle East Trade Agreement: A Circle of Opportunity*, Washington: Institute for International Economics.

Leffler, M.P., 1992, *A Preponderance of Power*, Stanford: Stanford University Press.

Leverett, F., 2005, *The Road Ahead: Middle East Policy in the Bush Administration's Second Term*, Washington: The Brookings Institute.

Lewis, B., 2002, *What Went Wrong: Western Impact and Middle Eastern Responses*, London: Phoenix.

Little, D., 2002, *American Orientalism: The United States and the Middle East Since 1945*, London: I.B.Tauris.

Lloyd, C., 1993, *The Structures of History*, Oxford: Blackwell.

Lofland, J., Lofland, L., 1985, *Analysing Social Settings: A Guide to Qualitative Observation and Analysis*, Belmont: Wadsworth.

Lovett, W.A., Brinkman, R.L., Eckes, A.E., Eckes, A.E. Jr, 2005, *US Trade Policy: History, Theory and the WTO*, Washington: Institute for International Economics.

Lowndes, V., 2002, 'Institutionalism', in Marsh, D., Stoker, G. (eds.), *Theory and Methods in Political Science*, 2nd edn, Basingstoke: Palgrave & MacMillan.

Lucas, R., 2005, *Institutions and the Politics of Survival in Jordan: Domestic Responses to External Challenges*, New York: State University of New York Press.

Macrory, P., Appleton, A., Plummer, M., 2005, *The World Trade Organization: Legal, Political and Economic Analysis*, New York: Springer.

Madfai, M. R., 1993, *Jordan, The United States and the Middle East Peace Process 1974–1991,* Cambridge: Cambridge University Press.

Malkawi, B., 2005, *Jordan and the World Trading System: A Case Study for Arab Countries*, Washington: American University, Washington College of Law.

Mansfield, P., 1992, *The Arabs*, 3rd edn, London: St Ives plc.

— 2003, *A History of the Middle East*, 2nd edn, London: Penguin.

March, J.G., Olsen, J.P., 1995, *Democratic Governance*, New York: Free Press.

Marsh, C., 1977, 'Problems With Surveys: Method or Epistemology?', in Hay, C. (ed)., *Sociological Research Methods: An Introduction*, London: MacMillan.

Marsh, D., Furlong, P., 2002, 'A Skin, Not a Sweater: Ontology and Epistemology in Political Science', in Marsh, D., Stoker, G. (eds), *Theory and Methods in Political Science*, 2nd edn, Basingstoke: Palgrave & MacMillan.

Marsh, D., Stoker, G. (eds), 2002, *Theory and Methods in Political Science*, 2nd edn, Basingstoke: Palgrave & MacMillan.

Marx, K., 1890, *Das Kapital*, Washington: Regnery Publishing Inc.

Maskus, K., 2000, *Intellectual Property Rights in the Global Economy*, Washington: Institute for International Economics.

Mayo, M., 2004, *Global Citizens: Social Movements and the Challenge of Globalization*, London: Zed Books.

Michaels, J.E., 1997, *The President's Call: Executive Leadership From FDR to George Bush*, Pittsburgh: University of Pittsburgh Press.

Michalet, C.A., 'From International Trade to World Economy', in Makler, H., Martinelli, A., Smelser, N., 1982, *The New International Economy*, London: Sage.

Miles, M., Huberman, A., 1994, *Qualitative Data Analysis: A Source Book*, London: Sage.

Mill, J.S., 1991, *On Liberty and Other Essays*, Oxford: Oxford University Press.

Milner, H., 1997, *Interests, Institutions and Information: Domestic Politics and International Relations*, Princeton: Princeton University Press.

Milton-Edwards, B., Hinchcliffe, P., 2001, *Jordan: A Hashemite Legacy*, London: Sage.

Moore, P., 2004, *Doing Business in the Middle East: Politics and Economic Crisis in Jordan and Kuwait*, Cambridge: Cambridge University Press.

Murphy, C., Tooze, R. (eds), 1991, *The New International Political Economy*, Boulder: Lynne Rienner.

Nathan, J., Oliver, J., 1978, *United States Foreign Policy and World Order*, London: Longman.

Nelson, D., 1991, 'Trade Policy Games', in Murphy, C., Tooze, R. (eds).

Newell, R., 1993, 'Questionnaires', in Gilbert, N. (ed), *Researching Social Life*, London: Sage.

Ohmae, K., 2005, *The Next Global Stage: The Challenges and Opportunities in Our Borderless World*, New Jersey: Pearson Education Inc.

Oren, M., 2007, *Power, Faith and Fantasy: America in the Middle East: 1776 to the Present*, London: W. W. Norton.

Padgett, D., 1998, *Qualitative Methods in Social Work Research*, London: Sage.

Page, J., 2003, *Structural Reforms in the Middle East and North Africa*, Washington: World Bank.

Page, S., 1994, *How Developing Countries Trade: The Institutional Constraints*, London: Routledge.

Parmet, H., 1972, *Eisenhower and the American Crusades*, New Jersey: Transaction Publishers.

Parsons, A., 1995, *From Cold War to Hot Peace: UN Interventions, 1947–1995*, London: Penguin.

Peters, G., 1999, *Institutional Theory in Political Science: The New Institutionalism*, London: Pinter.

Pigato, M., *et al.*, 2006, *Morocco, Tunisia, Egypt and Jordan After the End of the Multi-Fibre Agreement: Impact, Challenges and Prospects*, Washington: World Bank.

Pitt, W.R., Ritter, S., 2002, *War on Iraq: What Team Bush Doesn't Want You to Know*, London: Context Books.

Pole, C., Lampard, R., 2001, *Practical Social Investigation: Qualitative and Quantitative Methods in Social Research*, London: Prentice Hall.

Quandt, W.B., 1986, *Camp David: Peacemaking and Politics*, Washington: The Brookings Institute.

Quine, W., 1961, *From a Logical Point of View*, New York: Harper & Row.

Ragin, C., 2000, *Fuzzy-Set Social Science*, Chicago: Chicago University Press.

Read, M., Marsh, D., 2002, 'Combining Qualitative and Quantitative Methods', in Marsh, D., Stoker, G. (eds).

Renshon, S.A., 1995, *The Clinton Presidency: Campaigning, Governing, and the Psychology of Leadership*, Oxford: Westview Press.

Rhodes, R.A.W., 1997, *Understanding Governance*, Buckingham: Open University Press.

Richards, A., 2006, 'Long Term Sources of Instability in the Middle East', in Russell, J. (ed), *Critical Issues Facing the Middle East: Security, Politics and Economics*, Basingstoke: Palgrave Macmillan.

Rittberger, V., 1993, *Regime Theory and International Relations*, Oxford: Clarendon Press.

Robins, P., 2004, *A History of Jordan*, Cambridge: Cambridge University Press.

Rockmoore, T., 2004, *On Foundationalism: A Strategy for Metaphysical Realism*, Birmingham: Rowman & Littlefield Publishers.

Roper, J., 2000, *The American Presidents: Heroic Leadership From Kennedy to Clinton*, Edinburgh: Edinburgh University Press.

Rose, G., 1982, *Deciphering Sociological Research*, London: MacMillan.

Rosen, H., 2003, 'Free Trade Agreements as US Foreign Policy Tools: The US–Israel and US–Jordan FTAs', in Schott, J.J. (ed), *Free Trade Agreements: US Strategies and Priorities*, Washington: Institute for International Economics.

Rothbard, M.N., 1983, *History of Money and Banking in the United States: The Colonial Era to World War Two*, Auburn: Ludwig von Mises Institute.

Rothgeb, J. Jr, 2001, *US Trade Policy: Balancing Economic Dreams and Political Realities*, Washington: CQ Press.

Ryan, C., 2002, *Jordan in Transition: From Hussein to Abdullah*, London: Lynne Rienner.

Ryan, M., Shanebrook, J., 2004, *Establishing Globally Competitive Pharmaceutical and Biomedical Technology Industries in Jordan: Assessment of Business Strategies and The Enabling Environment*, Geneva: International Intellectual Property Institute Publications.

Rybczynski, T., 1976, *The Economics of the Oil Crisis*, London: Macmillan.

Sachs, J., Warner, A., 1995, *Economic Reform and the Process of Global Integration*, Washington: Brookings Institute.

Sadiki, L., 2004, *The Search for Arab Democracy*, London: C. Hurst & Co

Publishers Ltd.

Said, E., 1978, *Orientalism*, London: Clayes Ltd.

—— 2005, *Power, Politics and Culture: Interviews with Edward Said*, London: Bloomsbury Publishing.

Saikal, A., Schnable, A., 2003, *Democratization in the Middle East: Experiences, Struggles and Challenges*, New York: United Nations Press.

Schmidt, L., 2006, *Understanding Hermeneutics*, Birmingham: Acumen Publishing Ltd.

Schott, J.J., *Assessing US FTA Policy*, Washington: Institute for International Economics.

Schott, J.J. (ed), 2004, *Free Trade Agreements: US Strategies and Priorities*, Washington: Institute for International Economics.

Shlaim, A., 2000, *The Iron Wall: Israel and the Arab World*, London: Clays Ltd.

Silva-Jauregui, C. (ed), 2002, *Jordan Development Policy Review: A Reforming State in a Volatile Region*, Washington: World Bank.

Silverman, D., 1997, *Qualitative Research: Theory, Method and Practice*, London: Sage.

Simons, G., 2003, *Future Iraq: US Policy in Reshaping the Middle East*, London: Saqi Books.

Simpson, E. (ed.), 1988, *Anti-Foundationalism and Practical Reasoning: Conversations Between Hermeneutics and Analysis*, Toronto: Academic Printing and Publishing.

Singh, R., 2002, 'Liberalisation or Democratisation?: The Limits of Political Reform and Civil Society in Jordan', in Joffé, G. (ed), *Jordan in Transition: 1990–2000*, London: Hurst and Company.

Sjolander, C., Cox, W., 1994, *Beyond Positivism; Critical Reflections on International Relations*, Boulder: Lynne Rienner.

Smith, G., 1986, *Morality and Reason: American Diplomacy in the Carter Years*, New York: Farrar, Strauss and Giroux.

Spero, J., 1990, *The Politics of International Economic Relations*, 7th edn, London: Routledge.

Stempel, J., 1981, *Inside the Iranian Revolution*, Indianapolis: Indiana University Press.

Stewart, S., 1993, *The Impact of GATS in the Financial Services*, Manchester: Prentice Hall Ltd.

Strange, S., 1986, *Casino Capitalism*, Manchester: Manchester University Press.

—— 1988, *States and Markets, An Introduction to International Political Economy*, London: Pinter Publishers.

—— 1991, 'An Eclectic Approach', in Murphy, C., Tooze., R (eds.).

—— 'Political Economy and International Relations', in Booth, K.,

Smith S., 1995, *International Relations Theory Today*, Cambridge: Polity.

— 1998, *Mad Money*, Manchester: Manchester University Press.

Stubbs, R., Underhill, G., 2000, *Political Economy and the Changing Global Order*, 2nd edn, Oxford: Oxford University Press.

Talalay, M., Tooze, R., Farrands, C., 1997, *Technology, Culture and Competitiveness: Change and the World Political Economy*, London: Routledge.

Tashakkori, A., Teddlie, C., 1998, *Mixed Methodology: Combining Qualitative and Quantitative Approaches*, London: Sage Publications.

Thompson, E.P., 1978, *The Poverty of Theory*, London: Merlin Press.

Tibi, B., 1997, *Arab Nationalism: Between Islam and the Nation-State*, 3rd edn, London: Macmillan.

Todd, E., 2003, *After the Empire: The Breakdown of the American Order*, Birmingham: Constable.

Tooze, R., 1982, *World Political Economy*, New York: Continuum International Publishing Group.

Tschirgi, D. (ed), 1994, *The Arab World Today*, Boulder: Lynne Rienner.

Tussie, D., 1991, 'Trading in Fear?: US Hegemony and the Open World Economy in Perspective', in Murphy, C., Tooze., R (eds).

Usher, G., 1995, *Palestine in Crisis: the Struggle for Peace and Political Independence After Oslo*, London: Pluto Press in association with Transnational Institute and Middle East Research & Information Project.

Volpe, A., Weil, D., 2004, *The Apparel and Textile Industries After 2005: Prospects and Choices*, Cambridge, MA: Harvard Centre for Textile and Apparel Research.

Walker, M., 1995, *The Cold War: A History*, Birmingham: Holt Paperbacks.

Wallerstein, I., 1984, *The Politics of the World-Economy: The States, the Movements and the Civilizations*, Cambridge: Cambridge University Press.

Watal, J., 2001, *Intellectual Property Rights in the WTO and Developing Countries*, New Delhi: OUP.

Weingast, A., 1996, 'Political Institutions: Rational Choice Perspectives', in Goodin, R., Klingemann, H. (eds), *A New Handbook of Political Science*, Oxford: Oxford University Press.

Whitworth, S., 2000, 'Theory as Exclusion: Gender and International Political Economy', in Stubbs, R., Underhill, G. (eds).

Wilson, R., 1995, *Economic Development in The Middle East*, Oxon: Routledge.

— 1995, 'The Regional Economic Impact of the Gulf War', in Davis, M. (ed), *Politics and International Relations in the Middle East: Continuity and Change*, Aldershot: Edward Elgar.

Wittkopf, E., Kegley, C.W. Jr, Schott, J.J., 2005, *American Foreign Policy: Pattern and Process*, 7th edn, London: Wadsworth.

Woodward, B., 2003, *Bush at War,* London: Pocket Books.

Yergin, D., 1991, *The Prize: The Epic Quest for Oil: Money and Power*, London:

Simon and Schuster.

Zarouk, J., 'The Greater Arab Free Trade Area', in Hoekman, B., Zarrouk, J., 2003.

Zinn, Howard, 2003, *A People's History of the United States*, 3rd edn, London: Pearson Ltd.

Journal articles:

Al-Atrash, H., Yousef, T., 2000, 'Intra-Arab Trade: is it too Little?', *IMF Working Paper*, Washington: IMF.

Amin, A., Palan, R., 2001, 'Towards a Non-Rationalist International Political Economy', *Review of International Political Economy*, 8(4).

Amoore, L., 2000, Dodgson, R., Germain, R., Gills, B., Langley, P., Watson, I., 'Paths to a Historicized International Political Economy', *Review of International Political Economy*, 7(1).

Blyth, M., Spruyt, H., 2003, 'Our Past as Prologue: Introduction to the Tenth Anniversary Issue of Review of International Political Economy', *Review of International Political Economy*, 10(4).

Brand, L.A., 1991, 'Liberalization and Changing Political Coalitions: The Bases of Jordan's 1990–1991 Gulf Conflict Policy', *Jerusalem Journal of International Relations*, 13(4).

Brand, A., 1999, 'The Effects of the Peace Process on Political Liberalisation in Jordan', *Journal of Palestine Studies*, 28(2).

Brinkley, D., Spring 1997, 'Democratic Enlargement: The Clinton Doctrine', *Foreign Policy*..

Bromley, S., 1998, 'Oil and the Middle East: The End of US Hegemony', *Middle East Report,* 208.

Cohen, B.V., 1951, 'The Impact of the United Nations on United States Foreign Policy', *International Organization*, 5.

Cox, R., 1979, 'Ideologies and the New International Economic Order: Reflections on Some Recent Literature', *International Organization*, 33(2).

— 1981, 'Social Forces, States and World Orders: Beyond International Relations Theory', *Millennium: Journal of International Studies*, 10(2).

Das, D.K., 1998, 'Trade in Financial Services and the Role of GATS', *Journal of World Trade*, 32(6).

Deardorff, A., Stern, R., 2002, 'What You Should Know About Globalization and the World Trade Organization', *Review of International Economics*, 10(3).

Demir, O., Mustafa, A., Toprak, M., 2004, 'Anatolian Tigers or Islamic Capital: Prospects and Challenges', *Middle Eastern Studies*, 40(6).

Denemark, R., O'Brien, R., 1997, 'Contesting the Canon: International

Political Economy at UK and US Universities', *Review of International Political Economy*, 4(1).

Dickens, A., 2006, 'The Evolution of International Political Economy', *International Affairs*, 82(3).

Dobson, J., 2001, 'The Battle in Seattle: Reconciling Two World Views on Corporate Culture', *Business Ethics Quarterly*, 11(3).

'Editorial, 1994, Forum for Heterodox International Political Economy', *Review of International Political Economy*, 1(1).

El-Said, H., El-Said, M., 2007, 'TRIPs-Plus Implications for Access to Medicines in Developing Countries: Lessons from the Jordan–United States Free Trade Agreement', *The Journal of World Intellectual Property*, 10(6).

— 2005, TRIPS in Bilateral Agreements: The Jordan–US FTA, in *Manchester Journal of International Economic Law*, 2(1), pp. 59–80.

Farrands, C., Worth, O., 2005, 'Critical Theory in Global Political Economy: Critique? Knowledge? Emancipation?', *Capital and Class*, 85.

Fox, W., 1951,'The United Nations in the Era of Total Diplomacy', *International Organization*, 5.

Gills, B., 2001, 'Forum: Perspectives on New Political Economy: Re-orienting the New (International) Political Economy', *New Political Economy*, 6(2).

Golfer, W., 1954, 'GATT After Six Years: An Appraisal', *International Organization*, 8.

Goodrich, L.M., 1947, 'From League of Nations to United Nations, *International Organization*, 1(3).

Grabowski, H.G., Spring 1989, 'An Analysis of US Competitiveness in Pharmaceuticals', *Managerial and Decision Economics.*

Greenberger, R. S., 12 October 1994 'US Plans to Block Future Iraqi Moves On Kuwait Amid Signs of Withdrawal', *Wall Street Journal.*

Gresser, E., January 2002, 'Draining the Swamp: A Middle East Trade Policy to Win the Peace', a *Progressive Policy Institute* Report.

Grieco, J., 1988, 'Anarchy and the Limits of Cooperation: A Realist Critique of the Newest Liberal Institutionalism', in *International Organization*, 42(2).

Griswold, D.T., 6 January 2004,'Trading Tyranny for Freedom How Open Markets Till the Soil for Democracy', *Trade Policy Analysis*, 26.

Haggard, S., Maxfield, S., 1996, 'The Political Economy of Financial Internationalization in the Developing World', *International Organization*, 50(1).

Hall, P., Taylor, R., 1996, 'Political Science and the Three New Institutionalisms', *Political Studies*, 44(4).

Halliday, F., april 1991, 'The Gulf War and its Aftermath: First Reflections', *International Affairs*, 67(2).

Hay, C., Marsh, D., 1999, 'Introduction: Towards a New (International) Political Economy', *New Political Economy*, 4(1).

Hay, C., Watson, M., 1999, 'Globalisation: Sceptical Notes on the 1999 Reith Lectures', *Political Quarterly*, 70(4).

Hopkins, R., Puchala, D., 1978, 'Perspectives on the International Relations of Food', *International Organization*, 32(2).

Hosoe, N., August 2001, 'A General Equilibrium Analysis of Jordan's Trade Liberalization', *Journal of Policy Modelling*, 23(6).

Jessop, B., Sum, N.L., 2001, 'Pre-Disciplinary and Post-Disciplinary Perspectives', *New Political Economy*, 6(1).

Johnson, H.C., Niemeyer, G., 1954, 'Collective Security: The Validity of an Ideal', *International Organization*, 8.

Kanovsky, E., July 1997, 'The Middle East Economies: The Impact of Domestic and International Politics', The *Middle East Review of International Affairs*, 1(2).

Katzenstein P.J., Keohane R., Krasner S.D., 1 October 1998, 'International Organisation and the Study of World Politics', *International Organization*, 52(4).

Kennan, G., 1986, 'Containment Then and Now', *Foreign Affairs*, 65.

Kindleberger, C.P., 1951, 'Bretton Woods Reappraised', *International Organization*, 5.

Knorr, K., 1948, 'The Bretton Woods Institutions in Transition', *International Organization*, 2.

Kono, M., Low, P., Luanga, M., Mattoo, A., Oshikawa, M., Schuknecht, L., 2007, 'Opening Markets in Financial Services and the Role of GATS', *WTO Special Studies*.

Krasner, S., 1982, 'Structural Causes and Regime Consequences: Regimes as Intervening Variables', *International Organization*, 36(2).

— 1994, 'International Political Economy: Abiding Discord', *Review of International Political Economy*, 1(1).

Lapid, Y., 1989, 'The Third Debate: On the Prospects of International Theory in a Post-Positivist Era', *International Studies Quarterly*, 33(3).

Lindsey, B., 5 August 2003 'The Trade Front Combating Terrorism With Open Markets', *Trade Policy Analysis*, 24.

Lowndes, V., 1996, 'Varieties of New Institutionalisms: A Critical Appraisal', *Public Administration*, 74(2).

Maciejewski, E., Mansur, A., 20 May 1996, 'Jordan: Strategy for Adjustment and Growth', *IMF Occasional Paper*, 136.

March, J., Olsen, J., 1984, 'The New Institutionalism: Organizational Factors in Political Life', *American Political Science Review*, 78.

Martin, L.L., Simmons, B.A., 1998, 'Theories and Empirical Studies of International Institutions', *International Organization*, 52(4).

Matecki, B.E., 1956, 'Establishment of the International Finance Corporation: A Case Study', *International Organization*, 10.

Mearsheimer, J., 1994, 'The False Promise of International Institutions', *International Security*, 19.

Murphy, C., Nelson, D., October 2001, 'International Political Economy: a Tale of Two Heterodoxies', *British Journal of Politics and International Relations*, 3(3).

Niemeyer, G., 1952, 'The Balance Sheet of the League Experiment', *International Organization*, 6.

Peridy, N., September 2005, 'Toward a Pan-Arab Free Trade Area: Assessing Trade Potential Effects of the Aghadir Agreement', *Developing Economies*, 43(3).

Pierson, P., 1996, 'The Path to European Integration: A Historical Institutionalist Analysis', *Comparative Political Studies*, 29(2).

Randall, S., 1999, 'Insurance Regulation in the United States: Regulatory Federalism and the National Association of Insurance Commissioners', *Florida State University Law Review*, 26.

Rice, C., January-February 2000, 'Promoting the National Interest', *Foreign Affairs*, 79(1).

Rosamund, B., 2003, 'Babylon and On: Globalization and International Political Economy', *Review of International Political Economy*, 10(4).

Rudzinski, A.W., 1951, 'The Influence of the United Nations on Soviet Policy', *International Organization*, 5.

Ruggie, J., 1972, 'Collective Goods and Future International Collaboration', *American Political Science Review*, 66.

Ryan, C., 10 June 2005, 'Reform Retreats Amid Jordan's Political Storms', *The Middle East Report*.

Sasley, B.E., March 2002, 'Changes and Continuity in Jordanian Foreign Policy', *Middle East Review of International Affairs*, 6(1).

Stein, K., June 2002, 'The Bush Doctrine and Selective Engagement in the Middle East', *Middle East Review of International Affairs*, 6(2).

Strange, G., 2002, 'Globalisation, Regionalism and Labour Interests in the New International Political Economy', *New Political Economy*, 7(3).

Summers, L.H., 'Building an International Financial Architecture for the 21st Century', *Cato Journal*, 18(3), Winter 1999.

Swaidan, Z., Nica, M., Winter 1999, 'The 1991 Gulf War and Jordan's Economy', *Middle East Review of International Affairs*, 6(2).

Taylor, I., 2005, 'Globalisation Studies and the Developing World: making international political economy truly global', *Third World Quarterly*, 26(7).

Teti, A., Heristchi, C., 2004, 'The Middle East After the Politics of Certainty', *The Journal of Mediterranean Studies*, 14(1).

Tooze, R., 1988, 'The Unwritten Preface: "International Political Economy" and Epistemology', *Millennium: Journal of International Studies*, 17(2).

Underhill, G., 2000, 'State, Market and Global Political Economy: Genealogy of an (Inter-?) Discipline', *International Affairs*, 76(4).

Vale, P., 1995, 'Engaging the World's Marginalised and Promoting Global Change: Challenges for the United Nations at Fifty', *The Harvard International Law Journal*, 36(2).

Ward, A., January 2003, 'US Policy to the Middle East: Utopianism and Realism', *IISS Strategic Comments*, 1(1).

Watson, A., 2004, 'Seen But Not Heard: The Role of the Child in International Political Economy', *New Political Economy*, 9(1).

Webster, A., September 2005, Hardwick, P., 'International Trade in Financial Services', *The Service Industries Journal*, 25(6).

Worth, O., Kuhling, C., 2004, 'Counter-Hegemony, Anti-Globalisation and Culture in International Political Economy', *Capital and Class*, 84.

Yaqub, S., December 2002, 'US Assessments of Arab Threats Since 1945, in The Impact of 9/11 on the Middle East', *Middle East Policy*, 9(4).

Reports:

Abu-Hammour, M., 2006, *Letter from the Chairman*, The Executive Privatization Committee, Amman, Jordan.

Abuhassan, K.A., 2007, *Mission Statement*, Amman: Jordan Insurance Corporation.

ABJ, 2006, *Annual Report*, Amman: Association of Banks in Jordan.

—— 2007a, *Annual Mission Statement*, Amman: Association of Banks in Jordan.

—— 2007b, *Statistical Report 2007: Banks Rating Upon Their Assets*, Amman: Association of Banks in Jordan.

AMF, 2006, *Foreign Trade Statistics of Jordan 1993-2006*, Cairo: Arab Monetary Fund.

AFL-CIO, 2006, *Request by the American Federation of Labour and Congress of Industrial Organisations (AFL-CIO) and the National Textile Association (NTA) to the United States to Invoke Consultation Under the United States–Jordan Free Trade Agreement to Address Jordan's Violations of the Agreement's Labour Rights Provisions*, Washington: AFL–CIO.

ALICO, 2004, *Historical Background*, Wilmington: ALICO.

Anon, 2000, *Special 301 Report*.

Anon, 8 October 2003, *The Challenge of Political Reform: Jordanian Democratisation and Regional Instability*, Amman/Brussels: International

Crisis Group.

Anon, 2003, *Annual Report,* Amman: Delegation of the European Commission in Jordan.

Anon, 2005, *Jordan: National Indicative Programme: 2005–2006,* Brussels: The Euro-Med Partnership.

Anon, 2006a, *Regulatory Guide for Foreign Banks in the United States,* New York: PriceWaterhouseCoopers.

Anon, 2006b, *Insurance in the United States: Industry Profile,* Washington: Datamonitor.

Anon, 2006c, *International Crisis Group Report,* New York: ICG.

APM, 2007, *Annual Report,* Amman: Arab Pharmaceutical Manufacturing Co Ltd.

Arab Bank, 2006, *Annual Report,* Amman: Arab Bank.

— 2007, *Arab Bank Group Semi-Annual Report,* Amman: Arab Bank.

Arafat, A., 2001, *Pharmaceutical Sector Report,* Amman: Export & Finance Bank.

Armdt, H.W., 1986, *Measuring Trade in Financial Services,* Australian National University Research School of Pacific Studies.

Cassing, J., Salameh, A.M., 2006, *Jordan–United States Free Trade Agreement Economic Impact Study: Searching for Effects of the FTA on Exports, Imports and Trade Related Investments,* Amman: USAID, Jordan.

CBJ, 1994, *Fiscal Year Report 1994,* Amman: Central Bank of Jordan.

— 2006, *Yearly Statistical Series: Money and Banking,* Amman: Central Bank of Jordan.

— 2007a, *History of the Central Bank of Jordan,* Amman: Central Bank of Jordan.

— 2007b, *Research Department Monthly Report May 2007,* Amman: Central Bank of Jordan.

Citibank, 2005, *Historical Background,* New York: Citibank.

Citibank Bahrain, 2006, *Annual Report,* Manama: Citibank Bahrain.

Citibank Jordan, 2006, *Annual Report,* Amman: Citibank Jordan.

The Compulsory Unified Insurance Office, 2000, *Mission Statement,* Amman: The Compulsory Unified Insurance Office.

DADVet, 2006, *Annual Report,* Amman: DADVet.

Dar Al Dawa, 2006, *Annual Report,* Amman: Dar Al Dawa.

Dennis, A., February 2006, *The Impact of Regional Trade Agreements and Trade Facilitation in the Middle East and North Africa Region,* Washington World Bank.

The EFB, 2007, *Report on the Insurance Sector,* Amman: Export and Finance Bank.

The EPC, 2001, *Privatisation Newsletter,* Amman: The Executive Privatisation Committee.

— 2006, *Report on Privatisation Proceeds*, Amman: The Executive Privatisation Committee.

— 2007, *Types of Privatisation*, Amman: The Executive Privatisation Committee.

—2009, *Report on Completed Transactions*, Amman: The Executive Privatisation Committee.

The Federal Reserve, 20 July 2007, *Assets and Liabilities of Commercial Banks in the United States*, Washington: Federal Reserve Statistical Release.

HBTF, 2006, *Annual Report*, Amman: Housing Bank for Trade and Finance.

Hikma Pharmaceuticals, 2006, *Annual Report*, Amman: Hikma Pharmaceuticals.

The Insurance Commission, 2005, *Annual Report*, Amman: The Insurance Commission.

— 2006, *Annual Report*, Amman: The Insurance Commission.

Jardaneh, D., 2003, *US–Jordan Free Trade Agreement: Reaching the Finish Line*, Amman: Atlas Investment Group Report.

JIB, 2006, *Mission Statement*, Amman: Jordan Investment Board.

— 2005, *The Pharmaceutical Sector*, Amman: Jordan Investment Board Publications.

— 2006, *Invest in Jordan: The Textiles and Garments Sector*, Amman: Jordan Investment Board.

JIC, 2006, *Annual Report*, Amman: Jordan Insurance Company Ltd.

JIEC, 2006, *Annual Report*, Amman: Jordan Industrial Estates Corporation.

JIF, 2006a, *Annual Report*, Amman: Jordan Insurance Federation.

— 2006b, *Historical Background of the Jordanian Insurance Sector*, Amman: Jordan Insurance Federation.

Jordan Investment Trust, 2005, *Jordan: Growth Despite Difficulties*, Amman: Jordan Investment Trust plc.

League of Arab States, 1997, *Executive Programme of the Agreement on Facilitating Trade and Developing Intra-Arab Trade for Establishing the Greater Arab Free Trade Area (GAFTA)*, Cairo: Secretariat of the Arab League, Directorate of Economic Affairs.

Manneh, J., 2004, *Pharmaceuticals Sector Report*, Amman: Export and Finance Bank.

Ministry of Finance, 2002, *Government Finance Bulletin*, Amman: Ministry of Finance, Vol. 3, No. 12.

Ministry of Industry and Trade, 2006, *Implementation of the JUSFTA*, Amman: Ministry of Industry and Trade.

Ministry of Labour, 2006, *Report on the Status of Migrant Workers in the Qualifying Industrial Zones and Industrial Estates*, Amman: Ministry of Labour.

Ministry of Labour, 2007, *Labour Report*, Amman: Ministry of Labour.

NutriDar, 2006, *Annual Report*, Amman: NutriDar.

OECD, 1999, *Cross Border Trade in Financial Services: Economics and Regulation*, Paris: OECD.

Organon, 2000, *Annual Report*, New York: Organon.

Pfizer India, 2006, *Annual Report*, Delhi: Pfizer India.

PhRMA, 2006, *Industry Profile Data*, Washington: Pharmaceutical Research and Manufacturers of America.

Patten, C., 2006, *The EU–Jordan Association Agreement: Opportunities and Challenges*, Amman: The European Commission in Jordan.

Shaban, R.A., Abu-Ghaida, D., Al-Naimat, A.S., 2001, *Poverty Alleviation in Jordan in the 1990s: Lessons for the Future*, Washington: World Bank.

Sprague, R. *et al.*, 7 Nov. 1957, *Deterrence and Survival in the Nuclear Age*, Washington: Security Resources Panel of the Science Advisory Committee, Executive Office of The President.

Thomas, J.R., 21 December 2005, *Intellectual Property and Free Trade Agreements: Innovation Policy Issues*, Washington: Congressional Research Service Report.

USITC, 2004, *US–Bahrain Free Trade Agreement: Potential Economy Wide and Sectoral Effects*, Washington: United States International Trade Commission.

USTR, 2005, *The US–Jordan FTA Fact Sheet*, Washington: Office of the United States Trade Representative.

— 2006a, *The US–SACU FTA*, Washington: Office of the United States Trade Representative.

— 2006b, *The US–Andean Community Agreement*, Washington: Office of the United States Trade Representative.

— 2007, *The US–Middle East Free Trade Area Initiative*, Washington: Office of the United States Trade Representative.

— 2008, *Bilateral FTAs*, Washington: Office of the United States Trade Representative.

Vamvakidis, A., 1998, *Regional Trade Agreements Versus Broad Liberalisation: Which Path Leads to Faster Growth? Time-Series Evidence*, Washington: IMF.

Van Beuzekom, B., Arundel, A., 2006, *OECD Biotechnology Statistics*, Paris: OECD Publications.

World Bank, 1995, *Country Report – Jordan*, Washington: World Bank.

— 1996, *Structural Adjustment in Jordan*, Washington: The World Bank.

— 2006a, *World Bank Press Report*, Washington: World Bank.

— 2006b, *Jordan Quarterly Update: Third Quarter 2006*, Washington: World Bank.

WTO, 1997, *World Trade Organisation Press Brief: Financial Services*, Geneva: World Trade Organisation.

— 1999, *Report of the Working Party on the Accession of Jordan*, Geneva: World Trade Organisation.

— 2001, *GATS: Fact and Fiction*, Geneva: World Trade Organisation.

— 13 August 2001, *Review of Legislation: Jordan*, Washington: Council for Trade-Related Aspects of Intellectual Property Rights.

— September 2006, *TRIPs and Pharmaceuticals Factsheet*, Geneva: World Trade Organisation.

Yousef, T., 2004, *Intra-Arab Trade: is it too Little?* Washington: International Monetary Fund.

Database sources:

Eurostat Data

Jordanian Ministry of Industry and Trade: Trade and Investment Information Database

The CIA World Factbook

The OECD International Trade in Services Statistics Database

United Nations Comtrade

United States Food and Drug Agency

US Census Bureau: Foreign Trade Statistics.

Primary interviews:

Abu Rahmeh, H., Director of the Jordan Exporters Association, interview held in Amman, Jordan on 27 December 2006.

Al-Badri, K., Managing Director of JEDCO, interview held in Amman, Jordan on 19 December 2006.

Ali, M., Director of Foreign Trade Policy, Ministry of Industry and Trade, interview held in Amman, Jordan on 22 December 2006.

Al-Khassib, S., Director of Research at The Amman Chamber of Commerce, interview held in Amman, Jordan on 24 December 2006.

Al-Shamali, Y., Deputy Director of the Foreign Trade Policy Department of the Ministry of Industry and Trade, interview held in Amman, Jordan on 24 December 2006.

Al-Zu'bi, T., Communication Officer for the Jordanian Executive Privatisation Commission, interview held in Amman, Jordan on 24 December 2006.

Atmeh, M., Deputy CEO of The Jordan Industrial Estates Corporation, interview held in Amman, Jordan on 28 December 2006.

Bahous, G., Head of Operations for Citibank Jordan, interview held in Amman, Jordan on 14 August 2007.

Bastani, T., Evaluations Consultant at the United States Trade and Development Agency, interview held in Washington, United States on 24 March 2008.

Castro, J., Counsellor at the Legal Affairs Division of the World Trade Organisation, interview held at the WTO in Geneva, Switzerland on 23 April 2007.

El Hachimi, S., Head of External Relations Division of the WTO, interview held in Geneva, Switzerland on 24 April 2007.

Farraj, E., Chief Advisor to Maan Nsour, CEO of the Jordan Investment Board, interview held in Amman, Jordan on 24 December 2006.

Hazimeh, F., Lead Counsellor for the Jordanian Mission at the WTO, interview held at the WTO in Geneva, Switzerland on 25 April 2007.

Kress, C., Regional Director Middle East and North Africa, US Trade and Development Agency, interview held in Washington DC, United States, 24 March 2008.

Kwakwa, E., Legal Counsellor at the World Intellectual Property Organisation, interview held at the WTO in Geneva, Switzerland on 23 April 2007.

Munyaneza, S., Head of Trade Analysis and Information at the United Nations Conference on Trade and Development, interview held at the WTO in Geneva, Switzerland on 25 April 2007.

O'Laughlin, P., Public Affairs Officer at the United States International Trade Commission, interview held in Washington, United States on 20 March 2008.

Schott, J. J., Senior Fellow at the Peterson Institute for International Economics, interview held at the WTO in Washington, United States on 23 March 2008.

Zeud, A., Head of Public Relations at the Jordanian House of Senate, interview held in Amman, Jordan on 24 December 2006.

Zu'bi, T., Chief Communications Officer of the Executive Privatisation Committee, interview held in Amman, 21 December 2006.

Secondary interviews:

Al-Fayez, F., International Crisis Group interview, Amman, 13 May 2003.

Bahous, G., Head of Operations for Citibank Jordan, Amman, 14 August 2007.

Marto, M., International Crisis Group interview, Amman, 13 May 2003.

Muasher, M., International Crisis Group interview, Amman, 16 June 2003.

News articles:

Anon, 'Jordan's Privatization Programme is One of the Most Successful in the Region: World Bank', *Jordan Times*, 4 March 2002, Economy Section.

Anon, Sept. 30 2006, 'Jordan Regrets US Union Action', Al-Jazeera News.

Anon, 'Foreign Grants up by End of April', *Jordan Times*, 27 June 2008.

Gibson, D., 'Playing Second Fiddle in China', WA Business News, 13 October 2005.

Burns, J.F., 'Jordan's King, in Gamble, Lends Hand to the US', *The New York Times*, 9 March 2003.

Harrison, P., 'Jordan Rocked by Abuse Claims', Emerging Textiles.com: Textile and Clothing Trade Information, 5 May 2006.

Sparshott, J., 'Jordan Shutting Abusive Factories', *The Washington Times*, 17 June 2006.

Tate, P., 'Jordan Witnesses Investment Boom', *The Jordan Times*, 4 October 2006.

The Economist, US Edition, 9 June 2001.

Legal documentation:

Agreement Between the United States of America and the Hashemite Kingdom of Jordan on the Establishment of a Free Trade Area, 2000.

Article 6 of the Investment Promotion Law 1995.

Berne Convention for the Protection of Literary and Artistic Works, September 9 1886, 828 UNTS. 221.

Communication from the Hashemite Kingdom of Jordan, Schedule of Specific Commitments Under the General Agreement on Trade in Services, World Trade Organisation, 15/12/2000, GATS/SC/128.

Communication from the United States of America, United States Schedule of Specific Commitments Under the General Agreement on Trade in Services, World Trade Organisation, 27/02/2003, S/DCS/W/USA.

Draft Law on Political Associations, Jordan, 2005.

Jordan Insurance Law No. 9.

The Law of the Central Bank of Jordan, 1959.

Paris Convention for the Protection of Industrial Property, 20 March 1883, 13 UST. 1.

The Privatization Law 25/2000.

Treaty of Peace Between Israel and Jordan, 1994.

TRIPS Agreement Article 12.

US–Jordan Free Trade Agreement, Schedule of Specific Commitments.

WTO, 15 April 1994, *Understanding on Rules and Procedures Governing the Settlement of Disputes, WTO Agreement, Annex 2, Legal Instruments – Results of the Uruguay Round, Vol. 31, No. 33, I.L.M. 1226.*

Conference papers and speeches:

Adams, Q., 1821, *Seeking Monsters to Destroy,* s.i.: s.n.

Bush, G.W., 6 Nov. 2003, *Freedom in Iraq and the Middle East,* remarks at the 20th Anniversary of the National Endowment for Democracy at the US Chamber of Commerce.

Eisenhower, D.D., 5 Jan. 1957, *Special Message to the Congress on the Situation in the Middle East.*

Gause, F.G., 1999, *Systemic Approaches to Middle East International Relations*, International Studies Association Annual Convention, published by Blackwells.

Jessop, B., 18-19 December 2000, *Institutional (Re)turns and the Strategic-Relational Approach*, paper presented at the Institutional Theory in Political Science Conference, Ross Priory, Loch Lomond.

Watson, M., 25 Feb.–1 March 2003, *Constructing and Contesting Orthodoxies: General Equilibrium Economics and the Political Discourse of Globalisation*, 44th Annual Convention of the International Studies Association, Portland, USA.

Winters, A.L., April 1996, *Regionalism Versus Multilateralism*, paper presented at the CEPR Conference on Regional Integration, La Coruna, Spain.

INDEX